'The second edition of *Omnichannel Retail* is a ginger shot of retail marketing genius. Packed full of concentrated advice and case studies, it is utterly stimulating. I read it in one sitting and emerged fizzing with energy and ideas to boost our omnichannel strategy.'
Charlotte Lock, Partner and Pan-Partnership Customer Director, John Lewis

'Brilliant and, for retailers, most welcome! *Omnichannel Retail* nails its value proposition. Tim Mason, in providing a comprehensive and highly practical guide to harnessing digital technologies, urges retailers to rethink brand, upgrade customer experience, deliver loyalty and (for most) regain profitability. He provides an exciting vision for the role of retail in the 21st century.'
Seán Meehan, Professor of Marketing and Management and Dean of Faculty, IMD

'Customers live and shop digitally and physically now but they don't see the distinction that retailers make between the two. The retailers that will win in the future will be able to effortlessly combine physical and digital experiences and marketing. Taking the disciplines of digital marketing that deliver more targeted, more scaled and more interactive messages for customers now is a "must-do" to create that seamless experience. *Omnichannel Retail* helps to address how to deliver this.'
Rob Hattrell, Head of Digital, TDR Capital

'I worked alongside Tim Mason for 15 years and he is the best marketer I have ever worked with. While "success has many fathers", Tim can genuinely lay claim to many of the customer initiatives that drove the growth of Tesco over a remarkable 20 plus years. This book brings all that customer knowledge and focus to life for the digital age.'
Andrew Higginson, Chair, JD Sports

'Since the last edition, four years have flown by and a lot has changed. The principles outlined in the first edition of Tim Mason's excellent book have not only accelerated, but they have been enhanced in this new edition. By reading this book, you'll learn from a real master in the of the art and science of marketing. Tim and co-author Sarah Jarvis have brilliantly captured new and improved ways of winning in the connected world. *Omnichannel Retail* shows how to blend customer understanding, data and technology into a winning mixture. Tim proves that his innovative mindset keeps adapting and evolving to keep finding ways to compete. A good lesson for us all. Worth the read.'
Matt Atkinson, Non-Executive Chair, UNiDAYS

'*Omnichannel Retail* brings to life Tim Mason's unrivalled sense of customers the world over and how their lives are changing. It draws out his life-long retail experiences and his instinct for growth and is a must-read for all thoughtful and sustainable retailers.'
David Potts, CEO, Morrisons

'Clearly articulates how to bridge the online and offline gap by utilizing best practice digital marketing, data and loyalty approaches. A must-read from one of the original pioneers of retail loyalty.'
Max Savransky, CEO, Loyalty & Reward Co.

'There are very few people who have truly dedicated their entire professional lives to customer loyalty, but Tim Mason has done exactly that. His legendary expertise spans the online and offline worlds, giving him a unique perspective and command on the challenges and opportunities that omnichannel retail requires. In this insightful book, Tim and his co-author Sarah Jarvis make a compelling case for the power of culture, communications and connection, both online and offline, as tools that drive success, with clear and practical examples that make this book essential reading for every ambitious retailer in today's digital world.'
Paula Thomas, Founder and CEO, Let's Talk Loyalty

'In the omnichannel world we live in, it's so easy for retailers to get lost in the jargon and technology and lose sight of what really matters – understanding and serving your customers better. This book reminds us that customer-first thinking is more important than ever and is packed full of advice and case studies for building relevant, meaningful digital connections with your customers.'
Matt McLellan, VP Customer Planning and Proposition, Asda

'This book looks to highlight the real value of knowing your customers and the insights into realizing how powerful your customers are to the growth of your business. If you believe customers can be the spokes in your wheel of fortune, then read this book (especially the chapters on loyalty!).'
Adam Posner, Founder, The Point of Loyalty

'The whole idea of omnichannel has never sat right with me. Pushed by tech vendors and consultants, the concept of omnichannel has contorted into a confusing buzzword that creates unrealistic expectations for marketing leaders. The second edition of *Omnichannel Retail* gives us a fresh and perhaps better approach to the concept. It could not come at a better time for retail leaders as brands have to respond to cost-of-living challenges, a post-Covid 19 world and increased digital expectations from consumers. In *Omnichannel Retail*, Tim Mason and Sarah Jarvis have delivered a vision for what this confounding word should represent that I can finally get behind.'
Juan Mendoza, CEO and Editor-in-Chief, The Martech Weekly

'Tim Mason is a pioneer in the world of enterprise customer engagement – a genuine icon. And while you have to credit him for the incomparable work he has done for the brands he's consulted with over the years and how he has advanced the thinking and awareness of the critical human factors that underpin this industry, that's not why you should read this book. Read this book because Tim provides retailers with strategies and tactics that are not only practical but are actionable right now and which (unlike so many other current books in this genre) actually help to move the needle! Tim Mason has done it again!'
Mike Giambattista, Founder and CEO, TheCustomer

Omnichannel Retail

How to build winning stores in a digital world

SECOND EDITION

Tim Mason
Sarah Jarvis

KoganPage

First published in Great Britain and the United States in 2019 by Kogan Page Limited
Second edition published in 2023

2nd Floor, 45 Gee Street	8 W 38th Street, Suite 902	4737/23 Ansari Road
London	New York, NY 10018	Daryaganj
EC1V 3RS	USA	New Delhi 110002
United Kingdom		India
www.koganpage.com		

Kogan Page books are printed on paper from sustainable forests.

ISBNs
Hardback   978 1 3986 1274 7
Paperback   978 1 3986 1272 3
Ebook   978 1 3986 1273 0

British Library Cataloguing-in-Publication Data
A CIP record for this book is available from the British Library.

Library of Congress Cataloging-in-Publication Data
Names: Mason, Tim (CEO of Eagle Eye), author. | Jarvis, Sarah (Marketing professional), author.
Title: Omnichannel retail : how to build winning stores in a digital world / Tim Mason, Sarah Jarvis.
Description: Second edition. | London ; New York, NY : Kogan Page, 2023. | Includes bibliographical references and index.
Identifiers: LCCN 2023027069 (print) | LCCN 2023027070 (ebook) | ISBN 9781398612723 (paperback) | ISBN 9781398612747 (hardback) | ISBN 9781398612730 (ebook)
Subjects: LCSH: Retail trade. | Stores, Retail. | Database searching. | Electronic commerce.
Classification: LCC HF5429 .M329 2023 (print) | LCC HF5429 (ebook) | DDC 658.8/7–dc23/eng/20230627
LC record available at https://lccn.loc.gov/2023027069
LC ebook record available at https://lccn.loc.gov/2023027070

Typeset by Integra Software Services, Pondicherry
Print production managed by Jellyfish
Printed and bound by CPI Group (UK) Ltd, Croydon CR0 4YY

CONTENTS

LIST OF FIGURES AND TABLES

FOREWORD

I have worked with Tim Mason on and off for over 30 years. I have no doubt that he is the best marketing practitioner the retail industry has produced. In his early career he had a lot of success as pioneer of CPG product management in retail. Twenty-five years ago, he led the launch of Tesco Clubcard. This was at the birth of Big Data and he was ground-breaking in the use of digital customer data to enable targeted marketing and create customer loyalty. Back then, the customer data were digital, but the marketing response was analogue and disjointed. Price, promotion, gift, loyalty and customer service investments were all isolated from each other and not in real time.

In recent years, as CEO of Eagle Eye, Tim and his team have been able to offer a fully integrated digital marketing experience, through the evolution from pre-digital and part-digital through to fully digital, to write this book, and I think he has developed some important themes that are relevant to CPG brands, traditional retailers and digital businesses alike.

He highlights the importance of creating a bridge for the customer between online and offline. We know more and more about customers when they are online but lose them as soon as they shop offline.

Tim explores how you can find your customer online and engage them with marketing incentives that can be redeemed offline, providing a seamless record of the customer journey (with the customer's permission, of course!). This offers the possibility of truly effective customer targeting and acquisition with quantified return on investment, because it tracks the journey through to action. It allows the marketer to reallocate resource behind the incentives that are actually of value to the consumer. This results in much less waste of marketing dollars and offers more opportunity to do things that actually create loyal customers.

In addition, he reminds us that this is much more than about e-commerce. Of course, e-commerce is of huge importance to retailers and CPG brands, but it is only a part of the digital relationship that businesses can create with their customers. Today it is possible to find the customers that are right for your business and engage them with products and services tailored to their needs. The medium is modern, digital data and digital marketing; the foundation is old-fashioned trust and loyalty.

Sir Terry Leahy

ACKNOWLEDGEMENTS

I would like to acknowledge the help of the following people in making the man who wrote the book, or helped with the book itself, including Jeff Adams, Matt Atkinson, David Aylmer, John Bird, Carolyn Bradley, Richard Brasher, John Burry, John Gildersleeve, Colin Goodfellow, Grant Harrison, Al Henderson, Andrew Higginson, Sarah Jarvis, Jo Kennedy, Paul Kennedy, Miya Knights, Terry Leahy, Ian MacLaurin, David Malpas, Laurie McIllwee, Joel Percy, Marie Helene Pitteloud Turner, David Potts, Jonathan Reeve, David Reid, Steve Rothwell, Angela Santaniello, Lucy Sharman-Munday, Janet Smith, Anthony Stevenson, Simon Uwins, Malcolm Wall and Paul Weinberger, plus all of the contributors to the book.

LIST OF ABBREVIATIONS

AI	artificial intelligence
AP	access point
API	application programming interface
AR	augmented reality
CCPA	California Consumer Privacy Act
CEO	chief executive officer
CFO	chief finance officer
CMO	chief marketing officer
CPG	consumer packaged goods
CRM	customer relationship management
CSR	corporate social responsibility
EDLP	everyday low price
EPOS	electronic point of sale
FMCG	fast-moving consumer goods
GDPR	General Data Protection Regulation
GMV	gross merchandise value
GPS	Global Positioning System
IMEI	International Mobile Equipment Identity number
IoT	Internet of Things
IPO	initial public offering
IT	information technology
KPI	key performance indicator
M&S	Marks & Spencer Group plc
NFC	near-field communications
NFT	Non-Fungible Token
NPS	Net Promoter System
OKRs	objectives and key results
PDF	Portable Document Format
PED	PIN entry device

PIN	personal identification number
POS	point of sale
QR	quick response
R&D	research and development
RMN	retail media network
ROBO	research online, buy offline
ROI	return on investment
satnav	satellite navigation system
SEO	search engine optimization
SKU	stock-keeping unit
SMS	short message service
UX	user experience
VR	virtual reality

Introduction

I first realized the scale of the opportunity for technology to revolution-ize the way that businesses engage with consumers while at Tesco. It was during this time that I began to understand the benefits of direct customer marketing engagement.

Fast forward to today and the retail industry is under significant pressure. This is driven in part by consumers embracing technology throughout the shopping journey, where the influence of internet-based and mobile-enabled digital technologies is challenging the traditional role of the store, while today's average retail space is tantamount to a 'digital black hole' and one-hour delivery and kerbside pickup mean shoppers need never have to step inside a physical retail space again.

However, the fundamental principles of what matters in retail are unlikely ever to change: people will always need to buy stuff, and the store isn't going anywhere soon as a means of connecting merchants and their goods and services to customers who want to buy from them. The advent of digital has, however, radically changed the terms on which consumers connect and transact with consumer businesses.

In *Omnichannel Retail*, I make the case for the value of digital customer connection and explain how to harness it, both online and offline. Based on 30 years' working for one of the world's largest retailers, my case is founded on understanding what drives customer loyalty in the digitally connected 21st century.

I aim to demystify the art of one-to-one engagement where it meets the application of mobile in customer-facing physical spaces, so they are digitally enabled and data driven. My practical, experience-led approach is designed to help any consumer business harness the benefits of digital customer engagement and performance marketing technologies today.

Learning how to use digital to know who your customer is, decipher what's 'right' for each of them in any given moment – even if that moment is 'right now' – and delivering it to them in a personalized way that takes account of their preferences and purchase history, at speed and scale, is precisely why anyone specifically looking to grow a customer-facing bricks business should read this book. It is designed to help merchants and brands turn today's digital imperative into a physical advantage.

Omnichannel Retail deconstructs the benefits of digitally augmenting bricks-and-mortar stores, showrooms, coffee shops, restaurants and so on to deliver truly personalized customer experiences that can both compete with and complement e-commerce growth. It also demonstrates how digital connections can support direct performance marketing to engage and interact effectively with customers, and why retailers must facilitate the value and analyse the impact of these connections to run their businesses better and more profitably, while meeting and exceeding digitally empowered and heightened customer expectations.

I believe we are at an inflection point in history. Soon non digitally savvy businesses will become aware they are losing out on an opportunity to create competitive advantage. Retail has always been a tough and competitive industry and there will always be winners and losers. But it feels like carnage on the high street at the moment, with so many household retail names struggling or going under. So, *Omnichannel Retail* is written for the winners going forward, where a prerequisite of winning will be that you are data driven and digitally enabled.

That is why this book is designed to guide retailers, brands and indeed any customer-facing business in the use of digital connection to generate footfall, deepen levels of customer insight, improve service, enhance loyalty and, ultimately, drive more sales – regardless of the channel.

It is also about the opportunity of harnessing the power of digital in physical spaces. It is my manifesto based upon the transformation that I have experienced. I'm not an academic, but a practical, action-oriented marketer, and so my approach is designed to help any consumer business harness the benefits of digital customer engagement and performance marketing technologies today.

You are the product experts, the innovators, the evangelists, the playmakers, the curators; you are so much more than the landlord of a digital shopping mall and it is these strengths that you have to demonstrate to consumers. I hope the book inspires you to find your digital mojo and go on to win.

Introduction to the second edition

It has been four years since I wrote *Omnichannel Retail* and it's difficult to believe how much has changed in that time. At the end of 2019, Covid-19 struck and accelerated many of the trends that were already at play. Digital adoption accelerated at pace. Zoom saw its daily virtual meeting participants grow from 10 million to 200 million from December 2019 to March 2020.[1] QR codes enjoyed mass adoption. TikTok became available worldwide. Jack Dorsey's first-ever tweet sold as an NFT for $2.9 million. Facebook became Meta and brands such as Starbucks and Nike started to leverage Web3 technology. E-commerce grew, with McKinsey reporting US e-commerce penetration saw '10 years' growth in 3 months'[2] and millions more consumers became used to online ordering and home delivery. Large food stores and home improvement businesses enjoyed significant gains but, like e-commerce businesses, have had to readjust as consumer behaviours returned to their pre-Covid ways.

Household names continued to go to the wall. Topshop, Debenhams and House of Fraser in the UK all closed their doors, as did Lord & Taylor and Dressbarn in the US and Dimmeys and Harris Scarfe in Australia. Walmart sold Asda, Morrisons became private equity-owned.

Loyalty schemes came back into fashion with notable launches by McDonald's, Lidl, Asda, Pret a Manger, Pizza Express, Walmart and more, while we also saw a renaissance of existing market-leading schemes – Tesco switched on Clubcard Prices and Woolworths in Australia relaunched Everyday Rewards.

Fred Reichheld, the inventor of NPS, has written a new book, *Winning on Purpose*, which updates his thesis from *The Loyalty Effect*. I share his vision that it's only possible to earn customer loyalty through engaged and committed employees. I'd like to acknowledge the significant impact that Fred's writing has had on me over the years and, as he wrote his latest book while he was unwell, would like to wish him a full recovery.

More latterly, the world has changed, with a combination of the war in Ukraine, the resulting energy crisis, rising inflation and, in the UK, Brexit, combining to create a consumer economic crisis, the horrors of which have yet to play out.

In times of recession, it's the discounters that make gains as the savings they offer become more important for more people. The premium sector tries to steal share as the wealthy trade down from eating out to dining at home, and the middle gets squeezed. The result historically has always been more promotions, with marketing spend switching from above the line to below, and a greater focus on loyalty.

So, in summary, we have an even more digitally savvy consumer, desperately in need of value. All of this points to the need for better and more personalized omnichannel marketing. What do I mean by better? Marketing that delivers more perceived value to consumers with a lower delivery cost to you. Successful execution will deliver more bang for the marketing buck, and that is a virtuous circle.

This edition has been updated extensively throughout, and includes new chapters on:

- The fundamentals of loyalty
- The power of personalization
- Marketing in the moment
- Monetizing the customer connection
- The culture of loyalty

Finally, I'd like to introduce my new co-author, Sarah Jarvis, Communications and Propositions Director at Eagle Eye, who ensures that we live up to the very high standard we set ourselves when it comes to effective communication. I'd also like to thank Miya Knights once again for her help on the first edition.

Notes

1 Yuan, E (2020) A message to our users, Zoom, 1 April. https://blog.zoom.us/a-message-to-our-users/ (archived at https://perma.cc/DEB8-BLKG)

2 McKinsey & Company (2020) The Quickening, *McKinsey Quarterly*, Five Fifty, www.mckinsey.com/capabilities/strategy-and-corporate-finance/our-insights/five-fifty-the-quickening (archived at https://perma.cc/P66Q-75P3)

1

The digital imperative

This book describes what I believe it takes for physical stores to prosper in the age of Amazon, Google, Meta, Netflix et al. In a nutshell, there is a digital imperative that has to be embraced. Many businesses have recognized that e-commerce is going to become a significant channel and have therefore built .com versions of themselves. However, they have failed to recognize the omnichannel beast they were creating. In simple terms, the consumer expected them to be one business across all their facets – in-store, online, in-app, etc – but have largely found them to be incomprehensibly not joined up, with each channel feeling like its own independent business. With the advent of increased .com market share driven by the Covid-19 pandemic this problem has just got bigger.

Advertising was quick to jump on the digital opportunity, making fortunes for Google and Meta and others but decimating traditional print and TV channels. However, these digital shifts have largely passed the less consolidated world of marketing by. Sales promotion in particular lags woefully behind.

As I write in early 2023, the digital imperative as I see it is all about providing consumers with a convenient, personalized and unified shopping experience, wherever, whenever and however they choose to engage with you.

The analogue years

Having spent a large part of my career in senior management roles at Tesco, I have been frequently asked to speak about the Tesco phenomenon, under the heading of 'Customer-centred growth'. I would explain that Tesco was motivated by two psychological drivers: an obsession with the customer and paranoia about competitors. These two traits drove the hyperactivity that characterized Tesco as it grew at its fastest. By then, I had been with Tesco for over 20 years, and I had worked directly for Sir Terry Leahy for 18 of them.

The 1980s had been a decade of building out Tesco's infrastructure, ranges and talent, and taking advantage of the latest in technological automation, with new store systems that included electronic point-of-sale (EPOS) checkout systems. Everything was new and driven by a determination to catch Marks & Spencer (M&S), which was then the most profitable retailer in the world, and J Sainsbury, as the most profitable grocer in the world. In short, the 1980s was a decade of paranoia-fuelled benchmarking.

The trouble with benchmarking, though, is that you only improve as much as those organizations you're benchmarking improve. Once you start to catch them, the rate of improvement decreases and so does performance. This relative rate of improvement, that is, how much better my business is this week, this year, than my competitor's, is a key driver of performance improvement that means when you improve faster, you grow faster.

This catching of the competition coincided with a slowdown in the economy at the end of the 1980s – a nasty coincidence. For two or three years, Tesco kept reprising variants of the tried and tested techniques of the 1980s, but with limited success.

In 1992, Terry Leahy was appointed Marketing Director on the Tesco main board, and he appointed me Marketing Operations Director. He commissioned a major research study to understand Tesco's place in the market and its role for the consumer. This led to Tesco replacing the competition as the focus with the consumer, who became our new 'North Star'. This, in turn, led to the creation of the 'Every Little Helps' strategy, which drove a series of improvements in small things; none of these were in themselves life-changing, but each of them, added together, made Tesco a significantly better place to shop.

Our first initiative was to launch the Tesco Value Range in the corporate red, white and blue striped livery, which was a strident attempt to cover the 'entry point' pricing square and remove the need to visit discounters. It was a big, bold move, executed quickly, rapidly exceeding 100 core items. Featured on promotion ends, advertised in TV and the press, it was a major effort and not without risk to margin of course, but also to image. Some of the pundits opined that we were jeopardizing a decade of hard-won image gains and were returning the brand to Jack Cohen's pile it high, sell it cheap roots.

As it happened, the launch of Value stabilized trading and slowly, Tesco started to grow market share again. A while later, as the economy improved, we launched Tesco Finest, evidence that we were not going downmarket, but were a business that was for everyone. This ubiquity of appeal was essential for a business that was to push on to have a market share of over 30 per cent.

The reason I have recounted this story is to indicate the scale of the change necessary to meaningfully respond to changed circumstances. Big moves get big results.

Now, in 2023, circumstances are dramatically changed and 'big moves' are needed. But it is my firm belief that many of those moves can now be made at the stroke of a key rather than introducing what become hundreds of new items to a store with all the costs and effort that entails. This book will illustrate what I mean. The 'Every Little Helps' strategy reached its apotheosis in 1995 with the launch of the Tesco Clubcard loyalty scheme. By 1997 Tesco was able to bring a decade's work together in the short phrase 'To create value for customers to earn their lifetime loyalty'. It was this aim, informed by customer data generated by Clubcard and driven by its direct marketing connection to the customer, that delivered the next decade or more of growth for Tesco.

Powerful strategies that really drive companies develop over time. In Tesco's case, it took over a decade in the articulation and almost two decades of performance delivery.

Having started my career at Unilever in 1979, before joining Tesco from 1982 to 2012 and ever since, I have focused on working with and advising a number of companies that focus on the digital shopping trip. These include:

- Eagle Eye, CEO – customer connections, enabling digital promotions and loyalty;
- Yext, Advisory Board member – 'Near me' search and business listings;
- Purple, Non-Executive Director – Wi-Fi-based 'intelligent spaces' customer data and analytics;
- Digital Natives adviser – digital content creation;
- Gousto, Non-Executive Director – e-commerce meal kit home delivery subscription service.

The reason I outline this brief precis of 30 years at Tesco and beyond from the outset is because it enables me to declare my hand early: I believe in the power of marketing to drive exceptional performance; I believe in putting the customer at the centre of everything; I believe in developing customer loyalty and the power of customer data; and I believe in the effectiveness of direct marketing. Latterly I have come to believe that all of those things can be achieved better, more simply and more cheaply by harnessing the opportunity of digital connection and engagement.

This book is about these beliefs and the experiences that led to them, as well as the lessons learnt.

The importance of digital

Digital connection is essential in modern life. It has transformed how we work, navigate the world, communicate and, most importantly in the context of this book, how we shop.

Music, maps, media, messaging and even memories have all been digitized. Smartphones and tablets have replaced 35 mm cameras, satellite navigation systems, alarm clocks and innumerable other gadgets, consigning them to museums as exhibits. And of course, since writing the first edition, we have seen digital adoption grow even faster than any of us could have predicted as a result of the Covid-19 pandemic.

The significance of this transformation ranks, in my opinion, alongside some of humanity's outstanding inventions, including the printing press, steam and combustion engines, electricity, powered flight, and the telephone and television. These inventions were not just important in themselves. They changed humanity and our global social and macroeconomic development. In the same way, we cannot underestimate the internet's role as *the* fundamental enabler of digital connection.

The internet, as a globally interconnected computer network, first opened up access to digitized information and communications. Second, with mobile and location-based technologies, it helped us to establish connections with places and use online maps to navigate our world. Now it is enabling two-way communication between network-embedded devices, or 'things', so we can connect up an Internet of Things (IoT) to turn smart lights and heating on or off and track everything from our health to the temperature of our fridges.

The internet is undeniably the biggest and most relevant recent change in retail because of its impact on the way businesses engage with and serve customers. Where the average business traditionally operated a single, physical sales channel – the store – many now support multiple digital and physical sales and marketing channels, through the store and e-commerce websites and marketplaces to social media networks and traditional advertising media, including print, television and radio. Today, a business offering a blended physical and digital retail presence that can seamlessly adapt its offerings and services consistently across all channels would be named 'omnichannel', if you could find it on a map (see Figure 1.1).

This ability to digitally connect people, places and things represents a fundamental shift in the world, especially in our examination of the evolving role it plays in the average shopping journey. Technology analyst Forrester suggests that 60 per cent of all sales are now digitally influenced,[1] up from 49 per cent pre-pandemic,[2] which

FIGURE 1.1   Illustration of single-channel, multichannel and omnichannel organizations

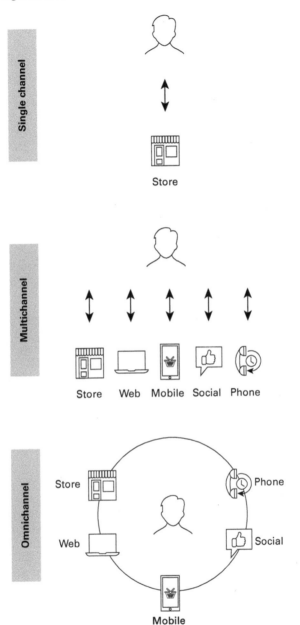

is why the need to forge a digital connection to customers of true competitive value is raising the stakes high enough to make it a top priority for retailers and brands alike.

In 2016 I joined the digital connection software provider, Eagle Eye, because I believed its time had come. The first task I set myself upon starting was to articulate the compelling reason for customer connection and digital marketing in modern, digital retail. The following is a digest of what our then Marketing Manager, Jo Kennedy, and I came up with – the characteristics of which you'll likely recognize from your own shopping experiences, just as much as from running your own consumer business.

THE EAGLE EYE STORY

The digital imperative describes the growing importance of digital in retail:

- Almost everyone is digitally connected 24/7. This has led to a fundamental shift in the ways in which businesses should engage and interact with consumers. But this digital capability significantly lags the opportunity.

Most stores, restaurants and other physical sales locations are now a **digital black hole**:

- Those that recognize the digital imperative are challenging the status quo, with their ability to establish a digital connection with customers wherever and however they choose to shop. Yet few capitalize on any digital connection with customers in-store.

The digital opportunity is open to any customer-facing business willing to embrace it:

- Retailers that build a consistent digital customer connection can use the insight it enables to know who their customers are both inside and outside the store. They use this insight to run their businesses better with the aim of acquiring, winning and retaining more customers and driving increased sales and loyalty from their engagement.

The digitally augmented store can connect with customers via mobile:

- Apply best practice for customers to embrace digital via mobile throughout their shopping trips, inside and outside intelligent spaces, to maximize the value of customer connection, marketing return on investment (ROI), data insight and loyalty learnings.

Performance marketing generates measurable returns, regardless of channel:

- Digital customer connection and consistent, compelling, cross-channel content are prerequisites for driving maximum marketing performance, traffic and sales offline, as well as online.

How Eagle Eye enables businesses to capitalize on the digital opportunity

1 Provides a real-time omnichannel customer connection by integrating to the till and all other points of purchase, as well as to the retailers' 'brain' or data analytics capability.

2 Through this connection, Eagle Eye enables all of the retailers' data-driven decisions to be actioned to the end customer via the full digital marketing toolkit, including real-time loyalty schemes, personalized promotions, subscription services, gifting/cashback programmes, charity donations, third-party partnerships, coalitions and much more.

3 We deliver to our clients in a 'Purple' way, which is acting in accordance with our core company values (integrity, excellence, passion, innovation, teamwork and kindness), caring deeply about our customers' success with a focus on long-term partnership.

The importance of connection

I was fortunate enough to learn about the power of customer connection many years ago, following the successful launch of Tesco Clubcard, but even on our best week, we knew we would never be able to associate 100 per cent of our sales to individual customers. This meant there would always be a gap, albeit small, in our understanding. At the time, this wasn't something we worried about too much as we still knew so much more than any of our competitors; however, the rise of e-commerce changed this dramatically. As a result of their business model, digital pureplay organizations like Amazon are able to tie every single transaction back to an individual, meaning they have a complete picture of who bought what and when.

Not wanting to stop there, in 2007 Amazon launched its now world-famous Prime proposition to enable it to deepen the customer connection, limiting the amount of cross-shopping members did outside of the Amazon network through offering exceptional convenience via its rapid fulfillment model. As of 2021, there were more than 200 million Prime members globally.[3]

Following Amazon's lead, there's been an explosion of subscription services over the last few years, with Barclaycard reporting that 81 per cent of UK households were signed up to at least one subscription in 2021, rising from 65 per cent in 2020.[4] These offerings exploit the e-commerce model to deliver cost savings and personalized shopping services to customers, while delivering recurring revenue and predictable demand to retailers. Examples can be found across all sectors from Birchbox and Liberty London in beauty, Pret a Manger in quick service restaurants, Stitch Fix in fashion, and meal kits with Blue Apron and Gousto, all of which chip away at the establishment.

A perhaps more surprising entrant to the world of customer connection via the subscription model is Walmart, which launched its Walmart+ proposition back in September 2020, offering customers free delivery, the opportunity to earn Rewards (loyalty currency), fuel savings, free video streaming with Paramount+ and other benefits, for an annual fee of $98. What I find particularly interesting about this proposition is how Walmart follows Amazon's lead by placing free delivery of online products at the heart of its proposition, rather than the value delivered to customers shopping in its stores, which means that its significantly smaller proportion of e-commerce shoppers receive the lion's share of value. The reason I call this launch surprising is because Walmart had, until this point, been famously outspoken about not wanting to move into the loyalty space as it believed it went against its EDLP business model; 'We believe that all of our customers deserve the lowest price possible, not just certain customers' said Walmart Executive Vice President and CFO Charles Holley back in 2013.[5]

This is what makes the positioning of the proposition so important – an additional offering on top of its core EDLP model – 'We have always been a champion for the right item at the right price, but now it's more than that. We have the right shopping solutions at the right time, too.'[6] Of course, for the end customer the promise is of additional savings and greater convenience, while for Walmart the opportunity is to become a data-driven and digitally enabled business that can, for the first time, work towards delivering personalized marketing to customers.

During a Q4 earnings call in February 2022, Walmart CEO Doug McMillon stated that that 'Walmart+ is important. It helps us grow our e-commerce business. It helps us deepen the relationship with customers and have more data.' However, only moments later, in response to questions regarding how many members the scheme has, he goes on to say 'I don't think it would be good if everybody gets overly focused on Walmart+.'[7]

The reason I call this out is because it is my fundamental belief that there is no such thing as being 'overly focused' on the end customer, particularly those customers who have displayed their loyalty to you by signing up to your premium subscription service. It seems clear that McMillon's major focus is on building a business that can compete with Amazon, which requires a greater focus on all things digital. However, I would suggest that the only way to do that would be to be relentlessly focused on understanding why, how and when individual customers shop, in order to deliver a better, more personalized and genuinely seamless relationship with them, wherever they chose to do business with you.

According to research conducted by CIRP in July 2022, Walmart+ has currently hit a plateau of about 11 million members, which suggests that perhaps the scheme does need more focus in order to stand a chance of standing up to Amazon Prime.[8] In my view, the greatest opportunity for Walmart, and so many other bricks-and-mortar businesses out there, is to stop looking only to e-commerce as the driver of future growth but to focus on how to run great stores in the digital age, something for which I don't think there is any benchmark as yet. This is the reason I chose to write this book.

Retailers have faced change on a near-equivalent scale before: take, for example, the car-borne shopper. Digital is merely this century's agent of change. In order to cope with it, the adjustment will have to be every bit as fundamental as the closure of thousands and thousands of high-street stores and their replacement with out-of-town shopping destinations. I contend that retailers are now facing a fundamental imperative to position their businesses in the digital world by establishing a customer connection that drives insight and can deliver growth. Most people get that they should learn from the likes of Amazon. What they are less clear on is what stores should look and feel like in the digital world. The digital customer connection lies at the heart of both.

One-to-one: a new reality

In 2003, Clive Humby, Terry Hunt and Tim Phillips wrote a book, *Scoring Points*, about Tesco Clubcard, which is still one of the world's largest grocery loyalty schemes. In it, they wrote: 'Tesco could theoretically create 10 million lifestyle segments of one household each, but there isn't an affordable way to communicate with those customers at that level. Until every home is constantly linked through digital media that one-to-one dream remains a dream.'[9]

It's worth noting that these super-smart trailblazers in digital marketing, with whom I had the privilege of working to launch Tesco Clubcard, thought it would be households, not individual customers, we'd be connecting with. Just four years after they failed to dream, Apple's iPhone landed and changed the game completely.

Since then, computing power has increased and become more affordable, data sets have become easier to handle and artificial intelligence (AI) has developed at breakneck speed. It has just got easier and easier, and cheaper and cheaper, to create a one-to-one digital connection.

Yet, I just don't see people forging customer-centred digital connections at the rate they could, or in the places they're needed. By the way, e-commerce, as a still relatively new way of doing business in comparison to the store, does this like breathing. It watches every move you make, every hesitation, every click and everything that you add, take out or abandon in your basket; it can all be tracked online, and offers can be redesigned in real time on the basis of not only who you are, but what you do while shopping online.

In this sense, if you're running a physical location and lack the ability to establish digital customer connection in that location, chances are you're flying completely blind. I would say that flying blind in the face of such competition is madness. It's like driving to a new location with the satnav switched off. Why would you? In fact, you wouldn't dream of it. So, retail has got to change.

This is why bringing the digital opportunity into physical retail spaces is as important as the urgency is real. The new generation of retail businesses is exploiting this digital connection online. They are displacing the established operators, who are caught in the headlights of a juggernaut driven by the likes of Amazon and Alibaba as the most successful retailers in the world, powered by their digital first-mover advantage. But there is one major thing these online-first players have in common with the Googles and Ubers of this world: they are all *digitally enabled and data driven.*

The value of digital connection

When it comes to the best way of understanding the true value of creating a digital customer connection, I think of Steve Rothwell, my colleague and founder of Eagle Eye. He first recognized the power of digital customer connection during his early work based on the development of short message services (SMS), as the first incarnation of one-to-one text-based chat in the early days of mobile. It's important to highlight here what he learnt from SMS about mobile communication back then: that these mobile devices could enable an instantaneous digital connection with a person that went beyond mass, broadcast advertising or direct mail. The connection established is also personal. It's personal in a way that is becoming more pervasive every day, as we rely on our mobiles to manage every aspect of our lives, from staying in touch with friends and family and tracking our health to doing our banking and shopping.

Even back in the pre-iPhone days, I remember a visit to Nokia's headquarters in 2003 where I was shown one of the first Nokia Communicators with its clamshell design and full keyboard. As the Nokia business manager handed it to me, he said: 'This is not a phone, this is a trusted personal device.' How right he was, as most of us nowadays would sooner lose our wallets than our smartphones, we're so personally invested in them (and how little he knew that it would be Apple and not Nokia that would unlock this reality). Indeed, one recent study actually found that we check our mobile phones more than 21,000 times a year, with the average person spending over three hours and fifteen minutes a day on their smartphone.[10] So mobile is the enabler of an unprecedented opportunity to open up a one-to-one digital connection to consumers wherever they go, including in both physical and online stores.

I discovered the benefits of the one-to-one customer insight that came with the data gained from consumers swiping their loyalty cards and the resulting performance marketing impact of a direct-mail programme in the early days of Tesco Clubcard. In the same way, new competitors are reaping the rewards of running their businesses in a world where it's possible to open up and rapidly scale a direct digital channel through which they can connect with, and market to, their customers via the very devices they carry with them everywhere they go. I suggest it would be competitive suicide for today's established players not to do so too, where the Amazons, Alibabas and JD.coms of this world are already raising the competitive stakes. While many of the established players have also made online gains and know that e-commerce is a vital piece in the strategic puzzle, few bricks-and-mortar businesses also capitalize by harnessing the true value of a digital connection with individual customers in a way that offers consistent competitive value – not just online, but offline too.

Many capture anonymized customer data, on baskets, store footfall or delivery location for instance, which can be useful for pricing and promotion decisions. But it is obviously useless in terms of personalization and direct marketing. If your anonymous customer insight tells you, for example, that consumers who have a propensity to buy organic products are also starting to buy organic for their pets, this insight can helpfully inform buying and ranging decisions. The natural requirement is then to inform the consumers in that target group of what you have done – but, without a direct channel and knowing who the customers in this channel are, how do you do that? Pureplay e-commerce businesses open up this free, personalized, digital marketing channel as part of their business model; and, at the same time, their online operations give them a real-time view of who their customers are, as well as what they actually do when they shop online with them. This insight gives them the advantage of being able to put the customer at the centre of everything. The customer can drive demand, dictate ranging decisions and have an inbuilt personalized shopping experience that responds to their preferences and every click and scroll, on the fly; and it's only made possible with that individual digital connection to each customer.

Bricks-and-mortar businesses must aim to achieve this same level of insight and agility from their digital customer connections in an effort to level the competitive playing field, if they are ever to foster truly customer-centred, and omnichannel-powered growth.

Winners and losers

The online giants are currently winning because they have embraced digital transformation. They are digitally enabled and data driven, capitalizing on their real-time, mobile-enabled and personalized customer connections. Those they are displacing have tended to avoid potential loss by sticking to the status quo, rather than risk any possible gain by adapting to the change. But change is a constant in retail and there have been winners and losers throughout my career. In the 1970s, for example, the UK retail landscape was dominated by the now long-lost grocery banners of Fine Fare, Gateway, Kwik Save, Safeway, Main Stop, Templeton and Galbraith, Presto, WM Low and Hillards... it's a long list, alongside Tesco, Sainsbury's, Asda and Morrisons. The last four still survive today, having capitalized and thrived on all sorts of disruption. However, I believe we are now at a tipping point.

Winning with omnichannel

This is why the term 'omnichannel' has gained currency, requiring an omnipresent physical and digital market proposition. With the Latin root 'omni-' meaning 'all or one', omnichannel reflects the fact that customers do not distinguish or, therefore, make allowances for differences between shopping online or in a store, particularly when under the same retail brand or banner. Retailers shouldn't be making this distinction between channels either. The bar is being raised so high by digital, e-commerce and mobile expectations that retailers have to operate connected omnichannel businesses with a consistent customer value proposition across offline as well as online, or fail.

It would be remiss not to consider the early evidence that speaks to the value of customer connection, just as the potential of digital to personalize that connection started to emerge with omnichannel requirements. Figure 1.2 shows the extraordinary acceleration in Tesco's performance when the customer became the business's North

FIGURE 1.2 UK grocery retail market share shows Tesco's dominance from the mid-1990s

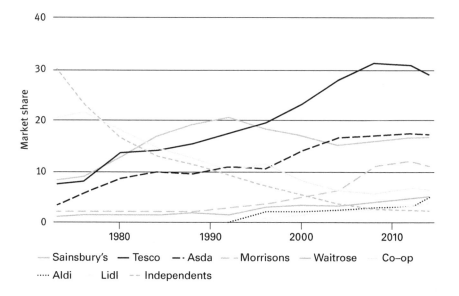

Star.[11] The launch of Clubcard in 1995 and the ensuing development of data-based direct marketing were at the centre of 15 years of industry-leading growth.

Today we are starting to understand the advantages that the winners in the current customer-facing landscape have. Amazon and Alibaba, founded on digital innovation, have rapidly climbed the ranks in terms of market capitalization (Table 1.1). This financial muscle gives them significant opportunity going forward. Amazon's acquisition of Whole Foods caused shockwaves, but what about Alibaba buying Costco or Tesco?

Despite Amazon being more than 2.5 times the size of Walmart, its closest competitor in terms of market capitalization, the majority of the list comprises leading retailers for whom the majority of their revenues still come from their physical stores, and so my advice to those businesses would be to push ahead and focus on everything they can do to enhance and unify the customer experience across all touchpoints.

TABLE 1.1 Market capitalization of the top 15 retail companies, as of January 2023[12]

Company	Market capitalization (US$ billion)
Amazon	945.31
Walmart	369.92
Home Depot	293.52
Alibaba	216.80
Costco	212.69
Lowe's Companies	119.62
CVS Health	98.87
Inditex	95.24
TJX Companies	86.62
Target	73.95
Jingdong Mall	71.71
Walmex	68.44
China Tourism Group Duty Free	56.75
Dollar General	48.61
Alimentation Couche-Tard	47.77

Adding further weight to the growing importance of omnichannel, the e-commerce-first giants already putting pressure on established global players are also now looking to exploit the very same power of bricks-and-mortar retail that many of these businesses, such as Carrefour, Tesco and Walmart, take for granted. This is because there are clear weaknesses in being an online-only or 'pureplay' operator: first, it is, and I predict will remain, the smaller part of the market, where consumers will still want the option of a physical retail presence; and 'going physical' is one of the few ways that Amazon (with its Amazon Go and Whole Foods banners) and Alibaba (with its Hema stores) can continue to scale their brands. (It is worth noting the significant number of ex-Tesco employees now working at Amazon. Could this suggest that Welwyn Garden City might twin with Seattle? Who knows. But Sleepless in Welwyn doesn't quite have the same ring to it.)

Second, while online pureplay retailers can analyse customer activity on their apps and sites, they still know relatively little about what these customers are doing in the physical world. So, the obvious way to raise the bar for pureplays is to create digitally enabled stores and become omnichannel operators. By applying online learnings to physical spaces, as these pureplays have started to do, I believe there is a massive digital dividend to be gained. This book seeks to spell out what that dividend looks like and how to access it.

Perhaps because of the store's inherent advantages of customer service, sensory selection, try before you buy and instant gratification, established bricks players think they can get by with their inflexible loyalty schemes, mystery shopper programmes and siloed e-commerce data to understand their customer shopping journeys. But this is not the case. The losers prove that change is the only constant. Businesses that have failed to adapt – of which there have been many, including Toys 'R' Us, BHS, McColl's, Missguided and Mothercare in the UK as well as Dimmeys and Harris Scarfe in Australia and Barneys New York, JCPenney and Lord & Taylor in the US – have fallen out of favour with today's consumers who are looking for convenience, relevance and value, delivered through an always-on digital connection.

The digital black hole

The internet and smart mobile devices have acted as catalysts in pushing the boundaries of not only how we live our lives but how we shop. But the race for digital connection with consumers has so far been limited to places and things, led by the likes of Google. This meets the huge demand to help us locate whatever we may need. Thanks to the increasingly sophisticated intelligence of Google's search algorithms, we can search for almost any product and easily find our preferred or most convenient storefront. This convenience is also responsible for a sharp increase in mobile 'near me' searching. According to Google, searches including 'near me' grew by 950 per cent in the UK from January 2018 to August 2022, showcasing the fact that proximity is a great proxy for relevance.[13] Search has been transformed as a result of this, and it is my firm belief that what 'near me' has done for search, 'now' will do for marketing, which is described in much more detail in Chapter 10.

So, a consumer can do a 'near me' search to find a product and navigate to the store, but the relevance and utility that come with having a digital connection via mobile ceases to exist once the customer is inside today's average store. They must either hunt for their chosen product themselves using analogue signage or find a customer associate to ask for help. On top of this, most retailers have Wi-Fi that is, at best, patchy and stores that, at worst, act like a Faraday cage, obliterating mobile data network signals when they don't bother to offer secure public Wi-Fi access. It's one of the few destinations where people put their phone back in their pocket because all digital enablement stops at the entrance to the store. A major project needs to be how shopping in its broadest sense can become a phone in the hand, not phone in the pocket activity. This is why in-store shopping is stuck in the past and the average store has become what I call 'a digital black hole'.

Yet it shouldn't be this way. There is no reason why all of this amazing digital change and opportunity to connect with customers should stop at the store, restaurant, bar and showroom door. Retailers are no strangers to using information technology (IT) for the benefits of automating their most manually intensive and error-prone store tasks. The digitization of sales, inventory and customer-related processes and information has enabled retailers to operate their businesses at scale; I include travel, leisure and hospitality, as well as quick service and food and beverage brands in this transformation. They all now use technology to centrally manage the information needed to run their often geographically dispersed, branch-based businesses; their digital presence can let you shop online; and they are even embracing IoT for increased operational efficiencies and ROI.

No one disputes that retailers know how to get the benefit from connecting up information about their products, places and things. However, they run the risk of overlooking the most important and increasingly accessible form of connection: to people, their customers. They risk knowing less about their customers than they do about their tills, lighting and fridges!

Creating compelling reasons to connect

Getting customers to engage digitally in-store needn't be difficult either. Thinking of the value of the one-to-one digital connection, bricks-and-mortar retailers should take a leaf out of the playbook of their online counterparts. They must use customers' mobile devices to make shopping in-store easier, faster and more convenient at the same time as obtaining data-driven insight into those customers' experiences during their online-to-offline shopping journeys in return. Take augmented reality (AR), for example. AR has made it possible to point the camera of your mobile device at an object, display or scene, and overlay an enhanced digital view that might include additional information or offers. AI-driven visual search technology works in much the same way, offering the consumer either some additional value or utility in accessing product information at the click of their smartphone camera shutter. These two buzzwordy digital features are very close to being readily available everyday realities.

Many grocers have now rolled out apps to encourage shoppers to use their mobile devices as they walk the store aisles, offering them convenience, speed of service and access to relevant information. The Asda Scan & Go app and Sainsbury's SmartShop in the UK as well as Loblaw's PC Optimum loyalty scheme in Canada are good examples of this online-to-offline integration, as are the apps of Rewe Group banner Merkur in Austria and Alibaba's Hema stores in China. But the point here is that there is still so much more scope to deliver an enhanced customer experience through this connection to the in-store customer.

It is an irrefutable fact that it is better to run a customer-facing business knowing who your customer is and what they are doing when they shop with you than not. Again, this may seem blindingly obvious. But what so many bricks-and-mortar businesses miss today is the fact that the digital world we live in has made it easier to gain that customer insight in their customer-facing physical spaces than ever before.

Most of the largest retailers and brands in the world are failing to capitalize on digital connections in-store quickly enough, in spite of the fact that they have armies of data scientists and analysts to help them better understand consumers and harness digital for competitive advantage. So, this book sets out to show shopkeepers, restaurateurs, publicans, salespeople and anyone with customer-facing operations how and why they must harness the power of digital in their physical spaces.

Bricks operators should exploit the fact that consumers want to engage digitally with retailers and brands. According to recent research by Klarna, 89 per cent of consumers have at least one shopping app downloaded on their mobile device.[14] Once this connection is in place, it becomes possible to open up a free direct marketing channel to them. E-commerce pureplays understand this, and that the best way to generate growth is not only through acquisition and conversion, but by increasing frequency to build retention. This is why we all receive so many emails from digital pureplays exploiting the free marketing channel they get as part of the condition of doing business with them.

So, based on lessons learnt using customer data to foster loyalty in the face of unprecedented change and, today, in my role as CEO of digital promotions and loyalty solutions provider Eagle Eye, I will share my first-hand experiences of the impact of developing the same opportunity through digital connection – both online and in-store, via mobile. As always, there will be winners and losers. But this book refines these learnings into the most important strategic steps every business must take to understand and win with digitally connected consumers, wherever they are, in-store as well as online, now and in future.

IN SUMMARY

- The digital imperative is about being digitally enabled and data driven in order that you can provide consumers with a convenient, personalized and unified shopping experience, wherever, whenever and however they choose to engage with you. In 2023 and beyond, this is table stakes.

- The majority of all sales are now digitally influenced and therefore there can be no denying the need to forge a compelling digital connection to customers.

- Digital enables better, simpler and cheaper marketing in our always-on, always-connected world.

- One-to-one is now a reality and omnichannel retailers must harness the power of personalization in order to compete with their pureplay rivals.

- Big moves get big results: we are at a tipping point and only the bold and focused will succeed.

Notes

1 Miglani, J (2022) Digital-influenced retail sales forecast, US, Forrester, 6 October, www.forrester.com/report/2022-digital-influenced-retail-sales-forecast-us/RES178197?ref_search=3544162_1674673148133 (archived at https://perma.cc/4YAQ-AE4S)

2 Kodali, S, Swerdlow, F and Wolken, S (2018) Digitally impacted retail sales in 2018: Still only half of retail, Forrester, 26 March, www.forrester.com/report/Digitally+Impacted+Retail+Sales+In+2018+Still+Only+Half+Of+Retail/-/E-RES122907; (archived at https://perma.cc/2WB2-UN6F)

3 Baxter, A (2021) Amazon Prime membership hits 200m, *Retail Leader*, 18 April, retailleader.com/amazon-prime-membership-hits-200m (archived at https://perma.cc/ZU4W-ABDE)

4   Barclaycard (2021) 'Subscription Society' surges as the average Brit spends
    £620 a year on sign-up services, home.barclaycard/press-releases/2021/08/
    Subscription-Society-surges/ (archived at https://perma.cc/J4NH-YFDU)

5   Seeking Alpha (2013) Wal-Mart Stores management presents at Bank of
    America Merrill Lynch Consumer & Retail Conference (transcript), 12 March,
    seekingalpha.com/article/1268861-wal-mart-stores-management-presents-at-
    bank-of-america-merrill-lynch-consumer-and-retail-conference-transcript
    (archived at https://perma.cc/4F4B-NNTS)

6   Walmart (2020) Walmart introduces Walmart+, 1 September, corporate.
    walmart.com/newsroom/2020/09/01/walmart-introduces-walmart (archived at
    https://perma.cc/2RJP-7B9H)

7   Motley Fool Transcribing (2022) Walmart Inc. (WMT) Q4 2022 earnings call
    transcript, 17 February, www.fool.com/earnings/call-transcripts/2022/02/17/
    walmart-inc-wmt-q4-2022-earnings-call-transcript/ (archived at https://perma.
    cc/T3QP-T68T)

8   Melton, J (2022) Walmart's paid loyalty program stops growing, but adds
    streaming video, *Digital Commerce 360*, 15 August, www.digitalcommerce360.
    com/2022/08/15/walmarts-paid-loyalty-program-stops-growing/ (archived at
    https://perma.cc/F6X2-C87H)

9   Humby, C, Hunt, T and Phillips, T (2003) *Scoring Points: How Tesco
    continues to win customer loyalty*, Kogan Page, London

10 Howarth, J (2023) Time spent using smartphones (2023 statistics), *Exploding
    Topics*, 9 January, explodingtopics.com/blog/smartphone-usage-stats (archived
    at https://perma.cc/75MN-JBSE)

11 Ruddick, G (2014) The rise and fall of British supermarkets, *The Telegraph*,
    27 August, www.telegraph.co.uk/finance/newsbysector/retailandconsumer/
    11057120/The-rise-and-fall-of-British-supermarkets.html (archived at https://
    perma.cc/8GW7-SDJB)

12 CompaniesMarketCap (2023) Largest companies by market cap,
    companiesmarketcap.com/retail/largest-retail-companies-by-market-cap/
    (archived at https://perma.cc/EX6P-H7T6)

13 Dearden, S and Massey, L (2022) The importance of an omnichannel strategy
    for peak season, Merkle, 24 October, www.merkle.com/emea/blog/importance-
    omnichannel-strategy-peak-season (archived at https://perma.cc/A2AK-YY9V)

14 Klarna Insights (2022) Mobile shopping report, Klarna, 15 March, https://
    insights.klarna.com/mobile-shopping/ (archived at https://perma.cc/ZJ7W-
    Z938)

2

Analogue learnings

I began my career in marketing at the consumer giant Unilever in 1979 and joined Tesco in 1982. But it was only in 1995, through the launch of Tesco Clubcard, that I saw marketing truly prove itself to be one of the key drivers of a business. Tesco discovered the power of customer connection and used the data it generated to drive insight and learnings that we used to drive business growth.

Clubcard's achievements changed the prevalent 20th-century conventional principle that consumers had to remain anonymous and marketing was aimed squarely at the masses. While digital communications were non-existent when the scheme launched, the use of direct mail enabled us to tap into that perennial desire to be recognized for one's custom and treated with a personal touch. So, the learnings from the successful execution and extraordinary success of Clubcard provided me with the knowledge of how to truly grasp the digital opportunity of building meaningful connections to customers.

Establishing customer connection

The most important moment on this journey of discovery was the day I had to get the Tesco Board of Directors to sign off the launch of Clubcard. Little did I know then that it would become one of my 'sliding door' moments. By that I mean it was one of those opportunities in life that can alter one's destiny.

It was 1994 and I was driving up to Brocket Hall for this board meeting. The grand, Grade I listed country hall, near Tesco's Cheshunt HQ in Hertfordshire, was where the full Board met once a year to discuss big strategic plans.

Even now I can recall how nervous I felt. Getting Clubcard signed off was a seriously big deal. I was trying to get the board to spend £100 million on what was, in effect, the UK's first data-based grocery loyalty scheme. Back then, that amounted to 20 per cent of the company's profits – as I said in Chapter 1, big moves get big results! But I wasn't going in there blind: we'd already trialled it for a year in 12 stores and the results were very encouraging. So, I wasn't quite betting the bank on Clubcard, but it certainly would have been severely career limiting if the first-year results had not at least matched the trial performance.

I do remember the fear that kept being expressed again and again during the trial period was that Clubcard and its 1 per cent discount would get us into a 'zero-sum game'. (We also trialled 2 per cent! But it didn't make much difference in uptake and participation levels.) The board was concerned that any gains Tesco might make by launching Clubcard would be wiped out by equivalent moves on the part of our competitors.

The final words in the discussion were from David Malpas, Tesco Managing Director and a hugely influential figure in the organization. 'We don't know how we will use the data [that Clubcard generates] or what value we will get from it,' he said. 'But we have to do this, because we can.' What he meant was that we could not profess to be a customer-focused business and yet pass up the opportunity to capture all of this information about who our customers were. I love that expression: 'We have to do this because we can.' It encapsulates what I would say to all business leaders about the digital opportunity available to them now. But that would make for a short book! So, Clubcard got the green light and it fell to me to make sure we extracted the maximum value from this new source of customer data over the subsequent years.

Soon after Clubcard's sign-off, Tesco management realized that fears of getting into a game where there would be no winners and losers were unfounded because of its first-mover advantage – just as those using digital customer connections have today. Tesco didn't invent the concept of loyalty marketing. But it created best practice to achieve new scale and levels of business sophistication with the application of customer data analytics by Tesco's Clubcard partner and now subsidiary, dunnhumby.

Clubcard also taught me an important lesson when it comes to creating a winning retail business: there is no such thing as an 'average customer'. The work I contributed to with Clubcard helped identify that many different types of customer shopped at Tesco. The mission of Clubcard was finding out how to be relevant to each of them.

Winning with loyalty

Officially launched in 1995, Clubcard was a one-point-per-£1-spent loyalty scheme, enabled by a plastic card with a magnetic stripe that was swiped at checkout. Points were collected, and rewards were paid out quarterly by direct mail (Figure 2.1). I led the project, reporting to Sir Terry Leahy. I'd been running the marketing department for

FIGURE 2.1 Opening Clubcard statement

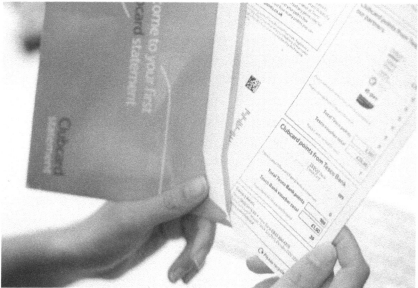

SOURCE © Tesco Plc

three years and he had been on the Tesco Board for the same amount of time. (Terry went on to become Tesco Deputy Managing Director in 1995, when I joined the Board as Marketing Director. In 1997, Terry became CEO.)

Within days of launch, more than 70 per cent of all Tesco sales – then some 3.5 million transactions – were being recorded and matched to Clubcard holders.[1] Within 12 months, Clubcard had gained 5 million members and Tesco at the same time acquired a panel of active customers who shared their feedback and shopping preferences. As Humby, Hunt and Phillips put it in their book about Tesco Clubcard, *Scoring Points*:[2] 'When Tesco said, "Thank you" to customers, they responded by opening wallets wider.'

When the first full-scale Clubcard statement mailing was sent out in the spring of 1995, Tesco saw a like-for-like sales boost of £17.8 million. Some 40 per cent of these sales were driven by Clubcard voucher redemptions and bigger member baskets.[3] This is why I am absolutely convinced that the customer obsession and innovation that Tesco fostered with Clubcard in 1995 drove the performance of the business for about the next 15 years.

Before Clubcard launched, Tesco's market share was about 25 per cent. By 2010, one pound out of every seven in the UK was spent with Tesco, when its share of the domestic UK grocery market peaked at 31.1 per cent and, in that year alone, generated £3.4 billion in profits across its entire business. As a measure of the contributing success of Clubcard, Terry (who led Tesco until 2011) has described it as the achievement in his Tesco career he is most proud of.

I interviewed Terry for this book. He reminded me that the brilliant thing about Clubcard was that, because it was first in mass grocery, and new and different, where UK consumers didn't at that point carry a wallet full of loyalty cards, its success in recognizing and thanking them for their custom also meant it was a great promotional engine. When same-store sales increased after it launched, Clubcard became self-funding.

Tim Mason (TM): Why did you pick Clubcard as the major achievement in your Tesco career?

Sir Terry Leahy (TL): I picked Clubcard because it was the beginning of the use of customer data when nobody else was using it.

If you look at industries like ours that have thin margins, slow growth, no patents and common economics, businesses don't really outperform each other. So, that unbelievable period of outperformance had to be driven by something. I know other things came in, around it and on top of it. But I think Clubcard was the thing that really drove it. If you remember the statistics, it was a huge shunt. I mean, it gave us 10 per cent like-for-like growth ahead of the industry for a period of time.

TM: I've only ever seen two things in my career which genuinely transformed performance. One was Operation Checkout in 1977 and the other was Clubcard. It's not that "One in Front" or everything else we did wasn't good for business. But it was all incremental by comparison and momentum maintaining. The extraordinary thing about Clubcard was, stores that had been in year-on-year decline for five straight years went positive. That rising tide was just amazing.

TL: The other thing about Clubcard, in contrast to Operation Checkout, is that it delivered incredibly high return on investment. There was also a first-mover advantage.

TM: Well, it paid for what it cost, didn't it? The other way I look at it, to get any business to spend 20 per cent of its net profits on one project is pretty brave. To some extent you can see why it took so long to reach the decision. I'm sure you can remember those interminable discussions about a zero-sum game? It taught me an interesting lesson, though: I think the zero-sum game is spurious, because people just don't see the world the way that you do. So, even though you may think a measure is worthwhile, they may not.

TL: In the end, there was a zero-sum reaction. Virtually every other retailer did end up having a loyalty card. But they weren't as effective, or it was a year, or two years later before they were able to launch them.

Below is a brief summary of some of the retailers in the UK that followed in Clubcard's wake by launching a loyalty scheme:

- February 1995 – Tesco
- October 1995 – Safeway, Sainsbury's
- 1997 – Boots
- 2008 – Iceland
- 2011 – Waitrose
- 2014 – Morrisons
- 2015 – M&S
- 2016 – The Co-op
- 2020 – Lidl
- 2022 – Asda

Note: I stated in the first edition of this book that 'It's just a matter of when, not if, for discounters and EDLP retailers to enter the loyalty arena' and it does feel good to be proved right with the examples above!

In my view this isn't a zero-sum game. I also believe that the energy and passion with which you do something you believe in far outweighs what you tend to invest in something you have copied. This is why, during its heyday, the Tesco strategy was typified by doing things for customers first, and therefore letting them set the agenda. On the rare occasions when Tesco had to fast-follow, we made doubly sure we owned it, otherwise there would have been no point in doing it at all.

Building business value

If my career has taken me on a journey to harness the value of digitally enabled and data-driven customer connection, Clubcard and its objectives were the beacons that guided my way. We'll examine Clubcard's objectives specifically in a moment. But it is first necessary to show you how Tesco got there.

Of course, it wasn't always the case that Tesco had clear, loyalty-led objectives. Some had questioned Tesco dropping the Green Shield Stamps savings scheme in 1977. But the need for Clubcard didn't emerge until after a number of years of building out Tesco's business under Terry's predecessor, Tesco Chairman and CEO, Lord Ian MacLaurin of Knebworth, to the point where it was in a position to place the customer effectively at the heart of everything it did.

I first met Lord MacLaurin in 1980. I was a Unilever trainee and he was the talismanic Managing Director of Tesco (having joined Tesco himself in 1959 as a management trainee). I remember the description of Tesco as a 'distinctly tacky operation' back in the 1960s that he used in his autobiography, *Tiger by the Tail*.[4] Then in 1977 he led Tesco to launch 'Operation Checkout', update the business and ditch Green Shield Stamps.

It was MacLaurin who led the board to abandon the Green Shield Stamps sales reward scheme. This saved £20 million a year and funded a move to cutting prices. Other than perhaps Clubcard, I doubt there has ever been a retail business initiative as successful as Operation Checkout. It enabled Tesco to really move the price list and slash prices by between 3 and 26 per cent on about 1,500 food items. In the period between 1977 and 1980, Tesco's market share went from 7.5 to 12 per cent, which was an unbelievable achievement. MacLaurin and his team had judged the grocery shopping mood of the nation perfectly.

But the business also nearly went bust. It couldn't cope with its new-found popularity. Straining every sinew to keep the business running meant it was in danger of becoming a victim of its own success. Unless it could be modernized in double-quick time, it would sink. The 'pile it high, sell it cheap' model had allowed very decentralized store management to do pretty much anything, as long as they turned a profit. So, this approach had to be replaced with more central controls and the economies of scale available with centralized ranging, buying and merchandising.

Tesco's management also looked at the likes of Sainsbury's and M&S, and asked: 'What do they do well that we don't do?' The strategy back then was very much about centralization of operational control that was competition-based and focused, with a heavy reliance on benchmarking, fuelled by competitive paranoia.

Distribution centres were built, and stores were told the products they should stock, the prices they should charge and the promotions they should mount. Systems were built to hold it all together and new people hired to do the work. The stores didn't always take kindly to handing over control to these upstarts in head office, and it was the start of a transformation that was far from certain to succeed. But MacLaurin won, principally because he had turned the best poachers into gamekeepers.

In parallel with all of this activity, Tesco's property strategy was reviewed. A modern blueprint was developed for a car-borne age. It featured the out-of-town superstore, with free parking and petrol forecourts. Hundreds of old, small stores were closed and the slack was more than picked up by these big, shiny new ones.

From competitive paranoia to customer obsession

By 1982, when I joined Tesco as a junior marketer, Tesco was not out of the woods. But at least it was out of the depths of the darkest forest. Having first been elected UK Prime Minister in 1979, Margaret Thatcher was still in power and consumers were becoming more aspirational. But Tesco didn't sell fresh poultry or sandwiches; the fruit and veg on offer in the local market were better; Chicken Kiev could only be found at M&S; and Tesco's own-brand ranges were sparse and of poor quality compared to Sainsbury's. New skills were needed to complement those of the gamekeepers and so marketers, pack designers and food technologists were hired. More progress was made, and then a restructure put the right leaders in place.

By the mid-1980s Tesco was revamping its infrastructure, systems, product range, employee skill sets and store estate all at the same time. When it got to the end of the process of modernizing the business, it was the end of the 1980s and recession had hit. The modernization process had run out of puff because, although Tesco did benchmarking very well, it wasn't really teaching the business anything new; it wasn't giving Tesco any new drivers for the business.

The customer quickly replaced Tesco's competition as the new North Star when Terry joined the board in 1992 during another restructure. Significantly at the time, he was the first marketing director to be appointed to the board of a UK retailer. It became marketing's role to bring the voice of the customer to the table and demonstrate it as being heard, underlined by the belief that, whenever Tesco could give customers more of what they wanted, it won. This laid the foundation for Tesco to become a more marketing-focused company through the rest of the 1990s and to start asking: 'What are Tesco customers actually doing and what do they want from their grocery supermarket?' The answer to that question led to the 'Every Little Helps' motto and the business tackled the things customers disliked, such as queuing. So, it took queues out with the 'One in Front' campaign: if there was a queue with more than two people in it (i.e. one customer in front of you), the store would open an extra checkout until queues had died down or every till was manned. This reduced queue length, but also differentiated Tesco from the competition by building up its reputation for understanding and addressing shopping pain points.

Tesco has always taken its lead from customers to give them more of what they wanted from the store experience in terms of store formats and range. While many customers were starting to shop at discounters, including Kwik Save, Aldi and Netto, it introduced the 'Value' lines in 1993. Many customers also liked to treat themselves. But it was hard to spot what they considered a treat, so Tesco launched its 'Finest' range. Then it returned to small, urban convenience stores, and so the first Tesco 'Express' store was launched at the end of 1994 in London; the chain of Dundee-based William Low stores was bought from under Sainsbury's nose to extend the Tesco footprint in Scotland in 1995; and, in the same year, it also really committed to online shopping via the internet with the launch of what would go on to become Tesco.com.

All of that activity worked really well. Such incremental change meant customers could see that Tesco understood their lives and was on their side. It got to the point where the business actually had such good visibility of Tesco customer activity that it then wanted to try to work out what was driving it. What it didn't know, however, was *who* was doing it. Tesco didn't know *who* its customers were. That

FIGURE 2.2 The front cover of *Tesco Today*, February 1995. Then Tesco Marketing Director, Tim Mason, and Chairman and CEO Sir Ian (now Lord) MacLaurin celebrate the launch of Clubcard with a store associate at Tesco Surrey Quays

was why Tesco launched Clubcard in 1995 (Figure 2.2). It put the *who* into the customer equation and spawned another 15 years of profitable product, promotional and marketing development.

It is also why Clubcard was not just the equivalent of 'electronic Green Shield Stamps', as David Sainsbury, former Chairman of rival J Sainsbury plc (1992–7), dismissed it as at the time.[5] Tesco overtook Sainsbury's to become Britain's largest grocer.

By the time MacLaurin retired in 1997, the Tesco team had built six drivers of growth:

- Tesco Extra;
- Tesco.com;
- Tesco Express;
- Tesco Personal Finance;

- Tesco Clubcard data-based marketing tools; and
- a nascent international business.

Customer curiosity

I've had some fantastic opportunities during my career thanks to marketing being my core discipline. But marketing services are, to be honest, rather dull. Good marketing, however, as we've begun to explore with Clubcard, can really make a difference to a business; and, if you want to do good marketing, either work for a business that is famous for understanding what good marketing is and how to do it, or work for somebody who gets it and has authority to do things differently.

Clubcard was the culmination of a number of customer-focused initiatives. It came out of the fact that one of Terry's great attributes is that he always wants to know more about the customer. He has a remorseless enquiring mind. Just as the Green Shield Stamps move in 1977 had its doubters, equally there were those for whom the logic of launching a new loyalty scheme in 1995 as the next step in Tesco's evolution wasn't exactly clear. Clubcard was the culmination of Tesco's strategic shift: 'To create value for customers to earn their lifetime loyalty'.

In a way, the two key reasons Tesco was able to make a major difference to its fortunes with Clubcard were: first, those traits in Terry that led him constantly to want to know more about customers; and, second, the industry environment the business was operating in. Tesco could write the playbook on deriving maximum value from data-driven customer connection and customer-centricity, and, for a period of time, it delivered exceptional performance.

> **Tim Mason:** Candidly, Terry, I think you are unusual in this: I think what's personally always fascinated you is, what do people do? And then how do I make money out of that insight? So, you went out to look for more and more ways of finding out what they do. You know, just trying to get an angle on what people do and why people do it.

Sir Terry Leahy: Good marketing is much closer to anthropology, being curious about people, philosophy, psychology and asking questions, as well as the freedom of thought. In traditional marketing roles, I don't think you get that freedom. You've inherited a legacy toolkit and you're just asked to use that toolkit. I don't think that's conducive to good marketing. I think, if you look at the best firms: a) the toolkit is usually pretty good; and b) there's also maybe a bit of extra room to think about new things and innovate.

With Clubcard, we had no toolkit to inherit. There was some new data. The first data that came in was barcode data [from the supply chain and EPOS] and that was terribly exciting. I mean, you previously had store deliveries. But that wasn't really accurate, and people didn't look at that data in that way. But, for the first time, we had item movements. Then, with Clubcard, we got shopper purchasing data.

Not so long ago, a former Tesco marketing colleague said to me, 'What people don't realize is that Clubcard was the pinnacle of Tesco's "Every Little Helps" strategy.' The strategy was: 'To create value for customers to earn their lifetime loyalty'. To deliver against that, we had to be absolutely clear about what we were aiming for – lifetime loyalty – and we had to be able to measure it using the customer data we were generating. So, very quickly, Clubcard became absolutely central to what Tesco wanted to do and how they wanted to do it, as it had authentically evolved out of the existing strategy, rather than it being more like: 'Our rivals have got something flash, we'd better get one too'.

This point about being true to yourself and being sure that what you do comes out in your strategy, rather than its being somebody else's strategy, is very important. Or, as Terry put it: 'You thought that the relationship between you and the customer was commercial, and it was, but you were also trying to be more useful to them, because you understood them better. That is marketing.'

The value of Clubcard's connection

The objectives of Clubcard were threefold:

1 To recognize customers and thank them for their custom.
2 To enable direct performance marketing in a way rarely used by a branch-based grocery business.
3 To capture data on customers' shopping behaviour that would enable us to run the business better.

One of the critical questions to answer for any loyalty scheme is how much is what you're offering the customer a 'thank you' that rewards continued custom and how much is it a route to performance marketing, which, by definition, is pretty transactional, that is, I will give you this, if you do that? What do you think the right balance should be in your business between using a scheme like Clubcard to encourage elasticity, that is, to buy more, and just to say 'thank you' to your customers?

The central tenet of the Clubcard scheme was that the idea of saying 'thank you' is very important. So, Tesco absolutely started from there. The points earned were themselves in effect a small 'thank you'. But so is money off on a product that you buy every week. Conversely, money off an item you have never bought or, even more so, an item from a category you have never bought is clearly stretching spend, which relies more on the mechanics of performance marketing. So, you need to strike a balance between emotional and functional loyalty.

To achieve this, we typically worked within a framework where we allocated the majority of our marketing budget to our very best customers, using it purely to say 'thank you'. With customers who were a little less loyal, we tended to do a blend of thanking and stretching, and with the customers who were a little bit less loyal than those in the second category, we were tempting and stretching and not so much thanking. If you imagine a spectrum of offers, you could have offers that are effectively thanking you for doing what you're doing: here's a treat, something that rewards you. It might be

FIGURE 2.3 Thanks versus stretch – the spectrum

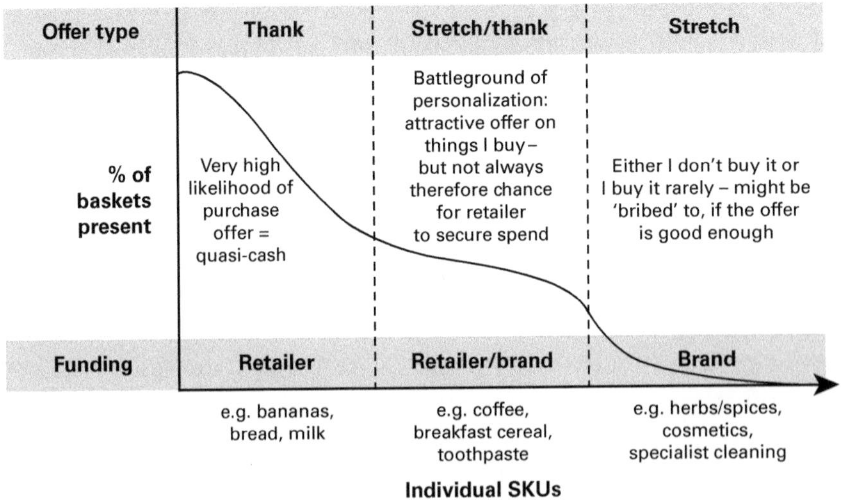

Offer type	Thank	Stretch/thank	Stretch
% of baskets present	Very high likelihood of purchase offer = quasi-cash	Battleground of personalization: attractive offer on things I buy – but not always therefore chance for retailer to secure spend	Either I don't buy it or I buy it rarely – might be 'bribed' to, if the offer is good enough
Funding	Retailer	Retailer/brand	Brand
	e.g. bananas, bread, milk	e.g. coffee, breakfast cereal, toothpaste	e.g. herbs/spices, cosmetics, specialist cleaning

Individual SKUs

money off or gift-like in its nature, like a privilege. Then you've got things that stretch you and encourage you to reach a little bit higher, such as enticing you to buy our Finest steak rather than our ordinary steak, or to buy a more expensive bottle of wine than the one you normally buy, or you could stretch customers to shop in more adjacent categories; so, I see you buy dry grocery, but you never buy fresh; so, how do I encourage you into that part of the store? (Figure 2.3.)

Of course, to the modern marketer for whom one-to-one marketing is a reality, this will seem a very crude approach, but it was a huge first step on the long journey to personalization, which enabled us to flex marketing spend where it was going to have the greatest impact.

The importance of frequency

One of my earliest lessons when Tesco turned on the data light was what an unbelievable indicator frequency was of a) customer loyalty and b) customer value. Almost overnight, our long-held beliefs were transformed when we saw that the £100+ overflowing trolleys belonging to the 'mother with two kids' weren't necessarily our most valuable when positioned against the 'convenience customer' who visited us five times a week, spending what we initially thought was an insignificant £20 a visit. Suddenly, when comparing monthly spend, the value equation stacked up very differently. With Clubcard, you could actually see that there was a whole group of 'can't stay aways' who were hugely valuable when their individual trips were combined. What this then taught me was – and it seems obvious with the benefit of hindsight – that frequency was the most significant driver of performance, because encouraging another shopping trip generates between £20 and £100, whereas encouraging the purchase of another product generates £2 to £5. Obvious, I know, but before we saw the customer data, we did not understand the scale of it. This is another reason why tapping today's digital connection to gain this kind of insight from a store – and not just online – is imperative.

Creating strategic advantage

In the move from mass, anonymized service to creating a customer connection, Tesco's Clubcard advantage was to quickly realize the value of the connection it provided. At that time, the difference between a physical and digital connection didn't really exist, let alone matter. The sale was tied to the customer ID and that was the key. So, I chose to direct mail the rewards, rather than build up an at-the-till rewards redemption capability, because of my desire to open up Tesco's direct marketing capabilities. I applied the logic that either the Clubcard Reward vouchers could go for free with direct marketing letters or vice versa.

In fact, a quarterly reward mailing created four trade-driving events a year. People chose to shop at Tesco on the next shopping trip after the mailing. Given that no customer is 100 per cent loyal, this was a huge fillip to trade. Subsequently, you could actually see Tesco's market share peak just after the mailing and then slowly decline until the next mailing, which kicked it up again. The impact of the mailing was palpable: sales went up, stock levels came down, store footfall and till throughput increased. Not a single person in the company could be in any doubt that Clubcard was good for trade, with the result that everyone was a supporter.

Here, I learnt that you are really on to something if you can create artificial 'seasonal' peaks in your business. Prime Day is an example of Amazon doing this for its business, earning it $6.8 billion in 2021,[6] a growth of 186 per cent since the 2017 figures I quoted in the first edition.[7] Alibaba's more established Singles' Day Shopping Festival hauled in an incredible $84.5 billion (underlining the growth of consumer spending in the East),[8] a 238 per cent increase since 2017, illustrating that these strategies are continuing to gain traction.[9] These sales events are also flanked by the global, multibillion-dollar shopping days, Black Friday and Cyber Monday, so nowadays there's no shortage of artificial, as well as seasonal, peaks. It may be a case of 'if you can't beat them, join them'. If it is, then best make sure you have a customer connection through which to communicate your great deals, special offers and new products.

The central point of this book is that *connection is king*; and the most valuable connection of all is connection to customers. Therefore, it pays to nurture and develop this connection. In my view, the advent of digital access and communication means it has never been easier to do, and more valuable to businesses and consumers alike.

IN SUMMARY

- The 'average customer' doesn't exist. Use data to understand individuals and use that understanding to endeavour to make their lives better and simpler.

- Frequency is the major driver of incremental value, which can be heavily boosted during artificial 'seasonal' peaks.

- If you agree that customer connection is king, find a compelling reason to create the connection and pursue it relentlessly. In my view, 'will' always outweighs 'skill'.

- If you really want to create value and lifetime loyalty, you've got to earn it. To know if you are being successful, you've got to measure it. You manage what you measure.

Notes

1 Humby, C, Hunt, T and Phillips, T (2007) *Scoring Points: How Tesco continues to win customer loyalty*, p 63, Kogan Page, London

2 Humby, C, Hunt, T and Phillips, T (2007) *Scoring Points: How Tesco continues to win customer loyalty*, Kogan Page, London

3 Humby, C, Hunt, T and Phillips, T (2007) *Scoring Points: How Tesco continues to win customer loyalty*, p 75, Kogan Page, London

4 MacLaurin, I (1999) *Tiger by the Tail: A life in business from Tesco to test cricket*, Macmillan, London

5 Lee, J (1996) Marketing focus: Does Tesco hold all the cards? *Campaign*, 15 February, www.campaignlive.co.uk/article/marketing-focus-does-tesco-hold-cards/58176 (archived at https://perma.cc/2V4B-QTUN)

6 Spangler, T (2021) Amazon Prime Day 2021 generated $6.8 billion in gross sales, up 9%: Analysts, *Variety*, 24 June, variety.com/2021/digital/news/amazon-prime-day-2021-revenue-1235004305/ (archived at https://perma.cc/7YCB-EUYR)

7 Ali, F (2017) Amazon Prime Day analysis in 5 charts, *Digital Commerce 360*, 20 July, www.digitalcommerce360.com/2017/07/20/amazon-prime-day-analysis-in-5-charts/ (archived at https://perma.cc/7EDR-ATZT)

8 Tan, H (2021) Alibaba posted $84.5 billion in Singles Day sales this year. That's a record high – but also its slowest growth ever, *Business Insider*, 12 November, www.businessinsider.com/alibaba-record-85-billion-dollars-singles-day-sales-2021-11?r=US&IR=T (archived at https://perma.cc/6UVR-QTPV)

9 Wang, H (2017) Alibaba's Singles' Day by the numbers: A record $25 billion haul, *Forbes*, 12 November, www.forbes.com/sites/helenwang/2017/11/12/alibabas-singles-day-by-the-numbers-a-record-25-billion-haul/#4677e8b81db1 (archived at https://perma.cc/9M4T-QQP9)

3

Is loyalty dead?

To create value for customers to earn their lifetime loyalty.
TESCO'S CORE PURPOSE, ARTICULATED TO CONSUMERS
AS 'EVERY LITTLE HELPS'

Periodically I get asked by journalists: 'Is loyalty dead?' This is a ridiculous notion, of course. Loyalty isn't about the mechanics of points, a coupon, stamp card or scheme. It's a feeling, as central a defining part of our human nature as the basic 'fight or flight' reaction; it's as irrational as love and as fundamental as breathing.

Fred Reichheld is a loyalty guru and the creator of the Net Promoter Score, now known as the Net Promoter System (NPS). His latest book, *Winning on Purpose*, is subtitled *The unbeatable strategy of loving customers* and continues to make a very strong case for why earning customer loyalty by following the golden rule – treating customers as they would like to be treated – makes absolute business sense.[1]

Thinking about loyalty in its truest sense, it is unlikely that consumers ever feel as loyal to a business or brand as they do to their family, school or sports team. That doesn't mean that trying to be someone's go-to grocery store or restaurant, or favourite fashion or tech brand isn't a worthwhile and, indeed, valuable thing to do. The question more accurately put that most businesses have is: 'Are plastic cards and points-based schemes dead?' Or, when the stripped-down, convenient offerings from limited-range discounters and e-commerce retailers are winning, have 25-year-old loyalty schemes had their day?

As the newly promoted team that were running Tesco in the early 1990s, we were very influenced by Reichheld's first book, *The Loyalty Effect*.[2] In it, he argues that having loyal customers, that is, a lower attrition rate than the competition, compounds pretty quickly over a remarkably short number of years to create a noticeably larger and more profitable business. He states that reducing customer defections by as little as five points – from, say, 15 to 10 per cent per year – can double profits. He also argues that loyal staff, those with longer tenure, are more productive than their seasonal colleagues. (Interestingly, I note the Aldi model is to keep store managers in place for many years. In judging a Store Manager of the Year Award for *The Grocer* magazine in 2017, I met Ade Ogbomoide, who had done 18 years as manager of Aldi Catford.)[3] Finally, Reichheld argues that loyal shareholders create a more stable foundation for running a business.

Inspired by Reichheld, Tesco's core purpose became: 'To create value for customers to earn their lifetime loyalty'. At the centre of this strategy was Clubcard. From the start, Tesco wanted the quarterly Clubcard statement to be perceived as the 'most valuable and popular piece of junk mail'. It was founded as a scheme that was just one part of an overall strategy around loyalty.

Having a strategy based on knowing who your customers are to serve them better seems to me to have as much relevance today as it ever did. Indeed, this is what many of the large e-commerce players are doing. There are other strategies that businesses use to connect with and deliver value to their customers, including discounting, promotions, aspiration, innovation, peer pressure and even fear. However, I, like Simon Sinek describes in his book, *Start With Why*, would describe these as 'manipulations':

> I cannot dispute that manipulations work. Every one of them can indeed help influence behavior and every one of them can help a company become quite successful. But there are trade-offs. Not a single one of them breeds loyalty. Over the course of time, they cost more and

more. The gains are only short-term… In any circumstance in which a person or organization wants more than a single transaction, if there is a hope for a loyal, lasting relationship, manipulations do not help.[4]

For a mass-market, added-value business, customer-centricity is a very good differentiator. If you agree with that, the strategic priority has become to establish a real-time connection to consumers that they use with sufficient frequency because of the value derived from regular engagement via that connection. How you create and maintain this connection is a life's work.

Analogue loyalty learnings

Before Clubcard, Tesco knew *what* was being bought but not *who* was buying it. As we've seen, the differentiator was knowing the *who*. Once you know the *who*, you are a step closer to working out *why*. The '*what–who–why*', that's real insight. So, if you really want to see what customers value, you had better measure it. Following the launch of Clubcard, Tesco couldn't know everything, but it now knew *who* its customers were, where they lived, *where* and *when* they shopped and *which* departments they shopped in. From here, the marketing team could make a start on understanding and targeting them with offers and rewards.

This is when the DIAL way of working (see Figure 3.1; and explained in more detail in the next chapter) became the standard 'go-to' Tesco methodology: it had invested £100 million to get the data, and at that meeting I referred to earlier, David Malpas had pointed at me and said he'd get us a return on our investment. So I insisted the data was reviewed, insights derived, action taken and the resulting impact on loyalty measured. Even from the very beginning, loyalty was *the* KPI for Clubcard – something that every data-derived activity was designed to achieve and measured against.

It was nearly 30 years ago that dunnhumby representatives presented the Clubcard pilot results at a board meeting in Cheshunt. Tesco's then Chairman, Lord Ian MacLaurin, famously said: 'What scares me about this is that you know more about my customers after

FIGURE 3.1 DIAL: the operating model for customer-centric, data-driven decision making

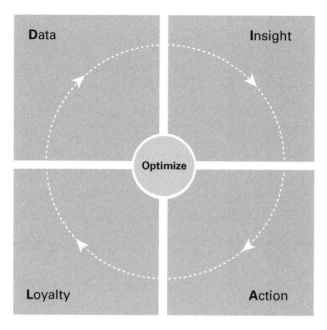

three months than I know after 30 years.'[5] It is this knowledge of *who* your customers are that makes the concept and dynamics of customer data so enduringly powerful.

Having established the value of knowing who your customers are, it seems pretty obvious to me that you might as well know who the best ones are. Furthermore, I believe that, by virtue of going digital, customer connection is more valuable than ever before when combined with good, creative marketing that is relevant, useful and acknowledges the person and/or shopping mission behind the purchase.

Clubcard was founded on a desire to say 'thank you' to customers and a belief that the business could be improved by using the data generated by the scheme. As a result, the decision was made that we would thank customers directly for their continued custom through the quarterly statement mailing, which included an array of rewards and offers as well as an individual update on the customer's value accrued through the scheme. It was an extremely successful use of performance marketing, where no one had done it before in the UK, so Tesco gained a first-mover and innovator's advantage. Tesco was the lead dog of the sled and the scenery only ever changes for the lead dog. As the effects of the promotions it delivered started to wain (as anyone in the business will know, lapping last year's extremely successful promotion this year is, at best, bittersweet), the direct marketing capabilities of the scheme started to improve, and the scheme itself was enhanced with additional rewards provided by suppliers and third-party partners, so momentum was maintained.

Thanking customers is about recognizing them as individuals and offering them something of value; it sounds self-evident, but it really was a strategy built upon politeness. It is a shared belief of Sir Terry Leahy's and mine that good marketing is good manners. Tesco hoped people would like its offer a bit better for being the only one that bothered to say 'thank you'. That's just human nature. The transactional element of the programme enabled the measurement of functional aspects of its operations, such as the performance of its stores and the products it sells, or 'data-based retailing' as I like to call it. More of that in Chapter 5.

Within the retail industry, loyalty-type schemes are often discussed within the 'give to get' framework, which refers to the fact that earning the privilege of connection to consumers depends on each one granting you access to their shopping data and personal information in exchange for the opportunity to receive better value. Following the launch of Clubcard, we learnt pretty quickly that if done well, this 'give to get' model can become a hugely valuable virtuous circle. The customer is incentivized to 'give' their shopping data to the business so that they can 'get' the value offered to them as part of the loyalty scheme (in Tesco's example, this was points). The data is then used by the retailer to generate insights to drive trade, fund greater marketing efficiency and run the business better. These data-driven activities improve the shopping experience for the customer, therefore improving their loyalty, meaning they shop more, which delivers more data, which can be used to generate more insights and so on.

FIGURE 3.2 The Clubcard Customer Contract[6]

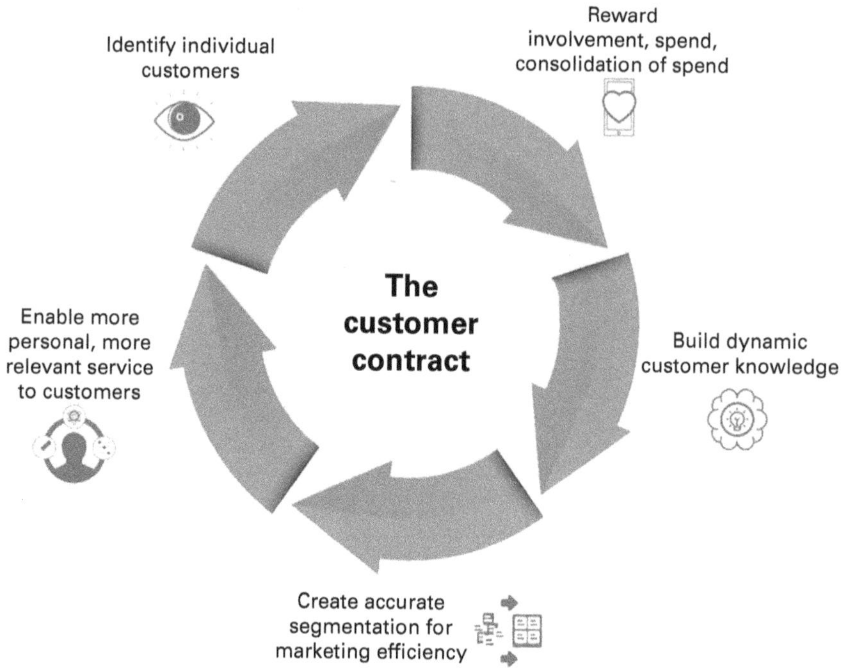

This became known as the Clubcard Customer Contract in *Scoring Points* (Figure 3.2).

Amazingly, nearly 30 years on, this model holds true today and reinforces the point regarding the virtuous circle. In this sense, Clubcard absolutely wasn't an acquisition strategy; it was aimed at retention, where Tesco could strike the right balance between emotional and transactional value. But the logic also followed that, if enough existing Tesco customers returned, this would support a self-sustaining organic acquisition strategy as well. Growth is fuelled when your best customers recruit new customers by being your best brand advocates. Reichheld calls it 'earned growth' which is the best growth of all.[7]

Customer-informed differentiation

Even in the 1990s the point about the Clubcard Customer Contract, which established the loyalty scheme's principles, was that Tesco was strategically clear on how it would manage this new 'give to get' relationship it was asking customers to enter. It showed the sort of people its employees were and therefore the values Tesco held. Tesco also developed a Customer Charter, which was a statement of how it would behave that was codified in the very early days of the scheme. The Clubcard Customer Charter came entirely from Terry.

What was it about a charter that caused Terry Leahy to be so focused on it and to make it so important, as well as making sure Tesco had one and that everybody in the organization knew, understood and followed it? He said:

> It was a completely innocent age. It wasn't discussed at all in the beginning – and, I don't mean just by us, but by anyone in the whole world. I think that the Charter came from a respect for customers we genuinely had, that we weren't going to peddle their data to a third party or sell them something they didn't want. So, at the beginning, it was a pure respect of true marketing, whereby you would only use the knowledge you had in order to serve them better in some way.

TESCO CLUBCARD CUSTOMER CHARTER, 1996

At Tesco we are committed to protecting the privacy of all our Clubcard members. And to make sure you know exactly what we do with your personal details, we have set out the Clubcard Customer Charter.

- We use your personal details to send your statement and any vouchers you've earned to your home without delay.
- This information also enables us to send you details and offers on things that may be of interest to you.
- And of course we want to make sure any coupons you receive are for products that you'd actually want. For instance, if you tell us you're a vegetarian, we'll make sure you're not sent coupons for meat products.
- Your personal details will not be disclosed to any other company unless it is necessary for the operation of the Clubcard scheme.
- We comply strictly with the terms of the Data Protection Act 1984.

- If at any time you would like all your details taken off the database, we will do so immediately.

- If you requested not to be contacted for research or not to be sent other offers and services through the Clubcard scheme, we will only send you your statement mailing.

- If you have any queries or would like to give us any additional information about yourself (such as your dietary requirements) phone the Helpline free on 0800 59 16 88.

Knowing your customer

As Terry suggests, the early Clubcard days were 'an innocent age' before the days of social media and retargeted advertising that follows you around the web. Yet, the concept of loyalty has, to varying extents, still proven a major factor in the fortunes of retail winners, then and now. All these years later, the founding values of Clubcard's Contract and Charter still apply: that is, I (the customer) *give* you (the retailer) my data because I trust you to make sure I *get* something good in return.

The issue nowadays is when it becomes a question of whether or not I trust Google or Facebook, for example. So, you must use the 'give to get' relationship customers enter into with your business or brand not only to give them incentives to get more of their custom by rewarding the behaviour you seek, but also to show the sort of business you are. I was recently asked what I recommended with regard to avoiding 'creepiness' from a personalized marketing point of view. My somewhat flippant response was 'it's amazing how creepy customers will let you be, providing you create enough value'. Although flippant, I do think it was directionally correct.

So, for the naysayers, who still proclaim that 'loyalty is dead', I say that knowing who your customers are, especially your best customers, and being able to communicate with them directly is an invaluable business benefit. The people who say loyalty is dead are the ones not doing it, or doing it badly. Meanwhile, there are huge amounts of ongoing activity and consolidation in the loyalty space, proving that those who know the inherent business benefits of loyalty are investing even more in it:

- Just as Tesco progressively increased its investment in dunnhumby during the 2000s, Kroger acquired its part of dunnhumby's US business in 2015 to bring its data analytics capabilities across the Atlantic and create a new consumer insights subsidiary called 84.51°.

- UK grocer J Sainsbury plc bought the Nectar loyalty scheme from Canadian marketing and loyalty provider Aimia in 2018 for approximately $85 million. Sainsbury's was a founding partner of the scheme in 2002. Explaining the move, Sainsbury's executives said it was taking Nectar back in-house to support its 'strategy of knowing its customers better than anyone else'.[8]

- In 2013 Woolworths paid $20 million for a 50 per cent stake in Australia's biggest data analytics company, Quantium. Quantium states that its personalization engine means customers are five times more likely to purchase a product than would be the case with standard marketing.[9] By 2016, Quantium was reported to be worth $400 million.[10]

- In 2017, Loblaw in Canada made a huge investment in loyalty by merging two existing loyalty programmes, Loblaw's PC Plus and Shoppers Optimum, with 8 million and 11 million members respectively, to become the largest loyalty scheme in Canada.[11]

- Following the acquisition of the Asda business from Walmart by TDR Capital and the Issa brothers in 2021, Asda went on to launch its Asda Rewards app following a significant investment in technology and digital capability in 2022. Just 3 months after launching nationwide, Asda reported it had amassed 2.7 million active app users.[12]

Across the world, retailers are just as interested in loyalty today as they ever were. Their continued investments and increasingly sophisticated data capabilities aim to harness the value of customer connection. Digital interaction enables a more complete view of who your customers are, and customer data can help you to infer why they buy from you. The rapid evolution of the retail analytics space means that through sophisticated analysis and by harnessing the power of AI and machine learning, businesses are more capable than ever of understanding what really matters to their customers and what motivates them beyond the purchase itself. So, for example, if someone is buying lots of vitamins and protein supplements, are they buying them because they're a cyclist and cycling is their real passion? Or is it perhaps that they are buying them because they are trying to gain weight? Depending on the answers to these questions, the product offered, creative editorial referenced and graphics used (i.e. the associated marketing) can either feel interesting and relevant or alienating and rather offensive. That's a big emotional difference.

The big advantage for the high-touch companies, such as grocers, is that they see so much of a person's life in the data that they can truly understand a lot about an individual just from looking at what they buy. Imagine a table loaded with every single product you've bought from a grocery store in the last year – it would reveal a lot about you wouldn't it? Generally speaking, customers' favourite brands tend to stick around, so in that way, customer data can reveal what really matters to them. Now, a customer can be very loyal to certain categories, and to certain brands in certain categories. Then, in other categories, they might buy on promotion or they will shop around. They might have a favourite beer, and so they buy that beer, or they might also shop around to find what's special or unusual or, dare I say it, cheap. That visibility gives the retailer the ability to understand where there's elasticity for the customer and where, effectively, the customer will only buy the product if it's there.

It may sound easy. But identifying that 'elasticity' – analysing customer data to understand customer preference and purchase intent – is a crucial marketing skill. Stretching spend is obviously valuable, and I think that many organizations believe that saying 'thank you' is giving money away, but that ignores the long-term value of the customer. It may be true that I may be giving money away in the first or second basket, but actually if the customer's emotional engagement goes up, the long-term value of that customer is more protected. It's a delicate balancing act. You don't want to be giving money away just for the sake of it, but at the same time, you don't want to be in a position where everything you're doing is trying to make the customer behave in an unnatural way.

In early 2023, Eagle Eye acquired a business called Untie Nots, a software as a service business that has built the best-in-class digital technology that enables grocers to unlock this 'elasticity'. By analysing customers' purchase data generated by retail loyalty schemes, Untie Nots can apply its proprietary AI to determine the best challenges to send to individual customers (e.g. promotions on brands they love), each containing personalized spend stretch targets for them to try to achieve in order to earn cashback. These challenges typically run for at least a month – as an additional layer on top of all the other loyalty-based activity that a retailer might be running – meaning that the potential for customers to earn significant cashback across multiple challenges is compounded over many shopping trips, making the proposition incredibly compelling. Not only this, but the challenges are funded by brands and the AI ensures they are profitable by design, generating $7 of incremental sales for every $1 of reward earned, while also growing share of wallet and driving digital participation. As an ex-retailer, the Untie Nots proposition stood out to me from the get-go because it really is a win–win–win for customers, suppliers and the retailers themselves. No easy feat!

When discussing the problem of 'giving money away for the sake of it', my co-author reminded me of the ASOS A-List loyalty programme, which ran across the pureplay fashion retailer's digital channels from February 2016 to October 2018. The scheme, in our opinion, was well designed – a generous points-based programme with clearly communicated tiers, which members could move up based on their spend and engagement levels. It ran points booster events, regular competitions, provided perks such as early access to sales as well as offering rewards through third-party partners. So, it had all of the elements required to make it a success but regardless of this, it was decided that the scheme should be taken down. Why? Because there was no 'give to get'. By the very nature of the business model ASOS operates, it knows every customer search, click, scroll and purchase, and so the loyalty offering wasn't providing the business with anything additional. At the time of closing the programme down, the business reportedly had 18.4 million active customers and an annual sales growth of 26 per cent[13] – fantastic figures that may have been at least in part achieved by making customer-centric and data-driven decisions, however it would have been able to do all of that with or without the costly A-List scheme.

Tim Mason: If you were starting today, as a retailer, what would you do? Would you create a loyalty scheme, with a 1 per cent discount?

Sir Terry Leahy: I definitely would seek to create loyalty, definitely. Thinking back to Fred Reichheld, it is true that different customers have hugely different levels of profitability, from hugely profitable to making a loss servicing them. The vast majority of marketing money, more than 90 per cent, is still going into acquiring new customers, whom you acquire for no profit; they're promiscuous, and they know their value, in that they know how to trade with you down to no profit or a loss. Whereas thinking about who drives your actual profit, you don't pay enough attention to them and don't reward them for their custom.

So, I absolutely would do loyalty, and I would try to use the new digital tools to listen to them better, get closer to one-to-one, and engage them in ways that interest them. I would reward them in the ways that have most value to them, because we know that some things have hugely different value. For some people, being able to buy a discounted theatre ticket to see a show might be the world's best thing. To somebody else, they might like something that helps them to treat their kids.

I also think online is rather impersonal and anti-social, even though it's convenient, and there will be an increasing demand among us, as social animals, to be recognized. So, being able to recognize a customer and thank them, and show that you know something about them, that you've listened to them, and that you've thought about how better to serve them, that's probably got to be more valuable now than ever before.

Long live loyalty

In spite of the evidence, the debate over the value of loyalty persists and not everyone is sold on its merits. Australian academic Professor Byron Sharp's book *How Brands Grow* contains a chapter entitled 'Why loyalty programs don't work'.[14] In it, he suggests, 'the key assumptions that underpinned large investments in loyalty programs are faulty' and 'it was also mistakenly assumed that targeting a brand's most loyal customers would generate the greatest return'.

> There is no evidence that outstanding business results are driven by loyalty programs.[15]

I would say that Professor Sharp reluctantly acknowledges some merit to a few of these schemes in a footnote: 'dunnhumby's work for Tesco and Kroger, among others, stands out for successfully building a useful database based on loyalty programme membership'.

But his argument perceives a loyalty scheme in isolation, not as part of an integrated strategy, and dismisses their value, in spite of admitting that they are 'useful' in building a direct marketing channel and customer database. I also know for certain that Terry would describe the stand-out creation of his unbelievably successful career at Tesco in rather more effusive terms than 'useful', and I suspect that Dave Dillion, who was also an extremely successful CEO at Kroger until 2014, would do the same. Kroger acquiring and creating 84.51° was motivated by more than usefulness!

Sharp and dunnhumby got into a small spat about Pareto,[16] the Italian economist who spotted in 1896 that 80 per cent of the land in Italy was owned by 20 per cent of the population. Pareto's general observation that, for many events, roughly 80 per cent of the effects come from 20 per cent of the causes, went on to become known as the Pareto Principle, or the 80/20 rule, and it applies to the ratio of sales to customers too. dunnhumby argues that this traditional 80/20 view of sales to top customers is more accurate for more businesses than the 50/20 view presented by Sharp in his book.

The differences have led to an argument over data sets, time frames and the merits or demerits of panel data versus loyalty card data. Both groups have data sets that have flaws, but there is no such thing as perfect data.

My take on it as it relates to loyalty being alive and well in this digital age is as follows: it is remarkable that a minority of customers – 20 per cent – account for somewhere between 50 and 80 per cent of sales. But, given that most retail and brand operators don't know who their best customers are, they also don't know where in the 50–80 per cent range they sit.

Tapping into emotional loyalty

I think it's also worth restating here what Tesco did, rather than getting drawn into a theoretical debate. Using relatively conventional research techniques, it set out to learn what customers liked and didn't like about Tesco and created a plan to make the customer experience better. (What's in a name? Symbolically, this was always referred to as 'The Customer Plan'.) Four years later, Tesco launched Clubcard, its 1 per cent discount reward scheme. This was applied by swiping a loyalty card at checkout, so it could track member behaviour against sales. It used the customer connection facilitated by Clubcard to meet the objectives of saying 'thank you', stretching spend via direct marketing, and using DIAL to inform ranging, pricing and promotion decisions and so run the business better.

Most importantly here, which I've not mentioned explicitly in the book before now, was that over time Tesco increased the attractiveness of the Clubcard programme by enabling more ways to *earn* points. It offered points on products, promotions and financial services, such as credit card purchases.

Tesco also developed exciting ways to burn points via Clubcard Deals, which later became Clubcard Boost, where Clubcard points could be worth four times their value for things such as a weekend away, a visit to a theme park attraction, a meal at a restaurant or an

Air Miles conversion.[17] As part of enhancing the burn, Tesco replaced Sainsbury's as the grocer whose points you could redeem for Air Miles and 300,000 customers switched to Tesco because of it. How many businesses know exactly how many new customers they have won as a result of a specific promotion and, more importantly, what their overall value is?

By flexing the way customers could earn and burn their Clubcard points, Tesco also noticed that those customers who saved for deals were at their most loyal just after they had enjoyed their visit to the theme park or weekend away thanks to Tesco. This clearly showed they valued the reward and wanted to continue to amass points by shopping with Tesco, so they could get something they wanted to do again. To spell it out, if the reward or, in loyalty scheme terms, the burn is attractive, people will behave in sometimes illogical ways to earn it. Think of those 300,000 Air Miles loyalists. If you really want your burn to be attractive, like everything else, it will work better if it's personalized because one size does not fit all. Customers who like the scheme find more ways to earn.

In not much more than a decade, the Tesco credit card, with which you could earn extra points, achieved a 15 per cent share of the UK market, which, although I say so myself, has always seemed a remarkable achievement and speaks volumes of what Tesco created with Clubcard.

It may, however, surprise you to know that, for all of the proven success attributable to Clubcard, I do actually agree with Sharp on two counts: loyalty programmes will only tangibly boost loyalty if the insight gleaned from the data is used to quantify the amount that should be spent on these best customers, and the investment should be targeted to reward the behaviour you seek. Put simply, delivering against this needs to happen across three broad areas:

1 'Thanks for shopping with us.'

2 'Please shop with us one more time.'

3 'Next time you shop with us, please enjoy this incentive to spend a bit more than you usually do.'

One of the key strategic skills is getting the 'give to get' balance right on a customer-by-customer basis. I would suggest that what really matters is how much of your business comes from your core customers and how much comes from occasional customers. If you look at the big supermarkets, they are still in a situation where the top 20 per cent of their customers are responsible for 50–80 per cent of their trade. If you think of loyalty as a ladder with 'one-hit wonders' at the bottom and 'can't stay aways' at the top, retailers are constantly adding customers in on the lower rungs. Getting someone from the bottom of that ladder all the way up to the top is quite difficult – unless their lifestyle changes, such as moving to a new house or having kids, or a store opens nearer to their home or work to make that customer now more likely to shop with you.

So, thinking about the very occasional customer, what can you do to market to them? They are effectively part of a prospect pool that you occasionally see. Clive Humby talks about suspects (or 'one-hit wonders'), prospects, customers and loyalists (or 'can't stay aways'). But, in reality, across that spectrum, at the bottom end – particularly in areas such as food – the difference between a prospect and a customer is very grey. But at least with a connection you know who they are, so you've got a way of reaching them.

Reichheld's point is that old-school mass marketing will cause you to spend as much on those customers termed 'suspects' – and probably more, given there are more of them – than you spend on 'loyalists', and this is a misuse of scarce marketing resource.

The great thing about a good loyalty scheme is that it gives you a lot of data about loyalists, customers and some prospects. This enables businesses to quickly reassign marketing budget to the customers on which it will have the greatest impact. Eagle Eye is working with a number of clients across the globe whose data analytics capabilities are now so advanced that they have a view of profitability per individual loyalty scheme member and therefore have an individualized marketing budget to spend on them, based on the primary objectives for that customer. This is true one-to-one marketing in practice.

What I find so exciting about marketing today is that there are so many opportunities to keep developing and adding to your toolkit to offer your customers more, while meeting your own objectives. Again, this is where the Untie Nots offering can be integrated into your current proposition as a new, additional layer for customers across the spectrum of engagement to participate in. Its personalized spend-stretch targets can be deployed within five weeks, unlocking new funds from suppliers while providing your customers with more reasons to be recognized and more reasons to consolidate their spend with you – so that they can hit the individualized purchase targets set to them.

Sharp is correctly adamant in pointing out the simple fact that loyalty schemes are useless at creating a connection with those who don't sign up. They aren't designed to do so – customers who don't join tend to come from the lighter customer, prospect and suspect segments. To address these groups, retailers still have to rely on their mass and in-store marketing efforts, with a longer-term objective to communicate the value of joining the scheme in order that they can begin to personalize marketing efforts to them.

Speaking to the founders of Untie Nots, Cédric Chéreau and Zyed Jamoussi, about this, they also said how their challenges can be a great way to getting customers who are currently less engaged to opt in to receiving more personalized communications, moving them up the engagement ladder. Zyed Jamoussi explained:

When we deploy challenges for our retail customers, the objective is to design these individually for each customer, which we do using our AI, which determines the right challenges to send to the right customers, and sets the spend stretch threshold at exactly the right level to motivate their behaviour within reasonable boundaries.

What we also do, however, is run some mass-appeal challenges that are available to all customers, including new customers as well as those who haven't given their permission for their data to be used for profiling purposes.

Due to the broad appeal of these challenges and the high level of reward offered, many customers choose to participate in these, which, once they start, they are compelled to finish!

For non-email opt-in customers, we can send them a notification when they start to engage with the challenge process, saying something like 'well done, you've got your first challenge on! If you give us your email address we can keep you informed about your progress and let you know when your reward is ready to redeem'. This can be a great way to generate this very valuable owned customer data, which you can go on to use to personalize the customers' experience further.

For customers who engage with these generic challenges but haven't given permission for their data to be analysed, we can send them a notification saying 'congratulations, you are halfway through your first challenge! If you want more of these on more of the brands you love, we need your opt-in so we can use your data to get you even better offers!'

Both of these methods have been extremely successful at driving increased engagement both with the challenges we provide, as well as with the retailers' wider digital engagement strategies.

Omnichannel loyalty

I remember a meeting in 2006 where Tesco's performance was below where the company wanted it to be. The marketing team and dunnhumby had done a full analysis of performance, and what was clear was that the Clubcard customer base was doing just fine and the underperformance was coming from the other 50 per cent of customers, accounting for 25 per cent of sales. This was a difficult problem because, for over 10 years, Tesco had honed its direct marketing skills to fix this sort of problem using the lever of loyalty. But there was no direct marketing capability to address these anonymous prospects and suspects.

The challenge Tesco faced then is the core reason for writing this book now: the advent of the internet, mobile and smartphones, bringing with them a means of digitally connecting to customers. I believe this has opened up the opportunity to develop a digitally enabled, data-driven approach to customers, prospects and maybe even some suspects as well as, of course, loyalists.

In light of this comment, it is obvious what a fan I am of Tesco's Clubcard Prices initiative, launched in May 2019 initially as part of its Centenary celebrations. Step back a moment and imagine its challenge. 'Our Clubcard customers are doing well, happy with us and our marketing is effective to them *but* our Clubcard penetration is in decline and our marketing to non-Clubcard customers is, at best, average. How do we increase Clubcard usage? What about if we took money we are already spending on promotions and said, here's an amazing offer – not points tomorrow but discount today but you have to have a Clubcard to enjoy it. Oh and by the way, Clubcard is super easy to sign up to, especially digitally.'

This was the first time a major supermarket in the UK had offered loyalty card holders lower prices at the checkout, with many items at up to 50 per cent off. To access the discounted prices, existing Clubcard holders simply had to tap their card or scan their app at the till, while non-members were encouraged to download the Clubcard app and register while in-store. E-commerce customers saw their discounts applied automatically.

Clearly it worked as, writing today, Tesco has recently announced that 100 per cent of all UK promotions, including its iconic meal deal promotion, are now exclusively available through Clubcard Prices.[18] The proposition has been a huge success thus far, rejuvenating a scheme that is fast approaching its 30th birthday, pushing Clubcard penetration back to near-record levels (86 per cent in large stores) – and driving rapid digital adoption.[19] This has been a brilliant strategic move as the entire proposition reuses existing funds to a higher objective and if it hadn't worked, that is, consumers couldn't be bothered to engage, it could have simply switched it off. No biggie.

I am asked regularly what the 'best' way to incentivize customers to engage digitally is and my answer is always that businesses simply need to reward the behaviour they seek. Clubcard Prices has done exactly that, and the results speak clearly to how well this strategy has resonated with consumers.

What is the next move for Tesco given their 9 million digitally engaged customers, 4 million of whom are already engaging with personalized offers in-app?[20] For me, the outstanding opportunity is 'marketing in the moment', which is described in more detail in Chapter 10.

I hasten to add here that I have no current inside knowledge, so this case study is based on my opinion, historical knowledge as well as what's publicly available, rather than fact. However, due to the great successes, Tesco has proudly spoken about the impact of Clubcard Prices on the business, some highlights of which include:

- Over 20 million households now actively using Clubcard (up 3.3 million year on year).
- 10 million customers are now using the Tesco Clubcard app, up 80 per cent since early 2021.
- Clubcard penetration in large stores is now 86 per cent (+7% pts) and has increased +21% pts year on year in Express stores.
- Clubcard satisfaction up +505bps.[21]

This is clearly a huge success story and if you think back to the virtuous circle mentioned earlier in this chapter, this will now be in full swing at Tesco with the business able to glean more insight on the omnichannel purchasing behaviours of its customers than ever before, largely funded by suppliers. This is exactly what businesses in this day and age need to focus on when they're up against businesses like Amazon that have the same direct digital connection with every single one of their customers, whether they have shopped with them once or a thousand times, all because they need to know who their customers are before they can ship their purchases to them. Winning omnichannel retailers have to address this disparity if they want to be able to offer their customers the seamless and value-added experiences they seek.

I suggest that today's opportunity around digital customer connection is not only about one catch-all loyalty scheme. Instead, it has to be about a mosaic of customer-facing initiatives that encourage the full spectrum of customers to make a connection to your business. This could include points, instant discounts, subscription schemes, games and challenges, charity and environmental propositions, third-party partnership programmes and so much more. In this modern world I would create a new marketing function responsible for collecting customers' IDs via a significant digital direct marketing acquisition effort.

One final comment on Sharp's views on loyalty programmes: he seeks to demonstrate that all brands behave according to certain rules or laws, driven to a large extent by his view that consumers are more similar than different. 'We know that loyalty metrics don't vary a lot between brands...' he writes. As I hope I made clear in Chapter 2, I completely disagree with this; it is my firm belief that there is no such thing as average. He continues, 'I call this the "my mum" phenomenon: "My mother is the best mother in the world, she's lovely. But she can also be rather annoying sometimes. Does that sound like your mum?"' I'm afraid the answer to that, Prof Sharpe is, 'No': my mum is dead. I hope you'll agree, that is just about the best argument for personalization I have ever heard.

Harnessing the power of digital connection

Customer transaction data and loyalty data are still absolutely essential to gain the insight needed for a strong marketing strategy. But there's a whole new world of digital data out there that can open the door to more insight into who your customers are and what they're likely to want and do in future. Imagine being able to overlay and enhance all that rich, functional, transactional data with knowledge of your customers' passions and intent to help you to give your customers the very best offers and experience possible. This is where the power of a digital connection is going at the moment. We are currently only in the foothills of this next great transformation but you've got to go through the foothills to get to the bright shiny uplands. You can see the start of the uplands and imagine what they might be like, but you've got to put in the miles to get there.

IN SUMMARY

- Be true to yourself and your brand and be sure that what you do comes out in your digital strategy.

- There's only one thing worse than not knowing and that's knowing and not doing.

- It is what people do that matters. What did a customer do and what action can you take to incentivize them to visit more or buy more? Use customer connection to answer these questions.

- Creating and maintaining the customer connection is a life's work, not a 'one and done' initiative. Do it, and then remember to keep doing it.

- Good marketing is good manners. Follow the golden rule and treat customers in the way that you would like to be treated.

- Reward the behaviour you seek.

- Measuring sales by customer requires knowing who your customers are, which is why forging digital customer connection through the mechanic of loyalty marketing is still such a powerful strategic tool today.

Notes

1 Reichheld, F (2021) *Winning on Purpose: The unbeatable strategy of loving customers*, Harvard Business Review Press, Boston, MA

2 Reichheld, F (1996) *The Loyalty Effect: The hidden force behind growth, profits, and lasting value*, Harvard Business School Press, Boston, MA

3 Mason, T (2017) A people person nails it, (online video) *The Grocer*, 6 August www.thegrocer.co.uk/people/people-news/a-people-person-nails-it-video/555099. article (archived at https://perma.cc/CTZ2-U3HX)

4 Sinek, S (2009) *Start with Why: How great leaders inspire everyone to take action*, Portfolio Penguin, USA

5 Marston, R (2010) Tesco's triumphs under Sir Terry, *BBC News*, 8 June, www.bbc.co.uk/news/10263953 (archived at https://perma.cc/K2BU-JVVT)

6 Reproduced from Humby, C, Hunt, T and Phillips, T (2007) *Scoring Points: How Tesco continues to win customer loyalty*, p 69, Kogan Page, London

7 Reichheld, F (2021) *Winning on Purpose: The unbeatable strategy of loving customers*, Harvard Business Review Press, Boston, MA

8 Vandevelde, M (2018) Sainsbury's buys Nectar reward scheme from Aimia for £60m, *Financial Times*, 1 February, www.ft.com/content/584f106e-0766-11e8-9650-9c0ad2d7c5b5 (archived at https://perma.cc/7KTC-SCAS)

9 Quantium (2016) How can I deliver more personalized offers to my customer? 3 November, www.quantium.com/who-we-work-with__trashed/how-can-i-deliver-more-personalised-offers-to-my-customers/ (archived at https://perma.cc/SX6T-BMS4)

10 Mitchell, S (2016) Woolworths sitting on big data goldmine, *Australian Financial Review*, 13 October, www.afr.com/business/retail/woolworths-sitting-on-big-data-goldmine-20161013-gs1cgw (archived at https://perma.cc/U5GZ-7SCK)

11 Evans, P (2017) Loblaw to merge Shoppers Optimum and PC Plus programs, *CBC News*, 8 November, www.cbc.ca/news/business/loblaw-shoppers-optimum-pc-plus-loyalty-programs-1.4392494 (archived at https://perma.cc/N235-97VK)

12 Asda (2022) Asda returns to positive like-for-like sales in Q3 and steps up support for customers affected by the cost of living crisis, 11 November, corporate.asda.com/newsroom/2022/11/11/asda-returns-to-positive-like-for-like-sales-in-q3-and-steps-up-support-for-customers-affected-by-the-cost-of-living-crisis (archived at https://perma.cc/YAM5-MPJA)

13 Hammett, E (2018) Asos A-List's failure shows you don't need a loyalty scheme to drive loyalty, *Marketing Week*, 24 October, www.marketingweek.com/the-failure-of-asos-a-list-shows-you-dont-need-a-loyalty-scheme-to-drive-loyalty/ (archived at https://perma.cc/VTZ9-XK2F)

14 Sharp, B (2010) *How Brands Grow: What marketers don't know*, p 172, Oxford University Press, Sydney

15 Sharp, B (2010) *How Brands Grow: What marketers don't know*, Chapter 11, pp 178–9, Oxford University Press, Sydney

16 Oakes, O (2018) Byron Sharp hits back at Dunnhumby's heavy buyers claim as 'dead-end' marketing strategy, *Campaign*, 25 January, www.campaignlive.co.uk/article/byron-sharp-hits-back-dunnhumbys-heavy-buyers-claim-dead-end-marketing-strategy/1455529 (archived at https://perma.cc/8GVF-32CR)

17 Formerly known as the 'Double Up', then relaunched as the 'Clubcard Voucher Exchange', the Clubcard Boost was the new name for Clubcard Rewards, launched in 2013. The Clubcard Boost in-store worked the same way as the previous schemes (for every £5 in Clubcard vouchers, customers received £10 in Clubcard Boost tokens). As with the previous scheme, only selected departments were included: Baby & Toddler, Cosmetics & Fragrance, Clothing, Opticians and Cook, Home & Dine. The in-store scheme has since ended, although the online scheme, where customers can exchange Clubcard vouchers for two times their value at other Reward Partner retailers is still available. Customers can 'boost' their Clubcard vouchers online to use for days out, restaurants and holidays. Examples of available Partner brands are PizzaExpress restaurants and Merlin Attractions.

18 Tesco (2022) Preliminary results 2021/22, *Tesco PLC*, 13 April, www.tescoplc. com/news/2022/preliminary-results-202122/ (archived at https://perma.cc/ P6ZJ-X2W4)

19 Tesco (2022) Annual Report and Financial Statements 2022, *Tesco PLC*, 1 June, www.tescoplc.com/media/759057/tesco-annual-report-2022.pdf (archived at https://perma.cc/ZE9N-4JEQ)

20 Tesco (2023) Q3 and Christmas Trading Statement 2022/23, *Tesco PLC*, 12 January, www.tescoplc.com/news/2023/3q-and-christmas-trading-statement-202223/ (archived at https://perma.cc/J57S-626Q)

21 Tesco (2022) Tesco Interim Results 2022/23, *Tesco PLC*, 5 October, www. tescoplc.com/media/759416/041022_interim-presentation-slides.pdf (archived at https://perma.cc/VM9W-4YD4)

4

The fundamentals of loyalty

So, you'll have gathered from the previous chapter that I believe loyalty marketing – that is, strategies businesses can deploy to understand more about their customers in order to use that knowledge to improve their experiences – is alive and well. This chapter will explore this in more detail with a focus on what makes a great loyalty scheme and how the data generated can be used to personalize every customer interaction, regardless of when or where they choose to engage with you. The next chapter, Data-based retailing, will continue on this theme but will instead focus on the ways in which customer data can be applied to all other areas of the business to help organizations move from a product-centric to a customer-centric view of the world.

My career since Tesco has been focused on how businesses can harness the power of customer connection to improve marketing and increase customer loyalty. The huge promise of the digital age is the opportunity it opens up to do it again, but in a better, simpler and cheaper way. It's why I joined Eagle Eye. Just as digital transformed music, maps and media, it also has the potential to transform marketing.

I describe Clubcard as a connection because, put simply, that's what it was. A way for us to connect to and understand customers, enabling us to serve their needs better. What Eagle Eye provides for businesses is that same connection, but built for the always-on and always-connected businesses and consumers of today. As my colleague and Eagle Eye founder, Steve Rothwell, put it: 'People are interested in relevant, timely content sent to them personally.' So, he developed a platform to enable primarily retailers, but also brands and aggregators to operate personalized marketing campaigns at huge scale in a digital world where one-to-one communication is now expected. Without this ability to get personal, a business will struggle to engender loyalty from its customers.

So, you need to get personal to get loyalty, but before you can get personal you need to create the customer connection. While loyalty programmes come in many shapes and sizes, in my experience, I believe all successful customer engagement schemes follow some core principles that should not be ignored (Figure 4.1).

Core principles of customer loyalty

Follow the golden rule

Treat people the way you would like to be treated. Why? Because it's the right thing to do. It's also the very essence of personalization and great things happen when businesses start to apply this way of thinking to their marketing efforts. What this means for every business will be different as for it to work and to be authentic, it must be consistent with your unique brand and values.

A common mistake that I see when looking at loyalty initiatives all over the world is businesses starting with 'what do I want my customers to do?' rather than thinking 'what would I want if I was a customer?' In a similar vein, I often find myself talking to businesses that claim to be customer-centric, when in fact the majority of their decisions are still product-centric, for example 'I have a product to sell, who are the right customers to sell it to?' rather than 'I have a customer I wish to delight, I believe offering them this product at this price is the best way to do that'. I was fortunate enough to see first-hand the enormous impact on Tesco's business when we started advocating for the customer and implementing strategies that followed this rule, so I urge you to always start this way round.

FIGURE 4.1 Eagle Eye's core principles of customer loyalty

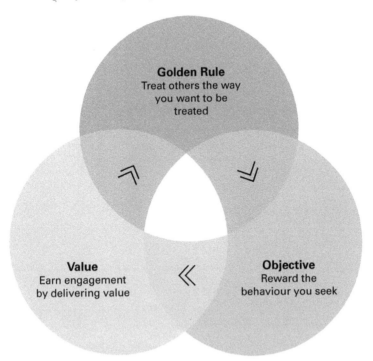

In his latest book, *Winning on Purpose*, Fred Reichheld does a fantastic job at succinctly explaining the business case for following the golden rule:

> When you put overriding emphasis on enriching the lives of customers, those customers come to trust that you will act in the best interests. When you earn your customers' trust, they openly share their needs and vulnerabilities. They provide honest feedback, which helps you design and deliver optimal experiences. They integrate your products and services into their daily lives and thus depend on (and contribute to) your continued prosperity. They treat your employees with dignity and respect. These factors turbocharge your loyalty growth engine, accelerating you past the competition, using the most efficient and sustainable fuel ever invested: happy customers coming back for more and referring their friends.[1]

Value

The value exchange that you offer the customer in return for their participation – referred to in the previous chapter as the 'give to get' is of paramount importance to get right, right from the start. The programme that you launch needs to be sufficiently attractive to persuade a significant proportion of customers to engage frequently. This can be a blend of both transactional (e.g. 1 point per £1 or $1 spent) and emotional drivers (e.g. perks including birthday gifts, tiers, charity donations, etc) but the value must be tangible for the end consumer. It is this value that earns you the permission to communicate with customers, and it is what keeps them coming back week after week to engage with the programme and pay attention.

Upon launch, Clubcard absolutely offered transactional loyalty, in that it gave customers discounts and special offers in exchange for opening up a direct marketing channel that Tesco could use to maintain a connection to its customers in return. As a Google representative said to me in 21st-century-speak not so long ago, running these schemes is 'the price of getting a consumer ID'. Looking at it this way, the cost of a 1 per cent reward was the price Tesco had to pay to get enough customers to consistently use their loyalty card and for them to share their data.

By contrast, the US model tends to be that the card provides access to lower prices on shelf. This is cheaper to run and drives a greater uptake: even if you can't be bothered to be part of a loyalty scheme, you won't willingly pay much higher non-club prices. As noted in the previous chapter, Tesco entered this arena +25 years on with the advent of Clubcard Prices, which launched in the UK in 2019 and has had a significant impact on Clubcard usage, with digital Clubcard users increasing from 2.2 million to 9 million in the 2021/22 financial year.[2] Quick to follow in the UK have been Boots, Sainsbury's and Morrisons, all of whom are offering lower prices for loyalty card holders, as well as Coles in Australia.

But the original Clubcard also proved that, if you do transactional loyalty in a thoughtful way (particularly if you do it first), it can demonstrate that you're offering customers something useful or of value too. The fact that a customer had to want to volunteer their details meant Tesco had to deliver what they expected from a decent partner. Then the customer starts to feel that you're 'on their side'.

In early 2023 I had the opportunity to interview Pano Christou, CEO of Pret a Manger, for this book. Having launched the YourPret Barista subscription scheme back in 2020, followed by its loyalty offering, Pret Perks in 2021, I was keen to find out his thoughts on how a business like Pret determined the right level of value to give to customers. He said:

> For me, the thing that is so important is being generous.
>
> There are so many examples within loyalty where companies have readjusted their loyalty programme to make it less rewarding for the customer and they get found out. When planning our initiatives, we look very seriously at the things we're putting in as we know that if we had to take them away, we'd be doing that at our peril. If, as a customer, you're giving something and being loyal to a brand, you rightfully expect that to be reciprocated.

For me, this is totally aligned with my belief that good marketing is good manners, and chimes true with a long-held tenet during my time at Tesco which was 'it's easy to give, but it's hard to take away'.

For both Tesco then and Pret a Manger now, the benefit of having first-mover advantage is that customers believe you are innovating for them, whereas they know the second mover is playing competitive catch-up. Launching something brand new means that people have to think about it before signing up in the knowledge they are giving data to get something in return.

Objective

In order to reward the behaviour you seek, you first need to understand exactly what you're trying to do in order to accurately assess whether you're achieving it or not. And don't forget that you're not the only one who needs to be clear on the objective – it needs to be exceptionally clear for customers too. There is no one-size-fits-all approach and as with the first of these core principles, it has to be authentic to your brand for it to fly.

Again, looking back at the launch of Clubcard, our objective was unmistakable. Our role was to create value for customers to earn their lifetime loyalty. And everything we did had to support that overarching objective. But this isn't the only valid objective, you have to determine what is right for your business. When interviewing Christou, I asked him if he could explain the core objective behind the YourPret Barista subscription scheme:

> For us this was absolutely a market share game. During Covid, what were once some of the busiest locations in the world became some of the quietest and our business literally disappeared overnight. As things started to open up again and hybrid working became commonplace, we had a decision to make. In urban centres, we could either sit back and lose between 40 and 60 per cent of our business because we knew consumers are only coming into the office two or three times a week, but clearly we weren't prepared to do that. So we decided it was all about market share. If there are fewer people coming into these locations, we need to now think about how we take share and how we incentivize people to come into Pret more often, rather than to our competitors. How can we encourage them to make more decisions to choose to visit us, not just during the week but even multiple times per day. How could we do this? We needed to put forward a too good to be true offer, something which had nearly zero barriers to entry.
>
> So, within 6–8 weeks we went from ideation to national launch with no testing whatsoever of our subscription scheme. We offered it for free for the first month as we decided we'd prefer to give coffee away and have traffic to our stores as this is what creates the buzz in any Pret.
>
> It totally outperformed any expectations we could ever have had – customers seemed to love it with 20,000 consumers signing up on day one and since then, it has totally transformed our business.

Other possible objectives could be that you're a low-frequency business that wants to maximize each visit, getting customers to spend that bit more every time they're in-store. Or perhaps you're a business that is renowned for a specific category, but your goal is to get customers to spend across a broader range of your product set. Whatever it is, ensure that you know what you are trying to achieve in order to design your proposition and then relentlessly optimize it in order to accomplish what you set out to.

Turn the DIAL

Once you have settled on the principles above, the next question is how you bring them to life. I would advocate for using the DIAL model introduced in the last chapter.

DIAL stands for: *Data*, leading to *Insight*, driving *Action* to promote measurable *Loyalty*. There are two common problems that I have seen in businesses when they do not use this approach. The first is that they confuse it with *data*, leading to *insight*, driving *awareness* and promoting *learning*, which is great if you're an academic institution but not if you're trying to beat competitors by winning with customers. The other problem is that businesses go straight from data to action. They don't really think about what insight they can generate that can tell them what actions might be successful. So, many organizations will look at their customers and say, 'these are our top customers, let's thank them', without thinking what the most appropriate form of thanks would be, or whether there should be multiple ways of saying 'thank you'.

The other possibility is that they have a lot of data and insight, but that they don't take very much action. They create an insight machine that's generating a lot of customer understanding, but there's then no one in the business charged with turning that insight into an outcome. It's about making sure you've got all four facets of DIAL in your organization. Don't try to go straight from data to action, and don't just do data and insight without having any tangible outcomes, because neither of those will deliver any increased value.

Without DIAL, Tesco would not have achieved the objective for Clubcard that David Malpas had set at launch: to use the customer data it provided to create a return by running the business better.

Building block #1: Data

As mentioned earlier, the starting point for any business wanting to launch a loyalty programme is to enable it to get access to its customers' purchasing data in order to use that information to understand and serve individuals better. So, if the crown jewels of the scheme are the data that's generated, a business needs to have a strategy for how to structure, store and utilize that data once it's got it.

The typical data sets that need to be structured and consolidated typically include (but are not limited to):

- EPOS data
- Customer demographic data
- Customer transaction data
- Product hierarchy
- Store hierarchy

Building block #2: Insight

Your customers have signed up to your proposition and are now connecting with you every time they visit, creating a rich source of data. But this has to be analysed and interpreted before it can be of any use. I don't profess to be an expert in customer data analytics but typically, I come across two choices in this space: conduct your customer analytics function in-house or partner with a specialist organization to run it for you. When this decision was mine to make, I chose to partner with dunnhumby, which developed its so-called 'win–win–win' model (Figure 4.2) by deriving insights from the data generated from Clubcard.

The typical functions conducted by the Insights function tend to include:

- Customer segmentation (lifestyle, life stage, value, loyalty, promotional sensitivity, profitability, etc)
- Customer KPIs

FIGURE 4.2 Dunnhumby's published 'win–win–win' approach for retailers, suppliers and customers[3]

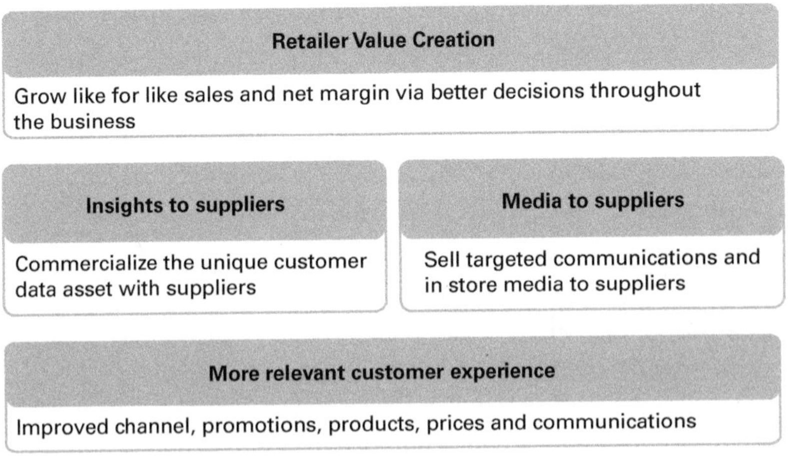

Retailer Value Creation

Grow like for like sales and net margin via better decisions throughout the business

Insights to suppliers

Commercialize the unique customer data asset with suppliers

Media to suppliers

Sell targeted communications and in store media to suppliers

More relevant customer experience

Improved channel, promotions, products, prices and communications

- Propensity modelling
- Predictive modelling
- Customer journey mapping
- Offer targeting/personalization
- Customer recommendations
- Category reviews
- A/B testing
- Measurement

Building block #3: Action

Data-derived actions can take many forms: loyalty marketing and communications, changing your pricing strategy, re-ranging a category, opening a new store and much more. Ultimately, it's about turning the data-derived insight into something of value for the end customer. Core to the ability to do 'Action' well, is the ability to communicate with customers wherever they are, because even if you're offering the greatest value in the world, if they don't know about it, it won't matter.

Businesses need to be able to showcase the value they are creating for their customers in a consistent, relevant and timely way. Often, this will take the form of an offer designed to drive a visit or a purchase or a particular product/brand/category, or a reward for displaying the behaviours you were previously incentivized to do. This could be done in the form of points, coupons, discounts, gifts, stamps, badges, etc – the 'currency' isn't relevant so long as it's possible to get it into the hands of your customers, this includes at the POS, on your website, in your app, via email, SMS, push notifications and more.

The outputs of the action phase typically fall within two areas, communication strategy and business strategy, outlined below:

COMMUNICATION STRATEGY

- CRM: acquisition, retention, growth, win-back
- Advertising
- Retail media

BUSINESS STRATEGY

- Pricing
- Promotions
- Ranging
- Availability

Building block #4: Loyalty

Because our objective at Tesco was to earn customers' lifetime loyalty, the final of our four building blocks was 'Loyalty'. Also, perhaps because DIAM doesn't have such a good ring to it. But really, the final block is all about measurement. Is your scheme delivering against the objectives you set for it at the start?

To do this, it is necessary to have processes and systems in place to enable you to evaluate the performance of your programme and to ensure that you are able to quickly make any adjustments needed based on what the data is telling you. This normally has two core parts:

1 You will want operational reporting on the offers you are sending out (e.g. email open rates, offer redemption rates). This is the tactical week-to-week measurement that allows you to figure out what's working and what's not in order for you to adapt quickly.

2 You will want programme-level metrics on whether you are achieving the overall goal defined in your loyalty strategy (e.g. are you effectively growing customer lifetime loyalty?).

This measurement provides more data, which feeds the engine all over again.

DIAL for 2023 and beyond

It is worth pointing out the obvious here – that the retail world is clearly more complex now than it was back when the DIAL model was created in 1995. Customers are generating more data, driven by more interactions with retailers across more channels and devices. Analytics capabilities including AI and machine learning have become much more powerful, moving away from analysis of customer segments to developing a true understanding of individuals and their specific drivers of behaviour. This means that rather than sending out – 'actioning' – perhaps three versions of a promotion to high-, medium- and low-value customers, businesses are now able to build genuinely personalized marketing strategies for individuals. And these strategies need to be actioned consistently, everywhere that the customer is – in your stores, on your website, in your app, on social media, etc.

One of the primary reasons I joined the Eagle Eye team back in 2016 was because I saw how the technology they'd built could enable modern, omnichannel businesses to run their business in accordance with the DIAL principles. How do we do this? (See Figure 4.3.)

1 We connect and consolidate customer **Data** using our Wallet service, enabling businesses to track every interaction that a

customer makes with them, regardless of whether they do so using a physical loyalty card, an e-commerce or app ID, a subscription membership, etc.

2 We create a real-time connection with a business's data analytics and/or AI services, ensuring that valuable customer *Insights* can be garnered ready for decisions to be...

3 *Actioned* into any connected touchpoint. We enable retailers to consistently present offers, rewards and other messages to customers wherever they happen to be – at the POS, on email, in the app, on the e-commerce website, on third-party sites, etc.

4 Due to our integration to all touchpoints, we can then track every customer response to every action that has been presented to them, enabling businesses to understand and track both the short- and long-term impact on customer behaviour and ultimately, *Loyalty*.

FIGURE 4.3 Eagle Eye powered DIAL for modern, omnichannel businesses

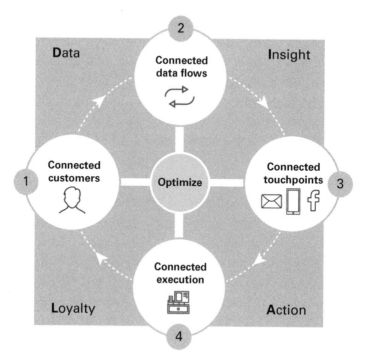

And although the world may have become more complicated in the last +25 years, the remarkable acceleration of digital means that not only are retailers able to turn the DIAL at much lower cost (digital communications versus direct mail), they can also do so in a much more sophisticated and impactful way by harnessing the power of real-time personalization.

Getting personal to get loyalty

I believe that personalization is the most economical way to drive the behaviour you seek – more about this in Chapter 6. But in a nutshell, it's good for customers, ensuring you show you care through the power of relevance, and it's good for business, reducing costs by funnelling marketing investment where it has the greatest impact. The ability to personalize means that you can incentivize and reward each customer for stretching their spend a reasonable and attainable amount from where they are today. It allows you to reward your customers who are actively engaged in your proposition, instead of just giving discounts away that customers may be engaging in passively. In 2023, personalization is a necessity for any loyalty scheme – regardless of channel.

To leverage the data generated by your loyalty programme to enable true one-to-one personalization (beyond simply 'hello {first name}), you have to have the right infrastructure in place. To explain this, I have included the image in Figure 4.4, which represents what we believe the core components of this connected ecosystem are, using an analogy of the brain and the nervous system.

The Eagle Eye Platform has been designed to sit at the heart of a retailer's' tech stack, acting as a central 'retail nervous system', which is connected to every customer touchpoint, both physical (e.g. the in-store till) and digital (e.g. mobile apps, e-commerce sites). Every time a customer interacts with these touchpoints (e.g. makes a purchase, redeems a promotion, signs up for a competition), the 'nervous system' feeds that information directly to the retailer's

FIGURE 4.4 The connected retail ecosystem, powered by one 'brain' and one 'nervous system'

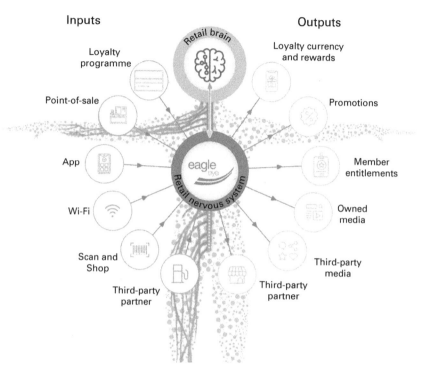

analytics function, (aka the 'brain') in real time. The 'brain' is then responsible for determining the next best action for each customer based upon analysis of that data, which it communicates back to the 'nervous system', which executes the personalized outbound action into all of the relevant, connected channels.

Without a functional nervous system, you are all thought and no action, meaning you are unable to complete the DIAL loop.

Putting it all together

It is my firm belief that to run a successful loyalty programme in today's omnichannel world, you need to embrace being a loyalty company, not simply a company with a loyalty programme. As Pano

Christou said when I asked him what he thought about loyalty, being a new entrant to the market with Pret Perks, 'Loyalty needs to be the whole essence of the brand, of what you're trying to do.'

Today's most successful loyalty programmes offer a mix of rewards and recognition that appeal to both the hearts and the minds of customers, and which are fully integrated with the business as a whole. Today, consumers have less time, and even less patience than ever before. They expect you to know what they want and to use that understanding to make their shopping experiences as simple as possible.

Therefore, to attract, convert and retain customers, you have to continually engage them with compelling experiences that are relevant, useful, desirable and valued. Businesses currently doing this well have a razor-sharp focus on their core loyalty objectives to make it easier and more rewarding for their customers to shop with them versus their competitors.

From a scheme design point of view, successful programmes of today combine the mechanics of frequency and value to ensure that they truly appeal to both the heart and the mind. They do this by offering customers a compelling reason(s) to sign up initially (e.g. a 'no brainer' welcome offer), a simple and rational reason(s) to continue engaging with the programme (e.g. loyalty currency, free delivery), as well as emotional features that are used to engender true long-term loyalty and advocacy (e.g. added value through privileges and perks).

My co-author, Sarah Jarvis, and I, have spent a lot of time thinking about what the features of world-class loyalty programmes are today. We have summarized what we believe the seven demands of customers are for loyalty programmes today (Figure 4.5), and have provided a number of high-level use cases to demonstrate best-in-class examples in each of these categories below:

Demand #1: Make it relevant

- **Why?** Customers want their experience of your business and your loyalty programme to be all about them. Pureplay e-commerce

FIGURE 4.5 Eagle Eye's seven customer loyalty demands

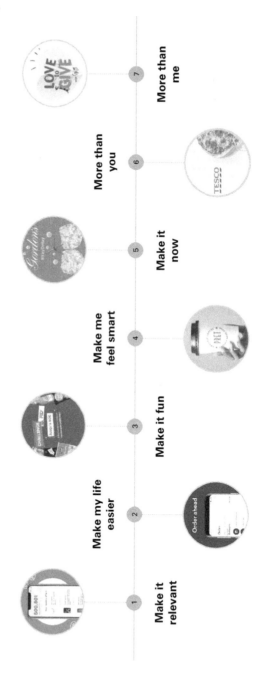

SOURCE Eagle Eye connected commerce 2023

businesses have made personalization at scale a reality online, so consumers expect the same offline. Omnichannel retailers need to ensure they are delivering a personalized experience across every customer touchpoint in order to satisfy customer expectations and to drive the valuable customer behaviours they seek.

- **Use case:** Loblaw PC Optimum is Canada's leading loyalty programme, comprising +15 million members who each receive entirely personalized offers from Loblaws each week, redeemable wherever the customer chooses to shop. In 2021, Loblaw customers redeemed more than $1 billion worth of points, which highlights the significant level of engagement that customers have with this hugely sophisticated digitally-enabled and data-driven programme.[4]

Demand #2: Make my life easier

- **Why?** We have seen that relevance and convenience are taking on more and more importance to customers – for many individuals these factors are now considered to be more important than price. Winners in this space are investing in removing any friction from the customer journey. The digital customer connection has to be used to offer customers utility over and above simply being able to access their loyalty balance. It should serve as the home of their relationship with you and should make it easier for your customers to choose to shop with you versus any of your competitors.

- **Use case:** Starbucks Rewards has been a leading scheme for a number of years with the Starbucks App being not only the home of the rewards programme, but also a place where customers can access a huge amount of digital utility, including mobile order and pay, pre-loaded balances with automatic top-ups, saved beverage preferences, access to free music and games, ability to send gift cards, access to seasonal promotions and more. All of this increases stickiness, ensuring that the end customer continues to see the value of keeping the app on their phone.

Demand #3: Make it fun

- **Why?** We define gamification as 'turning something boring into something fun'. It can be a great way to engage customers at different points in their journey with you and nudge them into 'more loyalty'. This can either be integrated as part of an always-on loyalty strategy or run alongside your existing scheme on a campaign-by-campaign basis, using gaming techniques to enhance and amplify existing programmes and to re-engage known customers.

- **Use case:** As mentioned in the previous chapter, the Untie Nots challenges solution does exactly this, creating profitable by design and totally personalized spend-stretch challenges for digitally engaged customers to participate in. Rather than offering customers generic, one-hit-wonder promotions, the solution here seeks to delight customers with brand-funded promotions on products that they love, and presents the promotion within an engaging UX so that each customer can track their progress against their own individual goals, monitoring the total amount accrued in their savings pot.

Demand #4: Make me feel smart

- **Why?** This is all about the customer value proposition. Successful engagement programmes should be a 'no brainer', making customers feel smart for participating due to the tangible value that they're getting out of it, whether that's financial, through convenience, exclusive access or anything else that has an inherent appeal to the end customer. The rapid rise in subscription services in the last few years has largely been powered by fulfilling this customer demand.

- **Use case:** Pret a Manger launched their YourPret Barista coffee subscription service in 2020, offering 'unlimited' (up to five times per day) barista-made drinks for the initial cost of £20 per month. For consumers who frequented Pret (or their competitors) more than twice a week, this became a 'no brainer', and subscription sign-ups grew rapidly, far exceeding Pret's initial expectations for the programme.

Demand #5: Make it now

- **Why?** Every action should have a reaction. Businesses need to move beyond personalization of content to contextual personalization – don't just send me an offer for a product you think I might like, send me an offer for a product that I need right now.

- **Use case:** Gordon's Gin ran their Yay Delay campaign across the UK, which monitored real-time train-delay data with customer location data and social activity to target disgruntled commuters while in a train station and give them a free Gordon's and tonic at the exact moment they were feeling most frustrated.

Demand #6: Make it more than you

- **Why?** In order to extend your offering and provide customers with greater flexibility in how they can 'burn' what they 'earn' through participating in your loyalty programme, we suggest that you look outside of your own network to be able to provide customers with added value through non-competing partners to diversify the loyalty offering and increase stickiness with customers.

- **Use case:** Tesco Clubcard pioneered this approach with its Tesco Reward Partners proposition, where loyalty members are able to double the value of their earned Tesco points by converting them into vouchers, which can be redeemed across a network of partners (restaurants, theme parks, streaming services, etc).

Demand #7: Make it more than me

- **Why?** Customers expect businesses to be drivers of positive social change in their communities. The best corporate social responsibility initiates are those that are closely aligned with the core values of the business, as well as with the broader loyalty proposition.

- **Use case:** Pets at Home achieve this brilliantly through their VIP Club. The focus of its scheme is all about giving back, with customers earning 'Lifelines', essentially points, which get donated to an animal charity of their choice with every purchase. Each customer receives a quarterly update to let them know how much has been raised, which drives increased engagement in the programme. In addition to the Lifelines proposition, Pets at Home has also bundled numerous other highly relevant features into their VIP programme, which includes their Puppy Club, 'find my VIP' – a service to enable you to alert the wider community to let them know a pet has been lost, as well as discounts for veterinary and grooming services.

I hope that the above clearly illustrates that one size doesn't fit all and that businesses need to create brand-relevant, multifaceted schemes to engage as wide a range of customers as possible. It's also pertinent to note that, as illustrated, there must be a blend of transactional and emotional benefits for customers, which both provide 'reasons to be recognized' – aka reasons for the customer to bother to swipe/scan/tap their loyalty card or other means of identification.

Loyalty for the future

One of the businesses I believe is wholeheartedly focused on delivering against these customer demands, as well as the needs of its specific customers, is Woolworths, Australia's leading supermarket chain. Its loyalty scheme, Everyday Rewards, encompasses all of the Woolworths Group businesses as well as external ecosystem partners, and currently has a membership base of 14.1 million, ranking it among the largest loyalty programmes in Australia.[5]

Although Everyday Rewards was already a successful programme, the Woolworths Group did not sit still but instead made the decision to upgrade its legacy systems to deliver a single real-time loyalty system and offer management platform. Woolworths Group CEO, Brad Banducci, emphasized the strategic importance of evolving in line with customer and business trends, 'There's a mega trend going on globally right now and it's primarily enabled through apps and capabilities like Eagle Eye... it's a space that I think will continue to evolve and we need to continue to evolve with it.'[6]

This project delivered significant advancements in digitization, establishing real-time connectivity with the in-store POS, e-commerce and scan-and-go functions, as well as individual customer wallets, powering an operational real-time single customer view. The main focus of the project was to enhance the customer experience through enabling the real-time redemption of a huge variety of offer constructs, including discounts, points, cashback, subscription entitlements, collectables, behavioural incentives, fuel vouchers, sustainability initiatives, gamification and charitable donations. Suddenly, a business that was constrained in how it could recognize and reward each of its customers, has unlocked the capability for all of these things at unrivalled speed and scale.

The upgrade also led to the centralization of all offers and loyalty functions into a unified system, delivering economies of scale for creating and delivering offers through any channel, and increasing automation through zero-touch offer creation from analytics capabilities and instant offer activation and redemption. In my view, this is modern-day personalized marketing at its best.

And the best part is that it's working. Within just a few months after launch, Kathryn Vaux and her fantastic team at WooliesX (Woolworths' dedicated digital division) were able to confirm some phenomenal results. They have been delivering up to 13 times more personalized offers to their customers, have seen record numbers of members redeeming bonus offers with a 14 per cent increase reported after launch,[7] and have automated and scaled offer creation – saving huge amounts of time and energy.

I was incredibly proud to see CEO Brad Banducci praising the work the team have done, stating that 'Our real-time loyalty platform is a re-platforming of our loyalty business to a system that is real-time... it can reconcile full history and it's not constrained in terms of the offers we can provide or how we can repurpose it.'

IN SUMMARY

- Design your loyalty proposition following the core principles and then use DIAL to continually optimize what you're doing for each and every one of your customers.

- Personalization is the most economical way to drive the behaviour you seek.

- There is no one-size-fits-all loyalty model – it needs to be authentically yours, with a variety of engagement tactics ranging from the transactional to the emotional in order to engage as broad a range of customers as possible, to enable you to create the richest data asset.

- Loyalty is not a 'one and done' proposition. To attract, convert and retain customers, you have to continually engage them with compelling experiences that are relevant, useful, desirable and valued.

Notes

1 Reichheld, F (2021) *Winning on Purpose: The unbeatable strategy of loving customers*, Harvard Business Review Press, Boston, MA

2 Young, R (2022) How do shoppers feel about loyalty schemes? *IGD*, 25 August, https://retailanalysis.igd.com/news/news-article/t/how-do-shoppers-feel-about-loyalty-schemes/i/30040 (archived at https://perma.cc/4ZYX-HXCB)

3 Humby, C (2009) Winning with dunnhumby, Tesco PLC, www.tescoplc.com/media/475966/winning_with_dunnhumby___clive_humby.pdf (archived at https://perma.cc/9AF2-65S2)

4 Loblaw Companies Limited (2022) Live Life Well: 2021 Annual Report, 23 February, dis-prod.assetful.loblaw.ca/content/dam/loblaw-companies-limited/creative-assets/loblaw-ca/investor-relations-reports/annual/2021/LCL_2021_AR.PDF (archived at https://perma.cc/E6ZD-V37L)

5 Woolworths Group (2023) Group Half-Year Results 2023, 22 February, www.woolworthsgroup.com.au/content/dam/wwg/investors/asx-announcements/h23/F23%20Half-Year%20Analyst%20Presentation.pdf (archived at https://perma.cc/Z4HV-5Q26)

6 Seeking Alpha (2022) Woolworths Group Limited (WOLWF) Q1 2023 Earnings
Call Transcript, 5 November, https://seekingalpha.com/article/4553775-
woolworths-group-limited-wolwf-q1-2023-earnings-call-transcript (archived at
https://perma.cc/E8NY-HQ5D)

7 Woolworths Group (2023) Group Half-Year Results 2023, 22 February, www.
woolworthsgroup.com.au/content/dam/wwg/investors/asx-announcements/h23/
F23%20Half-Year%20Analyst%20Presentation.pdf (archived at https://perma.
cc/34QP-V9ZT)

5

Data-based retailing

One of the most important lessons I have learnt in retail is that you manage what you measure. Variously I have been involved in initiatives to reduce queuing time, stock levels in branches, shrink, waste and so on; and, without fail, retail teams can tackle the objective successfully. The trick is making sustained progress on all fronts at the same time. Anybody who has ever had to manage the unintended consequence of an ill-judged change to a performance incentive will know that people manage what they are measured on and disregard the rest. So, if you don't want your store systems or staff depriving your customers of the best possible experiences, you must measure and manage their performance exactly as you would branches and products.

Now, retailers love data. Anyone who has ever worked in or managed a sales outlet will recognize the image of the store manager with a pocket organizer bulging with reports on daily sales, departmental sales, waste, wages, out-of-stocks, promotional availability and so on. However, it is unusual for them to be carrying any data about customers over and above their customer count.

What's required from the outset is to create a new lens: retailers are currently used to looking at their businesses through their products and stores, but they're not used to looking at their own businesses through the eyes of their consumers. I met the CEO of a major retailer recently, who told me in great detail about the performance of its stores in western Scotland and later in even more impressive detail about a particular product category, making me think this is a guy who really knows his business. But when talking about consumers, he referred to how his wife reacted to the brand. This is the classic behaviour of the vast majority of executives who don't live with customer data. Instead, they project their own experience onto their customers.

Generating data-based insight on who your customers are and what they're doing during their shopping trips, both while inside the store and before or after their visit, is a vital capability that every truly digitally enabled and data-driven sales outlet needs. You need to establish a real-time digital connection with customers to generate this insight and enhance their physical shopping experience, so it can better compete with, as well as complement, online. A particular skill of a retail marketing department is to bring this data to life for the business at large.

Linking customer insight to sales

The first step in becoming a customer-led business is to link purchases to individual customers. Wouldn't it be great if you knew who your best customers were? Who spends more than £50 per visit? Who visits three or more times a week? Who is visiting and spending more or less? Who has kids? Who buys clothing? Who has pets? Who buys booze? Who buys 'Free From'? Your value seekers? Offer junkies? Fine-food lovers? Who buys make-up? Who uses the pharmacy? Who takes part in your CSR initiatives? Who are 'greener' consumers? Who likes recipe suggestions? The list can go on and on, and each bit of insight derived from this new understanding may require a different approach to price, promotion, range and more.

The way to link as many transactions to as many customers as possible is to follow the core principles described in the previous chapter to create a valuable and brand-relevant proposition for your customers to engage with. As Tesco Clubcard proved, a 1 per cent discount in a high-spending, frequently bought category was once enough to capture the majority of transactions, but customer behaviour has changed over the years, with more customers moving away from the big weekly shop to instead conducting a number of smaller, top-up shops where the value equation of 'is it worth getting my loyalty card/app out of my pocket to collect points on a £10 basket?' is more difficult. That's why the value proposition has to be compelling, typically offering more than just points for tomorrow but more often than not these days, something for the here and now too.

Clubcard tied the customer connection Tesco had established with the benefits it offered back to the basket through to the point of sale, allowing it to start to know *who* was buying *what* and, in some cases, why. It is this connection at checkout that links what you sell to a view of who buys it, and this view plays an essential role in measuring any engagement with your loyalty proposition (digital and physical) and your wider mobile investment in the physical sales space. It is also exactly the role Eagle Eye now fulfils. Where Clubcard vouchers were delivered as paper vouchers every quarter by the postman, Eagle Eye is the always-on digital postman for offers and information in the 21st century. As an example, Loblaw's costs for sending personalized digital promotions to customers every week for three months are significantly lower than sending one communication per quarter in an analogue way, as we did in the early Clubcard days.

It is worth highlighting here that critical to the long-term desire for customers to 'earn' value with you is the attractiveness of the 'burn' that you're offering. I've said that it was Tesco's aim to make the Clubcard mailing the most valuable and popular piece of junk mail, which was achieved in part by adding branded offers and partner rewards, so there were lots of added-value goodies that came with it. It worked, as time and again consumer groups played back the same domestic cameo:

> The Tesco letter arrives, and it always goes in the same place in the kitchen; when I have a moment, I sit down with a cup of coffee and I go through it to see what I've got. It's amazing how much of the stuff they send me I put in my purse.

One of the earliest examples I can remember where I experienced the value of linking customer insight to sales was shortly after the launch of Tesco's Free From range. The range had been pioneered by Patricia Wheway, a Tesco customer who had written to Terry Leahy in the early 2000s to say that although she admired the 'Every Little Helps' strategy, she was disappointed that she could not buy the products she needed for her son, who suffered from food allergies, at Tesco, or any of the mainstream supermarkets. This wasn't very 'every little helping' her. Much to her surprise, he invited her in for a cup of tea and, having chatted to her for a while, offered her a job to come and fix it. This was much to Terry's credit and, much to Patricia's, she said yes.

Patricia joined the marketing department working for me and started planning Tesco's allergen-free range of products. Not long after, having worked with the relevant buyers, the Tesco 'Free From' range was launched. For me, this was a great example of good marketing enabled by knowing exactly *who* Tesco's customers were: there was a clear need on their part and we were going to make sure Tesco was there to meet it.

A few months later, I was visiting a store and asked the manager how 'Free From' was going. He replied that the numbers were disappointing, but he thought he might have picked up a few new customers. So much for 'good marketing', I thought. So, I asked the Clubcard team to do an analysis to see if they could find out what was going on.

The Clubcard 'Free From' data analysis showed that the manager was right and the 'Free From' category sales were a disappointing £50 million per annum. But, by tracking the Clubcards of people who were buying 'Free From', we were able to establish that 150,000 new members for whom this range was a priority had signed up to the scheme and that these new members were spending £100 million per annum across the rest of the shop. We also found that a number of the existing Clubcard holders who were shopping 'Free From' were shopping a bit more frequently, and that that was worth another £50 million per annum. What appeared to be a disappointing £50 million of product sales was actually a very creditable £200 million increase in customer sales.

Without the data that Clubcard provided through its connection to those customers, it would have been impossible to know this and, as a result, the 'Free From' range would have been cut back or even discontinued. Importantly, no one would have known what a positive impact it had had on the business. Without customer data, the only logical response is to pull back on the new range and that would have been exactly the wrong thing to do. Think how many retailers don't have customer data: every day they make ranging, pricing, promotional and a myriad of other decisions based upon product sales data, not customer data, and every day they risk hurting their business.

My co-author, Sarah Jarvis, shared an example with me recently, which reminded me of this story and made me fear for all retailers that are continuing to make important decisions in the dark without a data-based understanding of *who* their customers are. On a podcast published in early January 2023 entitled 'Why doesn't Trader Joe's have a loyalty program', Trader Joe's VP of Marketing, Tara Miller states:

> We don't collect any data on our customers. People see that as counterintuitive. Well, how can you possibly service your customers appropriately if you don't know what they want? Well, we do know what they want because they tell us with their purchases. We're not tracking individual customer purchases, but we are tracking whether or not a particular product sells well. And if it doesn't, that's our customers voting with their collective dollars, telling us, 'yeah, that's not something we love'. So we go and we develop something else. That's another example of our loyalty to our customers. We are trying to make sure we are offering the most interesting, delicious, and value-focused products that we can every single day.[1]

I have competed directly against Trader Joe's, it's a wonderful business but it would be a better business if it knew who was buying what and had a direct marketing channel where it could tailor messages to its customers.

As demonstrated in the Free From example above, making a decision based on pure sales or store data isn't enough. There could be a product in your range that is exclusively bought by your top 5 per cent of customers, a product that drives their entire visit to your store. Without knowing *who* is buying the product, you are at risk of discontinuing it thinking it won't have any impact, and suddenly your most valuable customers have taken their entire shop somewhere else. Decisions that impact the customer, in my view, must be supported by data that is viewed through the lens of the customer.

In the time since the first edition was published, EDLP giants Walmart and Lidl have both launched loyalty propositions as a layer to sit on top of their baseline customer offering – namely low prices. Their success has proven that you can be all about low prices and still find other ways to digitally engage with customers in order to provide them with additional value (e.g. rewards, discounts, perks, status, etc) in exchange for their data, which can be used to help you make better, more customer-centric decisions across every area of your business. Without the ability to connect with customers, to understand what's important to them and to use that understanding to serve them better, it simply becomes a race to the bottom.

Connecting to the point of sale

We know that digitally enabled and data-driven businesses are currently able to build the most profitable and customer-centric propositions. In order to capitalize on the opportunity to improve the customer experience and make significant retail productivity and efficiency improvements, businesses need to tackle the point of sale. The requirement is to create a real-time customer connection at the till to get sufficient data on who your customers are, as well as what they buy, so that category and marketing managers can drive more informed, customer-led decision making to improve the store experience as well as its overall offer. As explained in the previous chapter, you can do this by applying DIAL to the data generated from that customer engagement in the store: use the analysis to provide the insight needed to inform decision making that runs the business better. It is this 'operational' distinction that characterizes a data-based retailer.

By now, I'm sure you will have learnt that the DIAL model is something I passionately believe in. It's pertinent to note that it's also a model that works with or without customer data because, above all, it says, 'do it, measure the impact to see if it works and, if it does, do it again'. But it served me best at Tesco when we added customer Clubcard data into the equation. Even then, it took five years before Tesco had amassed enough Clubcard data to really analyse baskets for 'trigger' products and sophisticated segmentation.

The mechanics of the Clubcard customer connection allowed Tesco to harness the early benefits of data-based retailing, albeit delivered in a very analogue, direct-mail way. It met the early need for a more data-based retailing approach to customer engagement through a loyalty scheme that emerged from pre-internet shifts in the way people wanted to shop in stores. As mentioned in Chapter 2, the advent of out-of-town superstores and hypermarkets created huge economic value, creating a customer experience that was very modern, democratic and offered unprecedented choice, but that was also totally anonymous. The point here is that store ranging relies on the customer as their own search engine, picking from a range that is curated to serve more than the needs of any individual customer but, in aggregate, serves the needs of all customers.

Sir Terry Leahy made a good point about the Clubcard days on this subject. He observed:

> The thing I'd do differently or would've done harder if I had my time again was range editing. This is all linked to knowing individual customers better and building loyalty. I know now that more and more product options doesn't necessarily equal better choice for customers. The great flaw with category management I think, is the difference between duplication and choice. If there'd been a better understanding of what customers buy, it would've helped build a much smaller range that actually had much more choice in it.

The point that Terry picks up on is that, as stores got bigger, one of the things that category managers did was add more and more range into the stores – not really for customers' benefit, but to boost margins, with little understanding of the resulting impact on the cost structure of an operation carrying more and more slower-moving lines.

Meanwhile, you've got a competitor discounter, like Aldi or Lidl for instance, that comes on the scene and says: 'We've got one type of orange juice, it's really good and it's super cheap' and 'because we only sell one, we can buy it cost-effectively and pass those savings on to the consumer, so they get a great deal, but we actually make margin on it too'. This is why, nowadays, tighter ranging has become necessary to make bigger stores more productive and profitable.

Data-based ranging

Customer data is a really important asset to have at your disposal when it comes to ranging. Take sparkling wine as a category, for example. The most popular prosecco is the prosecco that is on promotion. There is very little brand loyalty, which means it doesn't matter so much what range you stock as long as you have an active promotional programme throughout the year. In my experience, the exception to this rule is Asti Spumante, which while not a great seller, sells consistently to the same group of people.

If you have basket-level data linked to anonymized customer IDs that you're using to help with ranging, you can see that there are a group of identities that, when they buy sparkling wine, always buy Asti Spumante, regardless of what other options are on promotion. When you're running a business that has real customer identities, not just anonymized ones, you actually know that those people tend to be over 60, and their brand loyalty suddenly makes sense because they're buying the brand they've always bought.

Without the data to provide such insight, if you're not careful, one of the things you can end up doing is ignoring your older customer base in the sparkling wine range. If you're ignoring them here, you could be ignoring them in the canned goods and frozen vegetable categories too; and, before you know it, you've taken five or six products out of your range that that group of customers are actually really loyal to. That can be quite a lot for those customers to swallow; so much so that, if those five or six discontinued products become

20 or 30, you are likely to face a real retention problem. The trouble is that without the data you don't know who and you don't know why. All you know is that your customer count is declining.

Thinking about smaller stores, the first time you range a smaller store, you say: 'What bestsellers from a big store can we fit into this smaller format?' Hopefully, you've got some sort of customer journey-related thinking that you apply alongside that, which reasons that the products should be appropriate in terms of size and occasion. Those kinds of ranging decisions reflect the fact that the consumer in the town-centre small store is on a completely different shopping mission from the one visiting the larger-format suburban outlet, mall or retail park. With data-based retailing enabling you to match customer segments to basket and SKU data, it's easy then to see that there are different customer groups on very different shopping missions, depending on the store's location more than its size or format.

A convenience store that is part of a fuel forecourt retail proposition will serve a very different type of shopping mission from an equivalent convenience store located on a main shopping street in the middle of a town centre. The former will be categorized something like 'on the go', such as an M&S shop on a BP site; the latter 'neighbourhood market' will look more like a convenience store. Following this approach, thinking about 'residential' and 'working lunch' as other filters, let alone household size, structure and affluence, and you end up with several different ways of ranging your 3,000 sq ft stores, depending on the location and customers they serve. This is important for two reasons: it maximizes sales based on relevance and frequency, and is a significantly more profitable approach than just taking an edited range of bestsellers from a big store and squeezing them into a smaller one. In simple terms, range proliferation to make up for a lack of customer knowledge isn't an option in a small store.

Data-based retailing takes away the customer anonymity, and although you still have to buy and range for the aggregate of all customers, you'll be in a position to start thinking about engaging target customer segments whom you now know more about because you have built a direct connection to them.

Data-based pricing and promotions

Traditionally, if retailers want to make a move on price, they'll usually involve staple products, including bread, milk, bananas and so on in grocery, or white cotton underwear and navy suiting in apparel. The issue with a price initiative constructed like that, though, is that you invest a huge amount of money in the price move on these products, which are bought by everybody. Instead, you could aim to understand what products are bought by the most price-conscious shoppers in your customer base. Top of the list of products that get into these customers' baskets will be the same staples or the basics. But there will then be a whole range of products they're also buying in order to stretch their spend as far as it will go to get the best value for their money. If you invest your price cuts into those products, you will actually be making a disproportionate difference for those customers who are on more of a budget, rather than investing a significant proportion of your available budget in people who are not as bothered about price. And once your data science capabilities extend to understanding individuals, you can take your pricing initiatives below the line and run personalized, item-level price discounts for specific customers on the products that you know are the most important to them. In 2021, Sainsbury's launched their Nectar Prices initiative, providing digitally connected customers with individualized discounts on a range of products, totally tailored to them. Mark Given, Sainsbury's CMO, stated at the launch:

> Our customers are at the heart of every decision we make. With more and more of them choosing to shop digitally, My Nectar Prices is designed to bring them the best prices on their favourite products. This is a really exciting step on in our plans to personalize loyalty and really reward customers with consistently great value.[2]

The objective use of the data is to plan and merchandise a better shop, to build a better price list and pick a better range – and so incrementally improve the customer's experience of the store. The way to think about it should almost be as though, invisibly – by a hidden hand – the customer is prompted to think: 'This shopkeeper seems to understand me and more about my life because the experience seems to get better.' Helpful nudges to the customer's phone can help demonstrate that this is not an accident, but as a result of thinking about their lives, in their shoes.

I remember a painful lesson early on in my data-based retailing days where Tesco really underestimated the power of the information it had at its fingertips. We'd worked out from the data that there was a clear opportunity to encourage customers to spend more in a new or adjacent category, and so we'd use the direct Clubcard channel to encourage customers to broaden their spend across departments. So, early on, we sent out a promotion for meat. Except then we received thousands of angry letters protesting, 'I'm a vegetarian!' We'd sent the promotion out to all of our light and non-meat-purchasing customers. Tesco knew only their names, addresses, where they shopped and which departments they shopped in. The marketing team saw the absence of meat in the basket as a great trading opportunity, not a potential personalization faux pas. But the customers' letters were clear: 'I swipe my card, you know everything about me, don't behave as if you don't.' A salutary lesson, and Tesco had to act on what it knew – this was all part of the unwritten 'give to get' we had in place with our customers. Back then, the business had to manually update the customer database with preferences like that. Of course, it was also the right thing to do, in the same way as ensuring it never offered Coca-Cola the opportunity to exclusively target Pepsi customers and vice versa.

Back to the Asti Spumante example: once you've got even an anonymized connection with customers, the next logical step is to have a rule as a business that says, when there's a disproportionate level of brand loyalty to a product from a group of IDs, we protect that product and its price; we don't discontinue it, we just take it on face value that there's something special going on with that particular product and we protect it. Again though, I would always advocate it being much better first to know who these people buying this product are. When you realize who the buyers are, at least you realize the logic of why you're protecting the product. The next element then becomes, once I know a certain segment are loyal to the Asti

Spumante brand, let's find them in the run-up to Christmas, Valentine's Day and other seasonal events, and run targeted promotions to them. But that can only be possible after mastering the data-based retailing basics as they apply to store space, range, merchandising planning and pricing.

Jim Noteboom, CMO at The Hudson's Bay Company, and former Senior Vice President of Loyalty & Analytics for leading Canadian retailer and Eagle Eye customer Loblaw Companies Limited (Loblaw), summed up the benefits of data-based retailing when I discussed the implications of the launch of Loblaw's PC Optimum loyalty programme with him:

> We get inputs through loyalty about how the customer interacts with us and we try to get more input from them through voice of the customer via different channels. We try to bring that holistic view around the customer together. That serves in making better planograms, store layouts, better pricing, better promotions, which we then serve up again to the consumer. We see how they respond again and what they say about it and that way, we get better and better and better. So, it's an ongoing learning circle.

It is this virtuous customer-data-driven circle that justifies the cost of having a loyalty scheme. Sure, you should design a scheme that promotes increased visits and spend, but when that scheme is mature, it is the use of the data in the running/improving your business that delivers the return on investment, and of course a wholly owned direct-to-customer performance channel.

Data-centric supplier relationships

One of the other ways in which retailers offset the cost of their loyalty programmes is through commercializing access to their new customer data and media assets, which they get simply as a by-product of having a connected and engaged audience.

Typically, there can be a lot of friction between retailers and their supplier partners as their core objectives are not always aligned.

However, by enabling suppliers to access the valuable customer data regarding how customers shop the categories they operate in can result in much stronger alignment and consequently, better results for everyone. Using the data, the objective for both the retailer and the supplier should become how to improve the overall experience for the retailer's customers, with the two partnering on what are the best, customer-centric decisions to make regarding promotions, pricing, product range, etc. Nowadays, it is relatively commonplace for retailers to mandate that their suppliers license access to their customer data as part of their trading agreement, with the argument being that the suppliers would simply be unable to make appropriate, customer-led decisions without it.

Once the supplier base are au fait with the data and have generated their own insights into the retailers' customers and specifically how they shop their category and brand, the second monetization opportunity for the retailer exists in enabling their suppliers to target customers with personalized offers, rewards, adverts and other information to drive the behaviour they seek. Back in my Clubcard days, this meant offering suppliers the opportunity to be the branded offer in one of the coveted Clubcard Statement slots, but today it can mean so much more. Reward types include brand-funded bonus points offers, price discounts, bounceback offers delivered post-purchase at the point of sale via the receipt, charity partnerships, continuity schemes, gamified campaigns – all available in-store and/or via every digital touchpoint – as well as the huge media advertising opportunity that exists now too (both retailer-owned media and via third-party sites).

Ultimately, what the data-based engagement with suppliers should lead to is a win–win–win situation:

- Suppliers win because they gain the ability to understand how consumers buy their brand and their category and can use that knowledge to run personalized, measurable marketing campaigns.

- Retailers win because they unlock a new revenue stream as a consequence of having a loyalty programme, can build a more customer-focused relationship with their supplier base who fund value-added traffic-driving and spend-stretching activities, targeted to their customers.

- Customers win because both the retailer and their suppliers are focused on improving their experience and personalizing the offers, rewards and content that are sent to them.

Data-driven in-store marketing

In the 'black hole' of a non-digital store, each special price, offer and promotion is potentially fighting for messaging space and share of voice, unable to reach targeted customer groups or segments. Every retailer has a legion of bright, energetic category managers with hundreds of stories to tell and nowhere to tell them. The marketing team are trying to weave an overarching message and themed look for the store. But they chart a tricky course between visual pollution, noise and chaos on the one side and bland sterility on the other.

The digitally augmented store creates a new marketing lens through which we want consumers to augment their shopping trip. This provides category managers with data-based insight on who is buying what, and marketing with a direct, real-time customer communications channel to target those customers. Viewed in the context of how much it costs to produce point-of-purchase material, including posters, flyers and other printed marketing communications costs, as well as the staff time and labour taken to manually update them, retailers spend a lot of money on these things.

Really good marketing is where the ad about a new product is on the press stands, billboards and social sites, some journalist's written an article about it, and it's the first message you see when you walk into the store because the shelves stocking the product have got a great big sign above them. You know, the idea being that you feel so surrounded by it that you've just got to try it. Today's retailers and brands must be slicker and sharper by having the ability to market for the moment, 'in the now', which is where real-time, identity and location-aware digital delivery comes in. In this way, as I have said but repeat because I think it is really important, I predict that 'now' will be to marketing as 'near' has been to Google, that is, transformational, because they are both huge signifiers of likely relevance. See Chapter 10 for more on this topic.

IN SUMMARY

- You manage what you measure – set the right customer-led strategy, pick your KPIs and track your progress through to success.

- To understand and be able to act on what customers are doing, you must seek to establish a real-time customer connection at the point of sale.

- Look at your business through the eyes of your customers, not through SKUs or store IDs. Use the data you have been given in order to improve every customer's experience.

- Use your investment wisely – you know who your customers are and can determine what they want – invest in price for the individuals who are on a budget, promote to bargain hunters, share recipes with budding cooks, etc.

- Use customer data as the foundation to build better, more effective relationships with supplier partners.

- Determine how you can cut out some of the noise in-store by offering customers a digitally augmented mobile layer that is personalized to them.

- Remember the learning never stops – every new data point should be used to feed your insight engine, creating an always-on, virtuous customer data loop.

Notes

1 Trader Joe's (2023) *Why doesn't Trader Joe's have a loyalty program* – ICYMI, 2 January, www.traderjoes.com/home/podcast?page=2 (archived at https://perma.cc/5FK4-7CDA)

2 Sainsbury's (2021) Sainsbury's gets personal with the launch of tailored My Nectar Prices, 16 September, www.about.sainsburys.co.uk/news/latest-news/2021/16-09-2021-sainsburys-gets-personal-with-launch-of-tailored-my-nectar-prices (archived at https://perma.cc/76XZ-B6MQ)

6

The power of personalization

Having looked at the fundamentals of successful loyalty programmes and illustrating how the customer data generated by these schemes can be used to run a business in a better, more customer-centric way, we're ready to look at direct-to-customer marketing. In this chapter I'll seek to illustrate how the DIAL model can also be applied to all of your customer communications, showcasing the power of personalization not just as a revenue generation tool but as a way to drive the behaviour you seek in the most economical way.

The concept of personalization is not new, and it's something that has been increasingly embraced by retail marketers and advertisers over the last four or so decades. All the way back in 1998, Jeff Bezos was interviewed by the *Washington Post* and stated, 'If we have 4.5 million customers, we shouldn't have one store, we should have 4.5 million stores.'[1]

He was, of course, talking here about the ability to analyse every customer's interactions across the Amazon website, and to use that information to create unique experiences for each of them, entirely curated to their needs. And it's not just Amazon that does this. Spotify, Netflix, Facebook – these digital pureplays are all experts in personalizing every stage of the customer journey through their deep understanding of how individuals interact with their businesses.

But personalization is not just something that e-commerce businesses need to worry about. Consumers are no longer satisfied by the 'hello {first name}', email campaigns that originated in the 1990s, and one-size-fits-all or even segmented marketing messages fail to reso-nate with today's empowered consumers who have become used to being treated like individuals by all of the digital platforms and services they engage with. In a world where we all have less time than ever before and where, for many, convenience and relevance hold as much, if not more weight than price, cutting through the noise and delivering tailored messages to individual customers that seek to make it better and easier for them to do business with you versus your competitors is the only way forward.

The value of personalization

From a retailer's perspective, personalization adds value in many ways. We know that different customers are motivated by different things at different times and so creating a framework where the business can act on this understanding is hugely important. The ability to personalize unlocks the opportunity for businesses to reward the behaviour they seek at an individual level. For one customer the objective may be to get them to visit more often, for another it might be getting them to download your app and you may want another customer to write a product review.

The capacity to flex sophisticated qualification and reward rules is an essential step in the progression towards being able to deliver a truly personalized experience, correctly incentivizing customers with the right combinations of stretch and reward. While this level of personalization creates compelling consumer experiences, the second crucial advantage for retailers is the ability to offer only what is essential to motivate the next best action for each customer.

While one customer may be motivated by a discount, another customer may require a non-monetary incentive on the same product to drive the same outcome. Not only should this drive emotional loyalty with customers as a result of them feeling known and under-stood, the savings to be made in giving away only what is essential – along with the ability to test this at scale – is where winning retailers are leveraging personalization to improve the customer experience and, ultimately, the bottom line.

Done well, I believe personalization should also help you to get closer to your best customers as it enables you to invest more heavily in them. As Reichheld pointed out,[2] if you spend too much money on mass broadcast marketing to appeal to non-loyal, irregular customers – who can also be characterized as a 'suspect/prospect', as per the 'suspects, prospects, customers and loyalists' classification – you may not have enough marketing budget left over to reward your loyal customers properly. One of my most strongly held beliefs is that businesses underestimate the potential for loyal customers to spend more. I have seen it time and time again over 30 years. The beauty of personalization is that it allows you to invest differently in different customers. Once you move away from mass promotions, your customers will expect to get something different from you versus their friends and then you can start to use multiple levers (number of offers, value of offers, frequency of offers, relevance of offers, etc) to ensure that the right customers are getting the most value. As Joel Percy, Regional Director for Eagle Eye, North America, said when I was speaking to him recently, 'this allows you to tilt the playing field towards where you want to invest, rather than having to give the same to everybody whether they drive business value for you or not... for me, this is the secret weapon of personalization.'

It's much cheaper to be relevant

Across the industry, grocers spend a huge amount of money on promotions and traditionally, all of this activity could be described as 'spray and pray' – one-size-fits-all price-cut deals that were marketed to the masses and impossible to measure. Reminiscing with Terry Leahy about our early Tesco days, he noted:

If you remember, with Tesco – and we weren't the heaviest promoters – we were spending about 4 per cent of our margin on promotion, and brands were funding a similar amount. So, arguably, about 8 per cent of sales were going into promotions – you know, analogue, money-off promotions. They were untargeted, with a very, very slow and clunky implementation. That's not counting the associated advertising and promotional costs, and coupons and things that go in support of all of that. Even just in Tesco, that's somewhere around £2.5 billion. Industry-wide, if you take retail, it's £20 billion-plus. It's massive and it's analogue and untargeted.

Thinking about this, it's crazy to think that even now, a sophisticated retailer with high levels of personalization still spends 90 per cent of the money in untargeted ways. The shift to targeting will continue for years to come.

Once Clubcard had launched and we had our hands on customer data, we became convinced of the opportunity to improve how we marketed to our customers and how we measured whether any of this activity was actually turning the DIAL and driving long-term customer loyalty.

As per the fourth step in the Clubcard Customer Contract (see Figure 3.2), we worked together with the team at dunnhumby to analyse the customer data we were generating via Clubcard to enable us to build a range of customer segments, which would go on to be used to help us tailor our marketing to different groups of customers to maximize its impact. There were segments based on value (recency and frequency), 'lifestyle' (you are what you buy), price and promotional sensitivity, propensity to lapse and many, many more. Very quickly, we were able to move on from simply 'spraying and praying', to creating targeted marketing messages for specific groups of customers that were designed to drive the behaviour we sought for each of those segments. This was a huge step forward, enabling us to get significantly more bang for our marketing buck by putting the right messages in front of the right people. Suddenly we were able to talk about Tesco Value with our price sensitive customers at the same time as talking about Finest with those customers who we could see had the propensity to trade up in the range.

For the first time, we were able to send out offers to our customers and could track the number of people redeeming that offer by making a purchase at the point of sale. Suddenly marketing could prove their impact. We knew whether we had generated a return on investment for every campaign. If the cost per sale or eventual return on investment was satisfactory, we did more of it; if not, we could tweak the mailing cell size or the offer level to arrive at a suitable return. This was DIAL in action!

At this time, the majority of our analysis was done at a 'household' level, and the idea of being able to entirely personalize a marketing message to an individual was a pipe dream. What you have to remember is that at this time, we were constrained by the data processing capabilities that were available back in the mid-1990s. Yes, we were capturing more than 70 per cent of transactions linked to a Clubcard ID but not to the same granularity as businesses are able to do now (in the early days we were unable to see product-level purchases by customer for example), and certainly not accessible in anything close to real time. In addition, due to the size of the data set we were working with, a statistically significant 10 per cent sample of the data was used to inform our decision making whereas now of course, technical infrastructure and advancements in analytical processes means that businesses are able to run analysis on 100 per cent of the data available and can execute marketing activity down to an individual customer level.

Delivering this at scale across all customer touchpoints is top of the priority list for all of the omnichannel retailers I speak with all over the world. Why? Because the potential upsides to personalization are huge. According to McKinsey:

> Personalization at scale often delivers a 1 to 2 percent lift in total sales for grocery companies and an even higher lift for other retailers, typically by driving up loyalty and share-of-wallet among already-loyal customers. These programs can also reduce marketing and sales costs by around 10 to 20 percent. Not only that, successful personalization programs yield more engaged customers and drive up the top line.[3]

The model in Figure 6.1 illustrates this, showing how as you move from mass marketing through to personalized offers, the level of discount required to motivate the behaviour you seek reduces

FIGURE 6.1 Eagle Eye's personalization model illustrating that personalization delivers higher rates of redemption for a lower level of discount

'Spray and pray'

Segmentation

Personalization

)% *OFF*

Offers available to all

Offers targeted to specific segments

Unique offers that are uniquely coded to individuals

Offer personalization delivers higher rates of redemption for a lower level of discount

Redemption rate

Offer discount

Low redemption

High discount

High redemption

Low discount

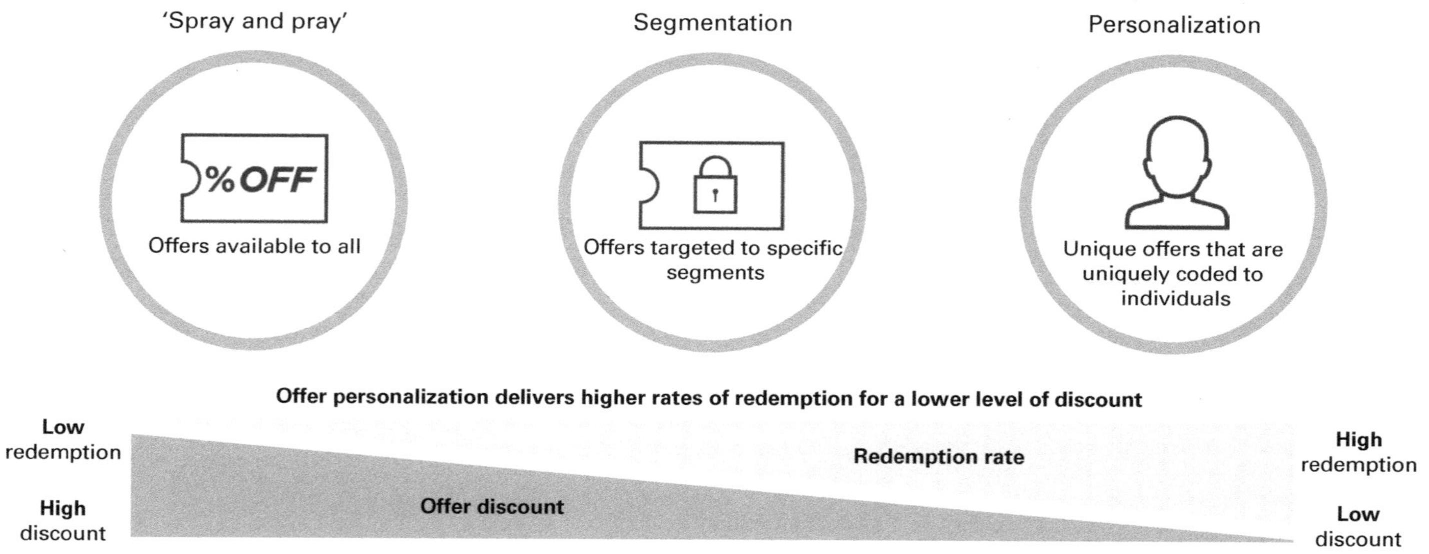

significantly, while the level of redemption grows due to the relevancy of the offer to the consumer it's targeted to. It's a win–win.

Getting personal to build emotional loyalty

With the benefit of even more hindsight since the first edition was published, I am clearer that the Tesco success of 1990–2010 was as a result of good marketing. We ran Tesco as best we were able as if it were one of the great FMCG/CPG houses (e.g. Unilever, P&G, etc). We were the first to do it and to date, I would say only, but hopefully marketing will rise again in the digital world.

I consider it one of the key observations of this book that good marketing fosters loyal customers, whether or not you use the mechanics of a loyalty scheme; and good performance-driven digital marketing enables you to estimate the returns on marketing investment before you make it, as well as track it in practice. Nowadays, with digital capabilities facilitating real-time engagement with the customer in the store via mobile as well as online, these techniques can be used to deliver personalized and entirely measurable marketing at any point where it may be relevant during the shopping trip, as well as while browsing beforehand or during any aftersales service delivery.

Just as there is a choice to make about how much value or utility to offer as an engagement incentive, there is also that balance you have to strike between the functional and emotional loyalty that any marketing engagement seeks to foster. Functional loyalty is very rational: I use it because it works, it's very convenient, it's local and it 'does what it says on the tin'. The very transactional nature at the heart of most loyalty schemes – 'I will give you this if you do that' – promotes functional loyalty.

Emotional loyalty, on the other hand, is more visceral, long-lasting and resilient to the ups and downs of a pure trading relationship, because it is generated by value that is inherently less transactional in its nature. People in the emotional loyalty world talk about the ability to 'surprise and delight' customers with a free coffee, a gift on their birthday, special recognition at a hotel check-in, or partnerships and events with charitable partners, to name a few examples.

It is a mistake, however, to believe that emotional loyalty can be derived only by these types of activities and events. Value plays arguably a more important role in supporting a brand's overall proposition alongside purpose. In that sense, it is wrong to believe that loyalty to a brand like Aldi is purely functional. What may start out as a purely price-based motivator can soon get supplemented by 'feelings'. This may translate to customer feedback that 'it's so easy to shop there', 'they don't tempt me to spend more on stuff I don't really need', 'their coffee is so good' and so on. I remember back in the day, studying Kwik Save as an early UK-based discounter, that it was remarkable to me how many qualitative attributes were attached to the brand. But these opinions only reflect human nature. What person is going to say of their regular supermarket: 'It's a dump, but I put up with it because I am on a tight budget'? So, price and value for money do have an essential role to play in creating effective marketing campaigns too, and demonstrating a great price on a product that is relevant to me is going to carry much more weight.

In September 2021, Sainsbury's launched its digital My Nectar Prices proposition, offering Nectar app customers shopping in-store using SmartShop access to lower prices on the products they love. These are a combination of branded and own-label products with the list being updated regularly to make sure it's relevant to each customer. This was described as 'the latest step in Sainsbury's strategy to digitise how customers shop, combining the best of online and in-person shopping to engage and reward customers'.[4] A year after launching, Sainsbury's reported that it had increased the number of app users to 10 million (from 8 million in 2021) and that the proposition is helping customers to save over £100 per year[5] which, in the current economic climate, is likely driving both transactional and emotional loyalty.

The goal for any business looking to deliver on its personalization strategy has to be to use the data to determine what matters to individual customers and to act on it. I was recently talking to a good friend who was extolling the virtues of an intelligent loyalty scheme. He explained that when his twins were born, the vodka, wine and ready meal offers disappeared from the very next Tesco mailing. Instead, it included a load of offers on stuff that was useful for the kids. Years later, he is still talking about receiving that mailing and what it told him about Tesco and how hard it was trying to do the right thing. It definitely increased his emotional loyalty to the brand. Even today, I think retailers the world over are missing a trick by not applying their now significantly advanced analytical and AI capabilities to watch for significant changes in customer purchasing behaviour in order to be able to act on that, to be as helpful to that customer as possible as they navigate the change. However, it is worth mentioning a cautionary tale here about a grocery customer who almost by accident bought a box of Matzo crackers and was then mystified by the ensuing Kosher food marketing they received.

Blending art and science

It is my firm belief that done correctly, personalized marketing should always be a blend of art and science. The data should always be your starting point, but I don't yet believe that an algorithm can replace a marketeer. A number of years ago, an Amazon search went viral when a customer was looking to buy a baseball bat and was recommended that they might like to buy a balaclava and knuckle dusters with it! To avoid situations like this, it's often wise to think before you act, and to potentially use what you've seen in the data as an opportunity to open up a dialogue with the customer to find out more. For example, if the data indicates the start of purchasing of foods that suggest a dietary intolerance, what about a message that says, 'Hi, we noticed you purchasing x and y and z. If this indicates a change in the dietary needs of you or someone you shop for, you might like to answer a few simple questions here, which will enable us to tailor offers and information to help you. Yours sincerely, Chief Nutritionist'. Setting this up in a way that programmatically repeats this process on triggers will create a much richer experience for customers and I'd predict an almost certain increase in loyalty and value for the retailer.

I think one of the great misses in personalization is that businesses are quick to make assumptions about their customers when they have the means to ask them what they'd like or what they think directly. A business that doesn't miss a trick here is Sephora. Rather than waiting for the customer-connected data to come through via relatively infrequent purchases (in comparison to grocery shopping for example), customers are prompted to complete their profile upon registering for the loyalty programme, informing the organization of their personal attributes and preferences (e.g. fine blonde hair, green eyes, problem skin) in order that the business can use this data to get personal from the very first communication the customer receives from it, driving very strong initial engagement with the scheme.

As I mentioned earlier, I believe that 'will' always outweighs 'skill' and building emotional loyalty through developing deeper relationships with customers is no exception to this rule. It takes energy and dedication but when done well, can absolutely become a key differentiator, particularly for a business's best customers.

Unlocking headroom with personalization

I had the pleasure of interviewing Matt McLellan, VP at Asda, responsible for loyalty, personalization, monetization, media and data partnerships, for the second edition of this book. Responsible for Asda's first ever loyalty scheme, Asda Rewards, launched in August 2022, Matt talked to me about how he is watching the business transform at pace as a result of its new customer data asset. He said that one of the biggest insights it's gained since launch is that there is still 'phenomenal headroom even amongst our most loyal customers', which the business plans to try to unlock by harnessing the power of personalization. Matt believes that 'using the data to be as helpful and as relevant as possible is what matters' and that can extend across all areas of the organization.

In order to achieve this goal, Asda has invested significantly in its Data Science team because, as Matt confirmed, 'building relevance is really difficult'. Asda, like many other leading retailers all over the world, has taken the decision to build its relevancy and personalization science in-house as Matt believes that 'if you can develop, own and protect how you can become more relevant for your customers then you should, as this will be your secret sauce'.

Matt explained to me that the Asda Rewards scheme is initially intended to be transactional by design – that is, there is an explicit data exchange with the customer – you give me your data and I'll reward you with 'Pounds not points'. However, the business plans to develop a deeper, emotional connection with its customers by genuinely understanding their individual needs and delivering against that. For some customers that will be value-based, with helpfulness manifesting itself as deep price-cut promotions or enhanced Rewards for buying certain products, while for other customers, Asda will become more useful by sharing recipes with them, introducing them to new products and services or potentially offering them experiences provided via third-party partners.

Saying 'thank you' versus stretching

When speaking to Matt McLellan, I recalled also significantly underestimating the headroom opportunity even in our most loyal customers when I was at Tesco and would therefore advise anyone reading this to never be complacent, particularly with those 'best' customers, as there is likely still a largely untapped opportunity to grow their share of wallet with you by, as Matt says, being more helpful and more relevant.

I would argue that the best way to address this is to focus on establishing a digital connection to as many customers as possible, ideally driven through the mobile phone, which will allow you to collect more data on more individuals who you can then seek to serve in a better, more personalized way.

I introduced the concept of thanking versus stretching back in Chapter 2, and I think that both mechanics can and should be used to help establish the customer connection and to address this headroom opportunity. In its most basic terms, the difference between thanking and stretching comes down to how much I try to make you deviate from your normal behaviours in order for you to get the reward. It could be purely a 'thank you', in the sense that I could give you something that I know you're going to want or buy anyhow. For example, I know you come in every Saturday, and I know you're going to buy milk because you always do, so I could say, 'this Saturday, the milk's on us'. It's not going to do anything to change those customers' behaviour in the short term, but it's a credit in the emotional loyalty bank, in the hope it will accrue interest by making the brand stickier in the longer term. By doing the 'thank you' well over the long term and giving customers relevant offers and rewards on the products they want, you should be able to see that they continue to visit your store, which translates to share gains over your competitors.

When it comes to stretching customers, the ability to personalize the stretch target is absolutely key to success. A one-size-fits-all approach here simply will not work. Imagine setting a generic 'Spend £100 in a single transaction this week to get £20 off next week's shop' – you risk upsetting and offending your lower-spending customers who will never be able to reach that target and you simply give margin away needlessly to customers who were planning to spend at least that amount, regardless of the offer.

Speaking to Cédric Chereau, Co-Founder and Managing Director of Untie Nots, now part of the Eagle Eye family, I asked him why he thought its proposition had proved so popular, with more than 60 per cent of the French grocery market already deploying their personalized challenges software to great success (Figure 6.2). He said:

> There are three main reasons why customers love to play the challenges: because it is fun, easy and generous.
>
> Why is it fun? Because there is a gamification component built into the way our challenges are designed and customers naturally want to hit their objectives and 'win'. The challenges are designed to nudge the customer in a direction they were already headed. Achieving the challenge seems doable and by being dared to do it, consumers are compelled to take action.

FIGURE 6.2 Examples of Untie Nots-powered challenges, seamlessly integrated into a retailer's app

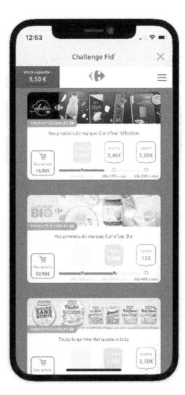

But that wouldn't work unless it was easy to participate in. I just said 'it seems doable', which is true only if you don't ask customers to reach thresholds that are disconnected from their natural shopping habits. At Untie Nots, we spend a large share of our R&D budget on that question: being able to predict the natural shopping behaviour of an individual customer (not a segment!) and modelling their headroom. Clearly this is working as we have recently run customer surveys with all our retail clients where the vast majority of customers declared that the challenges were easy to achieve, whilst they always generated incremental sales for the business!

And finally, generous. Customers won't participate in something unless they feel like the value equation is worth it. The beauty of continuity promotions means that the reward is cumulative. $10 at the end of the campaign feels much stronger than $1 per week for instance and drives really strong engagement. That's the other feedback we recently got from our participating customers: 'it is generous'. Well… on average the percentage discount we give is around 17 per cent, which is way below the discount you can find in promotional circulars. But the fact that you are cumulating the rewards gives an impression of greater generosity!

Performance marketing

Once businesses have set themselves up for success and have found a way to use their data to deliver a better, more personalized experience to their customers across all facets of their organization, there is also an opportunity to cast the net wider, moving into the pay-to-play world of digital performance marketing.

With digital delivery, you can know which investment created what impact. You can also see how much ROI it generated, which, versus general broadcast mass marketing, is very difficult to analyse and calculate. So, if I say to two customers, 'you spend £30 a week, so here's an incentive to spend £40 this week', and one of those customers doesn't use that incentive and still spends £30, it only cost a digital click to deliver that offer and, because one customer didn't play, you didn't pay. But the one that did meant that your promotional investment got an extra £10-worth of sales in a way that is extremely measurable. Set against cutting a load of prices that will or won't drive sales, and then measuring how such a promotion drives incremental sales or is purely substitutional without customer data-based insight, is very, very difficult because you just don't know who is buying what. Furthermore, if you continue to track the customer following their redemption, you can monitor to see if there is any post-promotion impact on sales.

Many retailers and brands are already taking full advantage of digital marketing channels and customer engagement touchpoints through e-commerce, online search and social media, where costs per click can be measured to the penny or cent and click-through attribution can be tracked from issuance right through to redemption. Programmatic advertising, for example, has automated the buying and selling of desktop display, video, social and mobile ads using real-time bidding engines that have audience buying criteria set according to the analysis of consumer online browsing and shopping data. Programmatic ad systems can be used to manage how online campaigns are booked, flighted, analysed and optimized using demand-side software interfaces and algorithms.

Eagle Eye works with lead generation experts at Driftrock in this space, so I spoke to its CEO, Matt Wheeler, about what was now possible with performance marketing and a digital customer connection. He said:

> The role of social media and search in contemporary marketing has an enormous impact on offline sales and I think people don't realize how much of an impact that is. When you've got 70–80 per cent of retail purchases happening offline and the rest happening online, marketing budgets have historically kind of been split like that too. But the reality is that somewhere in the region of 60 per cent of sales are influenced by digital,[6] while nowhere near the same proportion is spent on digital marketing.

Wheeler explained:

> The thing about digital marketing is that it's very measurable. If you're making even one penny on the pound, you'll spend as much money as you can. Social media and search platforms managed to solve attribution issues through e-commerce very easily in verticals where there's a 100 per cent online experience. Then they solved it in areas like mobile app downloads and brand advertising. But what they're really struggling to solve and where they've really been struggling is in proving offline attribution and sales.

Driftrock is working with retail operators, brands and agencies to deploy local, personalized campaigns at scale, with out-of-the-box offer issuance and synchronization through Eagle Eye. This allows advertisers to track and optimize ads from issuance partner through to redemptions, even with offline conversions. Wheeler said:

> Let's say, for instance, that they're advertising barbecues. But someone yesterday went into the store and bought a barbecue. They're no longer

in the market for a barbecue so, for them, seeing that ad on Facebook the day after is completely irrelevant; it's not useful. An experience like that is bad for the consumer, it's bad for the retail advertiser because they're now wasting their media spend on that person, and it's bad for Facebook, because the consumer and advertiser now don't trust the relevancy of the ads it serves. What we do at Driftrock is we help combine the data that the brands know about their customers and what they buy with the targeting capabilities of social or search advertising platforms. By doing so, you can deliver really relevant, useful ads to people that they're much more likely to engage with.

So, if they've just bought a barbecue, instead of advertising another barbecue to them, why don't we instead advertise some barbecue utensils? Or, if you want to engage with a message that has more of a CRM objective, you may target them with some interesting content on how to keep your barbecue in the best condition, or some recipes, for example. That's essentially what we do at Driftrock, and we believe that you can't deliver good, relevant advertising without having a clear view of the customer, and only the retailer or brand can truly understand their own customers. Facebook doesn't understand your customer, it doesn't have that data and nor should it.

Omnichannel personalization

To do great personalized marketing as an omnichannel retailer you need three things:

1 A rich customer data asset, which your analytics 'brain' can analyse to determine the next best action for every customer.

2 The ability to turn that insight into action via a 'nervous system' such as Eagle Eye, a platform that connects the output of the analytical 'brain' to every customer touchpoint (e.g. in-store POS, e-commerce, mobile app, email, third-party partners, etc).

3 The focus and determination to want to provide customers with the most relevant and most helpful content and experiences, knowing that this is a life's work.

IN SUMMARY

- Think about how best to deploy personalization's 'secret weapon' – flexing all of the levers available to you to ensure that you're investing the most value in your best customers.

- The best personalization strategies combine art and science. Look at what the data is telling you and think about what the best actions to take are. If you aren't sure what the customer wants or needs, ask them!

- Businesses that can offer both usefulness and relevance to their customers are the ones that will win in the personalization space.

- Don't be complacent – there is typically a huge headroom opportunity, even in your most loyal customers. Address this through personalizing every interaction with them to drive both transactional and emotional loyalty to your brand.

- Seek to have a balanced approach of both thanking and stretching customers, and ensure that when doing the latter, both the target and associated rewards are personalized to each customer.

- Capitalize on the performance marketing opportunity, not just in your e-commerce business but by measuring offline conversions to understand the total impact of any campaign. Relentlessly test and measure the results and optimize for success.

Notes

1 Walker, L (1998) Amazon gets personal with e-commerce, *Washington Post*, 8 November, www.washingtonpost.com/wp-srv/washtech/daily/nov98/amazon110898.htm (archived at https://perma.cc/R52M-TPFC)

2 Reichheld, F (1996) *The Loyalty Effect: The hidden force behind growth, profits, and lasting value*, Harvard Business School Press, Boston, MA

3 Lindecrantz, E, Tjon Pian Gi, M and Zerbi, S (2020) Personalizing the customer experience: Driving differentiation in retail, McKinsey & Company, 28 April, www.mckinsey.com/industries/retail/our-insights/personalizing-the-customer-experience-driving-differentiation-in-retail (archived at https://perma.cc/WY7J-ADPF)

4 Sainsbury's (2021) Sainsbury's gets personal with the launch of tailored My Nectar Prices, 16 September, www.about.sainsburys.co.uk/news/latest-news/2021/16-09-2021-sainsburys-gets-personal-with-launch-of-tailored-my-nectar-prices (archived at https://perma.cc/AP3Q-YLVD)

5 Sainsbury's (2022) Interim results for the 28 weeks ended 17 September 2022, 3 November, www.about.sainsburys.co.uk/news/latest-news/2022/03-11-22-interim-results (archived at https://perma.cc/GLB5-NWLS)

6 Miglani, J (2022) Digital-influenced retail sales forecast, US, Forrester, 6 October, https://www.forrester.com/report/2022-digital-influenced-retail-sales-forecast-us/RES178197 (archived at https://perma.cc/PPJ5-T3HD)

7

'Near me': the importance of place

In an era where the smartphone is an always-on device, capable of real-time tracking and one-to-one communication at extremely low cost, businesses no longer need to rely on the expensive plastic cards and direct mailings that were once at the very heart of loyalty propositions all over the world. What you do need, however, is a reason for someone to identify themselves and connect to you – most likely using their own mobile device – every time they visit your store.

In my opinion, the most important challenge facing retail today is the conundrum of what to do when you don't have a customer connection in the physical store. Even when you have an online connection, it likely does not extend consistently to your view of the same customer in a store. Quite a number of businesses are OK or even good when people are on their e-commerce sites, but as soon as customers get into their stores, they lose them into a digital black hole. It's very dangerous for you to know the online part of your relationship intimately and nothing about your in-store relationship. You may see me search but not buy and, every time I visit the site, you urge me to buy. But you don't know I bought it in the store two weeks ago! It makes you look daft. This happened to a friend of mine who bought one of those new-fangled Japanese loos that offers an optional extra of a wash and brush-up. Although he bought it six months ago, he is still being pursued relentlessly online to complete that sale. As he eloquently puts it, 'how many $3,500 loos do they think a man needs!' If Google can earn trust by reliably guiding you to a store entrance, why doesn't the shopkeeper own the relationship and take up the mantle as a reliable guide once inside?

The importance of place in the digital world

My focus is not e-commerce, but rather how physical spaces will evolve in the digital world. However, in 1995 I was the founding Chairman of Tesco Direct, which became Tesco.com. So, I have some experience of building an e-commerce business and clearly the title of this book, Omnichannel Retail, speaks to the strategic importance of e-commerce alongside physical stores today, but for now, I will focus on how digital can enhance trips to shops and visits to restaurants.

The growing sales and influence of e-commerce has impacted all aspects of the shopping journey, including the search and browsing phases particularly, digitizing previously analogue tasks such as price comparisons or compiling digital shopping or gift lists. It goes without saying that the Covid-19 pandemic accelerated the move to digital for businesses and consumers across the world at a pace that none of us could have anticipated. In 2021, e-commerce accounted for nearly 19 per cent of retail sales worldwide and forecasts indicate that by 2026, this will be closer to 25 per cent.[1]

Of course, many of the lockdown-driven rather than pure consumer-driven trends have started to abate with e-commerce spend in categories such as grocery declining as consumers return to stores. However, what is clear is that omnichannel is more important now than it has ever been.

To compete, every bricks-and-mortar retailer must ensure they are as easy to find online as their pureplay rivals. This is where search engine optimization (SEO) tools and techniques that govern organic search rankings and results can be the difference between making prospective customers aware that your business exists at all, and that you have a try-before-you-buy physical outlet too. Considering that e-commerce also enables borderless trade, SEO could also arguably offer smaller, regional or local organizations, without the same resources or reach of a multimillion-dollar international retail chain, greater potential of being found online, and so driving sales with customers who would otherwise never have shopped with them.

This book is not a guide on how to have a competitive, fit-for-purpose website, but you do need one, and some of the characteristics you need to consider are sophisticated search indexing capabilities and filters that can help a customer quickly find what they're looking for. Examples in this space would include the use of intelligent search, allowing a customer to perform a search using natural language, just as you would ask a question in a two-way conversation; or filters that can narrow the number of search results, by brand, colour or size. Visual search and recognition tools can also identify an image from the real world based on its unique visual features. So, a customer could upload a picture of a friend's favourite outfit to find similar items available to buy on a fashion retailer's site or app.

Customers will also appreciate it if you extend the ability to search effectively for products and services to ratings and reviews from previous customers. A recent study has found that when customers interact with ratings and reviews on a product page, it positively impacts conversion rates by 120 per cent.[2] Fresh, product-specific review content can also drive search traffic and keyword rankings, boosting awareness of your online presence.

You have to be expert in how Google ranks searches and ensure that you keep up with the changes it regularly makes to its algorithms. I once worked for a direct sales business that could track leads through to appointments and sales to a decimal point. Suddenly, the number of leads generated from traditional channels remained the same but leads from web advertising collapsed. At the time, it took three weeks to work out what had changed about Google's search criteria, but once discovered and corrected, normal service was immediately resumed. But they were three very painful weeks.

So, when it comes to your place in the digital world, there's a huge amount to keep IT and marketing busy before they even start to think about integrating an e-commerce presence effectively with their physical stores.

Location as a proxy for relevance

I used to be a Board Advisor to Yext, which is the global leader in 'near me' searching. Founded by Howard Lerman and Brian Distelburger, Yext launched its initial public offering (IPO) in 2017 as a unicorn. Its success has been built on the massive growth – 150 per cent year-on-year in 2017 – in 'near me' searches, proving that location is a proxy for relevance. This trend has only continued to gain traction, with Google reporting a 400 per cent growth in searches including 'open now near me' from 2020 to 2021.[3] One of Yext's key selling aids is to take a sample of, say, 100 branches from a prospect and scan the internet for information about those branch locations. The levels of inaccuracy they often find are shocking and include basic information, such as the wrong phone numbers and zip codes or out-of-date opening times.

Yet, the significance of accurate, 'near me' search today is analogous to the directional advertising hoardings of the analogue age. It's laughable to imagine that any self-respecting retailer would have put up with a sign that said turn left in 200 yards for the store when, in fact, the store was actually two miles away on the right. Yet there is something about the personal and hidden nature of a mobile search that means the same store managers do not expose mobile search results to the same rigour.

Ignoring its importance also belies the fact that most 'near me' searches are prompted after the shopper has been through (or doesn't need to go through) the item search and browsing phase and is now ready to discover where or how quickly they can buy. Using my own experience here, I once searched for my nearest John Lewis department store on Google and thought I would give them a call before paying a visit. I clicked on the telephone number included in the information results Google served me and it took me through to none other than its direct department store rival! Now I can say this because that was before John Lewis began using Yext, which is one of the few technology companies that has built a direct API into Google, so, of course, it no longer has any issue with its location data! But, it also just shows the dangers of your physical location not being accurate in the digital world, as it means you can't be found in the real world.

Blending physical and digital

This is why companies like Yext enable you, at a stroke, to change opening hours, reflect departmental changes, and accurately map any new or changed store locations in one place, at one time, everywhere on the web. Back in the day, there was always a photo of the store manager in each Tesco store, which was great, except that the managers were moved around so much it was hell's own job keeping the pictures up to date. Now this can all be done digitally and centrally.

'Near me' search is also a good indicator of immediacy and one of the reasons that the ability to be found digitally in the real world is gaining in importance. 'ROBO' – research online, buy offline – or 'webrooming' as it's also known, is the process that culminates in 'near me' searching and encapsulates digital's omnichannel influence on shopper expectations of a seamless transition from online to in-store that bridges online to offline. ROBO refers to the trend among an increasing number of shoppers researching online to qualify their buying decisions before making a purchase in-store. And recent research suggests the two often happen simultaneously, with 56 per cent of in-store shoppers reportedly using their smartphones to research items while in a physical store.[4]

It may have seemed that the store's role was being diminished and becoming less important when home delivery, enabled by e-commerce, grew in popularity. So, this initial online challenge is also the reason why most established retailers now have their own transactional, e-commerce presence. It's why a high proportion also now capitalize on their physical store networks to offer buy online, pick up in-store – or so-called 'click and collect' services – to better compete with the pure-plays and bridge the online-to-offline gap. The resulting 'bricks and clicks' model ensures that their digital presence online is operationally connected to the store, which has now become a hybrid fulfilment hub as a result.

Target is often touted as a leader in this space, having kicked-off an omnichannel transformation journey back in 2016 that reaped huge rewards during the Covid-19 crisis. During an analyst update in March 2021, Target CEO, Brian Cornell summarized:

> In 2016, our digital transformation was only beginning. We weren't even a Top 10 e-commerce provider, and we were just getting our same

day services off the ground. Today we have the most complete suite of same-day fulfillment services in the industry. We're one of the leading e-commerce players, and for click-and-collect same-day services, we continue to deliver industry leading growth and dollar volume as well as Net Promoter Scores over 80 per cent, despite record demand.

We placed the physical store more firmly at the center of our omni-channel platform and we created a durable, sustainable and scalable business model that put Target on a road of our own. Our goal was to use our proximity – nearly 1,900 stores within 10 miles of the vast majority of the US consumers – to offer the fastest and easiest digital fulfillment in retail. The capabilities we've built to become 'America's easiest place to shop' also cracked the essential question of how to grow our digital sales exponentially, while maintaining the overall profitability of our business.[5]

At a time when many other brands were paralysed by a fear that Amazon was coming to eat their breakfast, lunch and dinner, or were wholly focused on trying to adapt their traditional businesses to morph into something more Amazon-ian, Cornell and his team invested their money and efforts in a belief that:

> The key to guest preference and breakout growth lay in an unappreciated omnichannel asset called 'the store'. Many were skeptical, which is why we said from the beginning that we were playing our own game in creating a category of one. Many thought the inevitable drift was for our store guests to become digital guests and that the current only ran in one direction. We saw something different. We saw a future in which even the most committed digital-only guests would find the best and easiest shopping experience at Target because of how we connect that experience to our stores.[6]

As I summarized at the end of Chapter 2, it's my firm belief that will always outweighs skill, and this Target story is a real demonstration of this. When it started its business transformation back in 2016, it was significantly lagging the competition when it came to digital, but five years later through focus and determination, it was able to publish the astounding results shown in Figure 7.1. It achieved this

FIGURE 7.1 Target's omnichannel success story for the full year 2021[7]

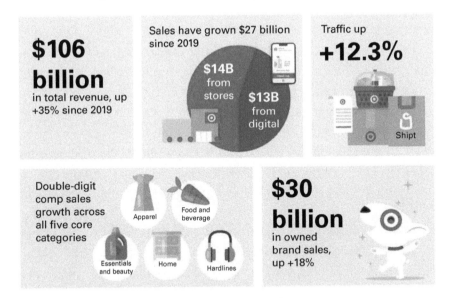

by building an organization that seamlessly blends digital and physical experiences, enabling it to meet its customers' needs wherever, whenever and however they choose to shop.

The value of utility

And it's not just Target that has seen huge successes offering online-to-offline customer services. Faced with the many challenges brought about by Covid-19, retailers around the world experimented with variations on the click-and-collect theme in the race over the last mile, using different online-to-offline fulfilment methods. Some of the most notable include curbside or drive-through pickup, which 'Uberifies' the collection process. Adopting the same name as the service it provides, US fulfilment firm Curbside, for instance, partners with retailers in order to enable shoppers to drive by the store and easily pick up orders placed through the Curbside app without having to leave their vehicles.

This was a trend that was accelerated by the pandemic but has continued to increase in popularity due to meeting consumers' needs relating to convenience and value (by removing fees associated to delivery). In early 2020, less than 7 per cent of the top 1,000 retail chains in the US offered curbside pickup, a number which exploded to 62 per cent at the end of 2021.[8] In the UK, click-and-collect now accounts for 40 per cent of sales for retailers that offer the service, with more than 8 per cent of the UK's total retail spending going through this channel.[9] But the work here isn't done. According to the 2022 Grocery Omnichannel Retail Index, only 13 per cent of retailers offer curbside returns,[10] something I expected to be more mainstream by now – a service which absolutely would offer increased utility to customers. Following a successful trial, Target has recently announced it will be offering their Drive Up Returns service across almost its entire estate this year, which means that customers can process a return from the comfort of their car.[11]

Physical spaces have always had the advantage over the e-commerce channel of being able to offer human interaction via customer service, sensory selection, try before you buy and instant gratification, where online just can't compete. This is despite advances in virtual 'try-on' systems, virtual reality (VR) headsets and 3D.

The main point about the proliferation of online-to-offline fulfilment methods is that, in the face of many competitive challenges, including e-commerce and discounters, stores are not going anywhere soon. In 2021, nearly 80 per cent of global retail sales were made in physical stores.[12] Internet shopping is reportedly most popular in the UK compared to any other country, with 82 per cent of the adult population having made a purchase online in 2021, but even here, e-commerce still only represents 30 per cent of the retail market.[13] As the functional utility of digital's influence on shopping journeys matures, more malls and stores are being refurbished to satisfy the increased need for more experiential physical retail, combined with hospitality and leisure spaces, which integrates into a pleasant physical experience not replicable in the digital world.

It is pertinent to note that investing in omnichannel makes good business sense as we know that shoppers who engage across channels are the most valuable. According to the IGD, omnichannel customers spend between twice and three times the amount a single-channel shopper does.[14] In order to engage as broad a range of customers as possible, businesses need to deploy different solutions whether it's in pricing, promotions, loyalty, subscriptions, etc, which appeal differently to different customers but when combined, create a mosaic of digital attraction.

What this means to me is that your store, restaurant, bank, motor dealership or any other physical business needs to fit into a digital ecosystem, which starts with a website, then probably has 'near me' searching and local ads, so you can get to the physical space; then, when you get there, instead of losing digital connection and having visitors put their phones in their pockets, the digital connection is maintained and enhanced. Once you have all of that, what do you do while they're there that makes them think: 'I'm really glad they've got all of this information on me, because it makes shopping more valuable, relevant, interesting and fun'?

Another crucial fact about the real-time nature of the store touches on one of the things we don't talk about enough in retail, and which I think is becoming much more important now that we're all leading such busy, always-on lives. That is, when is the right time to talk to someone? Not just what do I communicate, but whom do I communicate it to and when? These questions rightly recognize that the digital connection, geofenced in the physical space, unlocks a whole new dimension of taking your insight from being post the fact, or just hindsight if you will, and allows you to act on the customer connection during the fact, in the now, in real time. That's a big breakthrough and something I dive into in much more detail in Chapter 10.

Locating customers in-store

To find out more about the impact of connecting to customers in-store, I turned to the best expert I know on the subject, Gavin

Wheeldon, CEO of Purple, which is a Wi-Fi-based customer data and analytics firm. I chatted to Wheeldon when writing the first edition about what we could learn from Amazon's then recent moves into physical spaces. The e-commerce giant's activity came up when I asked him who, in his opinion, was doing the digital part of omnichannel well in-store.

He answered the question in the same way I would, which is that there are just not that many examples of retailers doing what we've already suggested they should do to make the most of their digital presence in the real world. This is what led me to ask him what difference he thought Amazon's ownership of Whole Foods would make to the Whole Foods shopping trip. He predicted it would become more personalized with Amazon aiming to remove a lot of friction from the customer journey:

> Friction is one of the reasons I and a lot of other consumers don't particularly like physical shopping. When I say 'friction', I mean finding things, for instance, and then when I find them, queuing to check out. Those two things alone cause me a lot of grief and neither of them need exist. I mean, Amazon could just suggest my shopping list to me before I walk in the door of Whole Foods and then just show me where everything is in the store via the shortest route, so I can pick them up and walk straight out, as you can do in its Amazon Go stores. Just achieving that would be an immeasurable number of steps forward, and it would make physical shopping a much more pleasurable experience.

In the time elapsed since this interview took place in late 2017, Whole Foods has become more integrated with the wider Amazon business, but certainly not in all areas. Amazon Prime members have been able to engage with Whole Foods benefits since 2018, Prime Day now includes Whole Foods promotions and, as Wheeldon predicted, Just Walk Out technology and Amazon dash carts were implemented in a limited number of US stores in 2022.[15]

As Whole Foods no longer directly reports earnings, it is difficult to truly measure its performance, however, I think it is safe to say that many, including me, think that it has missed an opportunity in the five years since being acquired to truly differentiate both from a technology and a positioning point of view.

As I stated in the first edition, there was so much executional risk in Amazon's acquisition of Whole Foods. Even if it could get its digital store experience fully integrated with Amazon – which hasn't happened yet – it needs to focus on the positioning of the Whole Foods brand with its core consumer. At the time of writing this second edition in January 2023, Jason Buechel has just taken on the role of CEO and will be watched closely by the industry to see what decisions he makes to move the brand forward in such a rapidly evolving industry. Experts predict that one of the key focus areas will include reconnecting to the brand's purpose-driven roots.[16] In my view, there is a significant opportunity for Whole Foods to successfully achieve this by harnessing the power of digitally connecting to customers, adding value at every stage of their shopping journey by communicating with them on a range of topics from product provenance to sustainability, promotions and recipes, all while they shop in-store.

For the bricks-and-clicks operators as a whole though, there does remain a significant problem. They are stuck in the headlights of the Amazon truck. They're not talking about why they exist and how they should go to market. They're just terrified, asking each other, 'What are we going to do?', instead of saying, 'We have to be personalized, digitally enabled and data driven – because we can'. It becomes easier to decide what to do once you've been through that process of embedding a DIAL type of customer leadership in your business.

Wheeldon also made the great point that, from a technology perspective, competing with the likes of an Amazon-enabled Whole Foods is very achievable. 'It's not like other, more traditional retailers can't fight back, and that Amazon and the others have a secret sauce that only they can ever use,' he pointed out. 'They just need to bring their digital expertise together from other places. But, absolutely, if retailers don't move, and they sit staring in the headlights, they'll get run over. They'll either get acquired by one of the online players, or they'll go out of business.' So, we're back to the lessons that the winners can capitalize on and the losers fail to learn.

Tim Mason (TM): Certainly, and I don't know if you're going to agree with this, but it's a lot easier to be Amazon than it is to be Whole Foods. Having spent my entire life retailing food, Whole Foods is an unbelievably sophisticated and complicated retailer, and they're in a class of one. There are probably some smaller, regional number twos who can match them. But, in terms of being able to do all of those different things under one roof, pretty much replicated from store to store, they really are unique.

Gavin Wheeldon (GW): Don't forget that Amazon gets more money from its Marketplace (65 per cent gross merchandise value (GMV) in 2022)[17] than it does from selling its own stuff. It gets more money from other people selling on Amazon, so they're already plugged into that network and you'll probably get some crossover between the two, I suspect.

   The fact is, though, that everything is moving digital. So, you can be the best baker in the world but, if you're not digitally proficient in winning and keeping customers, you'll be the best baker in the world out of business.

TM: My point is that the largest online retailer in the world is in effect saying: "I've got unbelievable scale, capabilities and skills. But, in fact, I'm going to buy a supply chain, I'm not going to build it." That's because it's just so hard to build a supply chain.

GW: It is. Although, often the online businesses are predicated on not having as complex a supply chain as store-based retail chains, where there's often disintermediation between the various parts. They take the middle, which is the most profitable part. I would think that Amazon, Netflix, Alibaba and all of the others that have grown rapidly online are looking at the offline world and going, "wow, that's all so inefficient", where they measure everything to within an inch of its life and, if they did the same offline, what could they achieve.

   They say ~80 per cent of sales are still completed offline, and I don't believe that will dramatically change over the coming years. So, if I'm Amazon or similar and I want to significantly increase market share, then I need to start chipping into some of that offline, ROBO spend.

TM: You're absolutely right. The point I was leading to with that was that both bricks-and-clicks retailers and pureplays are on the same journey, but they need each other's smarts. The question becomes whether a Tesco or a Kroger can add the digital skills to their very highly honed merchant curation skills. They're much better merchants and curators, and they're actually much better users of customer data than Amazon. They use it much more to benefit the customer, I think. If they could put the tech on top, with that, they could be a formidable force.

Why place matters

I think my colleague, Steve Rothwell, summed up how important place is to customer-facing businesses in the digital world best when he said:

> The world of retail has to appreciate that their beautiful world of the last 40-odd years, where they've got the best position on the main shopping street in town, which means they're going to make a load of money, does not exist any more. Therefore, the mentality of going 'well, we'll worry about it in two years' time' should not exist any more, because the pureplay e-commerce guys who are going to eat their lunch are making customer-centric decisions every day. They don't care that you've got a 15-year lease, because they never need that building. They can just hammer social media or the digital world around you and destroy the competition.

So, the average store, restaurant, mall and any other customer-facing physical space needs to digitally augment its offer, both inside as well as on the journey to the store to deliver personalized experiences that can both compete with, as well as complement, e-commerce growth, which is what we study in the next chapter.

IN SUMMARY

- Omnichannel is more important now than it has ever been. E-commerce represents 21 per cent of the total retail market and this is growing. To compete against pureplay rivals, physical retailers need to build a strategy that incentivizes customers to identify themselves every time they engage with you, especially when shopping in your physical stores.

- Location is a great proxy for relevance – use this to your advantage and harness the power of knowing where your customers are in the physical world in order to serve them better and drive the behaviour you seek.

- The Covid-19 pandemic accelerated the digitization of the physical retail store, with the ones that have been the most successful being those that have removed friction from the customer journey while offering customers tangible value – saving them time, money or both.

- Omnichannel customers spend more than single-channel customers and so investing in the customer connection across every touchpoint makes good business sense.

- As there is no such thing as an average customer, this will likely require a mosaic of digital attraction.

Notes

1 Coppola, D (2023) e-commerce as share of total retail sales worldwide 2015–2026, Statista, 20 February, www.statista.com/statistics/534123/e-commerce-share-of-retail-sales-worldwide/ (archived at https://perma.cc/NQ6U-42W4)

2 Fischer, A and Zuckerman, A (2021) The impact of review volume on conversion: Is more really better? Power Reviews, 15 June, www.powerreviews.com/blog/review-volume-conversion-impact/ (archived at https://perma.cc/MN29-UCYN)

3 Thygesen, A (2022) 2022 Marketing Guide: Increase foot traffic and in-store sales, Think with Google, April, www.thinkwithgoogle.com/intl/en-gb/consumer-insights/consumer-journey/increase-foot-traffic-and-in-store-sales/ (archived at https://perma.cc/3HF3-TU3Y)

4 Think with Google (2019) In-store smartphone research statistics, www.thinkwithgoogle.com/consumer-insights/consumer-trends/in-store-smartphone-research-statistics/ (archived at https://perma.cc/EBL4-JAPU)

5   Lauchlan, S (2021) How Target's omni-channel leap of faith 5 years ago set it up for retail's COVID crisis and beyond, Diginomica, 3 March, diginomica. com/how-targets-omni-channel-leap-faith-5-years-ago-set-it-retails-covid-crisis-and-beyond (archived at https://perma.cc/3UM5-V7MD)

6   Lauchlan, S (2021) How Target's omni-channel leap of faith 5 years ago set it up for retail's COVID crisis and beyond, Diginomica, 3 March, diginomica. com/how-targets-omni-channel-leap-faith-5-years-ago-set-it-retails-covid-crisis-and-beyond (archived at https://perma.cc/RAX3-YCBK)

7   Rug News (2022) Target reports fourth quarter and full-year 2021 earnings, 3 January, www.rugnews.com/news-archives/target-reports-fourth-quarter-and-fullyear-2021-ea-8559 (archived at https://perma.cc/E7BU-GW29)

8   Melton, J (2021) More than 50% of large retail chains offer curbside pickup, *Digital Commerce 360*, 27 April, www.digitalcommerce360.com/2021/04/27/ more-than-50-of-large-retail-chains-offer-curbside-pickup/ (archived at https:// perma.cc/NEG4-GV5N)

9   Johnson, K (2022) What's in store for retail? Barclays, October, www. barclayscorporate.com/content/dam/barclayscorporate-com/documents/ insights/Industry-expertise-22/whats-in-store-for-retail.pdf (archived at https://perma.cc/Z6VD-AMSP)

10   Rothschild, C (2023) Day two at NRF 2023: Retail's Big Show – Retailers tap tech to streamline the consumer journey, Coresight Research, 17 January, coresight.com/research/day-two-at-nrf-2023-retails-big-show-retailers-tap-tech-to-streamline-the-consumer-journey/ (archived at https://perma.cc/ GBA8-AB6Z)

11   Target Corporate (2023) Coming to a Target near you: Return a purchase *Without Leaving Your Car*, 28 February, corporate.target.com/ article/2023/02/drive-up-returns (archived at https://perma.cc/387B-4NTY)

12   Coppola, D (2023) e-commerce as share of total retail sales worldwide 2015–2026, Statista, 20 February, www.statista.com/statistics/534123/ e-commerce-share-of-retail-sales-worldwide/ (archived at https://perma.cc/ PMY9-77KY)

13   International Trade Administration (2022) United Kingdom – eCommerce, 12 September, www.trade.gov/country-commercial-guides/united-kingdom-ecommerce (archived at https://perma.cc/U27U-3SBK)

14   Wright, J (2021) Winning in omnichannel, IGD, March, retailanalysis.igd.com/ presentations/presentation-viewer/t/winning-in-omnichannel/i/10702 (archived at https://perma.cc/SR9Z-PM8F)

15   Retail Technology Innovation Hub (2022) Amazon's Tony Hoggett discusses 2022 in-store and rapid delivery innovations, 21 December, retailtechinnovationhub. com/home/2022/12/20/amazons-tony-hoggett-discusses-2022-in-store-and-rapid-delivery-innovations (archived at https://perma.cc/KZV4-GEYC)

16 Grocery Dive (2022) What should Whole Foods' new CEO prioritize? 1 September, www.grocerydive.com/news/what-should-whole-foods-new-ceo-prioritize/630985/ (archived at https://perma.cc/8WPV-3VBH)

17 Marketplace Pulse (2022) Amazon GMV reached $600 billion in 2021, 4 February, www.marketplacepulse.com/articles/amazon-gmv-reached-600-billion-in-2021 (archived at https://perma.cc/TAU2-CJ36)

8

The digitally augmented store

We all live in the digital world, so the store, restaurant and showroom should too. In mapping the average customer shopping journey and its many permutations via online and offline touchpoints, we have seen how physical retail locations must maintain an attractive and accurate presence in the online world to serve one or more of those touchpoints. But when customers are actually in the store, it becomes necessary to transition them to a digitally enabled and augmented physical store experience designed to help them get the most out of the fact that they've paid a visit. It's my contention that nobody really yet knows how to run good stores in the digital world. If you look at how smartphones have changed our world beyond recognition, shopping in a physical space is still often exactly the same as it was, and it doesn't need to be.

With a one-to-one connection to customers through their own personal devices in the store, you can start to capture more data, personalize messages, move much more into performance rather than broadcast marketing, and you can take a 100,000 sq ft box with 50,000 or 60,000 SKUs in it and actually make it feel an awful lot more manageable and more relevant. Giving the store digital context, so that it can infer and respond to shopper intent in real time, will provide a reason for customers to engage via mobile once inside, providing an opportunity for the retailer to enhance their shopping experience and increase conversion.

According to recent research conducted by Deloitte Digital, one-third of consumers report 'often' shopping both in-store and online during the same purchase occasion. We know consumers use their digital view of the world to find the nearest store or available item. They join their e-commerce view up to their final in-store shopping journey through ROBO, but two-thirds of shoppers also use their mobile phones while in-store, often to compare prices at the shelf edge with the aim of buying items cheaper online.[1] So, if they are looking to use their phones while in-store, why don't the store operators capitalize on this as a means of timely engagement instead of letting these showroomers try before they buy elsewhere?

The benefits of data in-store

It's incredibly important to make that digital connection in-store because developments in technology are making it much easier to gain more insight into customers compared to the Clubcard data that Tesco prized so highly back in the day. Customers are still willing to swipe their loyalty cards at checkout if it offers them sufficient value, so why wouldn't they be willing to engage via their phones in a store? By further connecting with and linking that in-store customer back to their e-commerce identity online, bricks-and-clicks retailers can capture a truly 360-degree view of who their customers are. They can use this view to run their businesses better and attract more customers who shop both online and in-store. This strategy should deliver significant gains, especially when it's known that omnichannel customers spend two to three times more than those customers who shop exclusively in one channel.[2]

I spoke to Gavin Wheeldon, Purple CEO, about the challenge from online pureplays moving into bricks and mortar, as Amazon has done with Whole Foods and its Amazon Go store concepts, and Alibaba and JD.com are doing in China. When I said that both customers' and retailers' expectations of in-store had been raised by the speed, ease and convenience of online, forcing a reassessment of the role of physical space in the digital world, Wheeldon commented:

> First of all, an e-commerce business would know how many people were visiting. You'd be able to find out how long they were staying, where on the site or app they went, or did they bounce? Then you optimize to improve all of those metrics. Then you try and capture people's information by encouraging them to sign up for a newsletter or register for an account, or whatever it might be. Then, you start doing personalized campaigns to drive more loyalty from those customers, you measure the impact with A/B testing, and go back through the loop again. That's exactly what people need to do offline.

To get a feel of what Gavin means, you could watch, or may have already seen, *The Social Dilemma*, a documentary released by Netflix in 2020. In it, there is a dramatization of how a social website continually A/B tests to drive the key outcome of dwell time. It's well done and as a lifelong retail marketeer, exposed me to a way of working that was vastly ahead of anything I had ever practised.

Using connection to erase friction

You can perhaps understand why so many traditional retailers are worried when the Amazon Go store format has made 'just walking out' without having to check out your goods a reality. It has digitally augmented the traditional convenience store customer experience by eliminating the friction of queuing and payment. The thing that interests me is that this store won't even let you in until you've downloaded the app, registered payment information and then identified yourself to gain entry to the store. This ultimate digital in-store connectivity gives Amazon an enviable view of its Go customers' activity online and offline. In the first edition, I noted that,

> by contrast, Tesco has decided to go 'back to basics' by opening Jack's, a store banner that owes more to a German discount retailer than it does to a digitally enabled Amazon Go, Alibaba Hema or JD.com 7FRESH store.

> Only time will tell if the current Tesco management's decision to forsake the value of customer data will pay off by opening a store without it.

As I write now in January 2023, time has indeed told. In January 2022, Tesco announced it was closing Jacks, and in October 2021 it opened its first checkout-free 'GetGo' store in partnership with Trigo, who power the frictionless technology, offering customers an experience akin to Amazon's Go model.[3]

The checkout-free function of these stores is an interesting area of development in terms of the fusion of digital and physical to augment the store experience. The less friction there is – specifically here, the functional time customers must spend queuing and paying – the more likely the customer is to digitally connect in-store for the utility of convenience and speed.

My co-author shared an interesting story with me recently, which detailed the Twitter storm that erupted after a Tesco customer detailed his 'distressing experience' trying to enter the first Tesco GetGo store without having the required app or Clubcard membership, now known as #sandwichgate:

After work, Jonathan Rowson received a text asking him to get a sandwich for his son's packed lunch. He saw the Tesco store and thought he was in luck but found out that he could only enter the store if he downloaded the app and signed up to Clubcard. Jonathan downloaded the app but said no to the Clubcard – he was still unable to buy the sandwich and leave, and so asked staff for help. The staff member took Jonathan's phone and changed the options to 'accept Clubcard', and told him that without doing this, you can't get in. Despite Jonathan not wanting this, the staff member went on to say that this was store policy now, and that soon all stores will be like this. Jonathan deleted the app and vowed not to shop at Tesco, as he felt shocked at the compulsory data cost to buy a sandwich.[4]

What struck me here was that the same rules just don't apply to traditional, primarily store-based retailers as they do to the likes of Amazon. When you look for news stories relating to Amazon Go, you come across a lot of content akin to '5 Reasons why Amazon Go is already the greatest retail innovation of the next 30 years'.[5] When Tesco does it, it opens itself up to being accused of alienating customers all over social media and in the national press. I suppose the lesson here is to move cautiously and to always lead with the value proposition you've created for your customers, as well as of course remembering to personalize your message wherever possible as you can't please everyone all the time with a one-size-fits-all message.

Another way grocers are successfully capturing data in-store by removing friction is through mobile scan-and-go apps, which are increasing in popularity. According to recent research, the number of stores offering mobile self-scanning globally will grow by nearly 250 per cent between 2021 and 2027.[6] Across Europe, 38 per cent of retailers are already offering a scan-and-go service with another 21 per cent working on deploying such solutions.[7] In my opinion, and according to reported customer preferences, mobile ultimately provides a vastly better alternative to a purpose-built handheld scanner.[8] For one thing, we as consumers pay to change, maintain or upgrade our own hardware, whereas retailers must amortize the cost of their inflexible scan-and-go device estates over years and absorb their total cost of ownership.

For me, the big opportunity in this space is for retailers to offer a scan-and-go app that encourages engagement beyond the functional utility of faster payment, where it becomes stickier by playing a fully integrated role in the shopping trip: offering the ability to compile a shopping list, use in-store wayfinding, access offers, product suggestions and information in real time, and to also shop with the retailer online as well as in-store. In doing this, physical retailers could employ many of the incremental sales-driving tactics used by e-commerce businesses such as 'did you forget?', 'incomplete offers', 'you might like' and more. But don't forget, in the physical store these nudges will have to be delivered in real time to be useful. Recent research has shown that more than a third of European retailers offering scan-and-go are already reporting basket size increases for customers using self-scanning,[9] with this being something that has the propensity to grow significantly as the ability to engage with these consumers on a one-to-one level as they shop through the physical store improves.

Recent research has shown that 60 per cent of consumers want to use this kind of technology in order to access more detailed product information to enable them to make more conscious purchase choices[10] – I expect leading grocers to start to use this form of digital engagement to communicate with customers regarding the associated carbon footprint of products, for example.

In response to increasing labour costs and general costs pressures, more and more retailers are opting to introduce more unmanned customer self-scan checkouts. These are not great for big shops and so I recommend that retailers offer a combination of self-scan and scan-as-you-shop going forward. While consumers have chosen manned checkouts over self-scan historically, I am not sure they would make the same choice if the alternative was an unmanned checkout.

Building physical connections

Going back to the concept of connecting people, places and things, there are many other friction points that can be addressed with a direct digital connection to your customers in the store. This chapter is about working out a way for the consumer to naturally use that connection to help throughout every point on their journey. There are some systems that encourage retailers to use the credit or debit card PIN entry device (PED) that faces the customer to gather feedback after the transaction, just as swipe cards are still used for loyalty schemes at the point of sale. But nowadays the advantages of having it all go back to the phone that most people always have with them, linked by digital connection at the POS, far outweigh any alternative.

Picking up on Wheeldon's point about having visibility of who is visiting your store, he said that the starting point for digitally augmenting your store is to measure what's going on in physical spaces and try to collect data, even if you do nothing else. Providing secure public Wi-Fi has become basic hygiene in this sense. He confirmed:

> 90 per cent of the time, it's likely that the store has got Wi-Fi because store operations will have it for management reasons, but they won't have enabled it for guests. Most will, but some won't. The trouble is that retailers have bought secure public Wi-Fi systems that serve as basic

hygiene that they've had for years. But that gives you nothing more than a utility. So, if I had a website and didn't know which pages people visited and how often, I certainly wouldn't be in business for long. The first step has to be measuring what's going on. Then, second, you need a way to get your visitors to consciously opt in to a conversation with you.

I can see why Wi-Fi is one of the primary ways for retailers to digitally connect with customers in physical spaces. It is a foundational piece of any strategy that gives customers' phones a useful or enticing enough role in the store for them to consider seeking out such engagement every time they visit. Wheeldon added:

> The issue with other [customer store tracking technology] alternatives, like infrared footfall trackers or cameras, is that they don't understand repeat from new, or dwell, because of the way they count; and the key thing is they are never going to collect data on engaged customers. So, Wi-Fi can replace all of those types of technologies too. It can take you on that digital journey of: first, measuring customer activity in-store; second, collecting data on their habits and preferences by incentivizing customers to sign up for more regular engagement; and, third, using that data to improve the business's understanding of the behaviours of those customers, so you can personalize the next engagement and measure, rinse and repeat.

Speaking to my co-author about this, the point we made in the previous chapter regarding the mosaic of digital attraction that's needed to engage a broad range of customers was reaffirmed, with Sarah's journey to in-store digital connection detailed below:

> I had never felt the need to log in to my local supermarket's Wi-Fi before. Yes, it was annoying that the store was a digital black hole, as if I ever wanted to research a recipe or something to check I had all the items I needed in my trolley, I had to run to the front of the store to get the 3G to work! But this wasn't happening frequently enough or irritating me enough to take the necessary steps to sign up to the Wi-Fi that was available in-store, although not well advertised.

However, after having a baby I suddenly found myself in this supermarket nearly every single day (often multiple times a day!) and obviously it's impossible to push a trolley around as well as a pram. Also, my needs had rapidly changed with my wanting to get in and out of the store with as little friction as possible – queuing while a baby screams at you is not for the faint hearted! So, I signed up to the retailer's Wi-Fi (which was somewhat cumbersome for the first time but I'm now automatically logged in every time I enter the store), downloaded the retailer's scan-as-you-go app, and have never looked back as it makes every visit to the store – pram or no pram – significantly easier for me.

So for Sarah the trigger point for registering with the Wi-Fi and creating a digital connection was wanting to use scan-as-you-go, but for other customers it could be to access product information, to unlock reduced prices, to play games, etc. We will provide more detail on what these engagement tactics could look like for your business at the end of this chapter.

Developing intelligent spaces

At Purple, Wheeldon talks about Wi-Fi enabled buildings as 'intelligent spaces'. 'The reason the term "intelligent spaces" came about is that, right now, physical spaces are very, very dumb,' he explained. 'We are on a mission to make spaces intelligent; in just the same way as I might get a personalized experience on a website, I want a personalized experience when I walk into a physical space.'

By his definition, an intelligent space should know if I'm already in it; it should know who I'm meeting if I'm in an office block, and it should be able to facilitate the journey through that building. It should tell the person I'm meeting that I've arrived and allow me to know where they are in the building, so I can use the mapping functions on my mobile to navigate straight to them using wayfinding. Wheeldon added:

That's intelligence that you'd expect online, but that is also perfectly capable of being replicated offline. Similarly, using a retail example, I often go into a retailer, get frustrated and leave because, although

I know what I want, I may not be able to find it quickly enough. Whereas, again, if the retailer had known I'd walked through the door, understands the type of preferences I have, so that they know, for example, that I'm probably likely to buy another pair of a particular brand of jeans, then they can tell me where they are.

It's worth considering here what Sir Terry Leahy, who also serves on Purple's Board of Directors, said about why he backed its proposition:

> The reason for my involvement with Purple was down to the same thing as it was with Eagle Eye, and that was the use of customer data in a new dimension – the physical space. Purple offers the prospect of intelligent space: space that you can learn something about, in terms of location. You can watch how a store is navigated and how a display is shopped; or how a shopping centre or hospital was used. You can know something about the person on that mobile phone.

Terry's point about knowing who people are when they come into a space you operate and being able to locate them in that space is a prerequisite for such intelligence. Although Wheeldon started Purple because he was frustrated by long-winded sign-up and log-in processes for public Wi-Fi, he soon realized the benefits of the data that Wi-Fi network operators could glean from users, in much the same way as Google knows something about you from the digital breadcrumbs you leave in the places you visit, and Vodafone, AT&T, Apple and Samsung know where you've been from the cell towers your phone pings to confirm its location.

Wheeldon describes the benefits better than I do:

> I very quickly realized that there's all this data being thrown off by Wi-Fi that everybody's ignoring because they only see it through an IT lens. When you looked at the data, we could start re-creating the same metrics that you get online, but offline. That includes footfall, bounce and dwell, and all of those e-commerce-type metrics – we could replicate them all from Wi-Fi data when nobody had thought to do it. It was then that I realized there was a journey to go on where we could recreate many of the advantages of the e-commerce world in a physical space.

Technically, you don't even need your customers to connect to Wi-Fi in-store. The capability Wheeldon describes is based on the same data connection that carriers, including Vodafone and AT&T, use to lock access to their network from a registered device that has been lost or stolen, or that you can use to track your device. The International Mobile Equipment Identity (IMEI) number is used to identify a device that uses terrestrial cellular networks, supplying the bandwidth for your and my mobile data plans. In terms of the tracking capability, only your carrier can attach a name or some form of personal identification to your IMEI number, because you registered the device when you purchased it.

Now, over an open and public secure Wi-Fi network, IMEI can provide very basic location information if the location of the Wi-Fi router access point (AP) you're using is known. This is why Google may prompt you to 'turn Wi-Fi on to improve accuracy' when using its Maps service, and why it can provide some location information in this way. But when a customer registers for free Wi-Fi in-store, they will associate some personally identifiable information with their device IMEI in return for internet access and automatic logins when they return. If, in addition, they're using your app in-store, some location information can be also shared (for example, if the app reads GPS and other sensor data generated by the phone), which can be used to match their shopping journey in the physical store against how they may use the app. So, it's back to that 'give to get' principle again, where the lesson is: give your customers a reason to get their phone out and engage while in-store. Even if you don't know who is using the Wi-Fi, you can still gain visibility into how a store is navigated and how a display is shopped. Footfall, dwell time, queuing and conversion through checkout areas can all be measured and used to create heat maps that can be used to inform store layout, merchandising, customer service and marketing decisions.

But, again, without opening up a dialogue using the connection that throws off this information, how do you tell customers about all of the great things you've done to improve their experience in that store?

Knowing the customers you have and when they come back is extremely useful in terms of basic recency, frequency and value data that can be used to drive extra visits. But it gives you no insight to move towards personalization and increased relevance, which is increasingly the digitally connected consumer's expectation and desired experience.

With the objective of driving extra visits in mind, we've already seen how loyalty schemes will seek to put a combination of offers in your hand that get you to visit and then to buy more when you do visit. But any traditional loyalty insight has been gained historically using rear-view mirror analytics based upon knowledge built up from studying many shopping trips. In the grocery category this works pretty well; the frequency of shops and number of items purchased (a lot) create a pretty good and regularly repeated picture. However, this doesn't work nearly as well for other sectors with fewer products that are bought less frequently, where additional data sources could add an extra layer of context to the types of shopping journeys taking place in a store.

> Gavin Wheeldon shared a great example of how the utility of free public Wi-Fi can shine a light on customer frequency:
>
> > We have just got past a year's worth of data for a major fast-food chain in Europe. It's a decent amount of data, at around 100 or so stores. One of the things we measure is return rate: what percentage of your customers are one-time-only customers or return at least once within a 13-month period. The results are pretty staggering. We've analysed this across the board, with all of our clients – that's 50 million users and 1.2 billion visits, including anonymized visits – and 75 per cent are first-time only; they never come back again. For this particular Belgian chain, which I thought would be way at the lower end of that, it was 53 per cent. A lot of people operating physical businesses wouldn't even know that, because they can't even measure return rates and frequency. There's actually a 9 per cent improvement if people log in to Wi-Fi versus not logging in and, where they send customers campaigns to drive return visits, that jumps to 24 per cent.

Frequency boosts visibility

As I mentioned before, one of the great learnings from the early days of Clubcard was the importance of frequency as a measure of loyalty. In grocery, visit frequency to superstores can be 50 visits a year, and if you add in convenience store visits as well, that can get to 100 or more! This level of frequency obviously demonstrates loyalty, and means that a business that has a customer connection in place is able to track its customers' purchases every time they visit meaning it has an incredibly powerful and valuable data asset that it can use to draw very clear inferences about what matters to that consumer when they are shopping, and consequently use that understanding to drive more value from that individual.

In Chapter 3, we demonstrated how Tesco has been able to keep its swipe rates up in the last couple of years through its Clubcard Prices initiative, which encourages a customer to identify with their Clubcard every time they shop, regardless of basket size or store format. This initiative has particularly addressed the issue of low swipe rates in convenience stores. As I travel around the world, I mention the simplicity and impact of Clubcard Prices. When speaking to Brits they will often say, 'Oh I know. I had to get a Clubcard/ download the app last time I was in the UK as the pricing difference without one was too great.'

The new opportunity and, I would argue, requirement to compete with digital pureplays is to add other contextual data to your shopper data so that you understand more about the consumer as a person. This is particularly important in lower-frequency categories such as fashion or restaurants where you are looking for a personalized hook, which could be based upon attributes such as location, time of year or day, life stage event and/or recent browsing or purchase history. I provide much more detail on the topic of 'contextual personalization' later on, in Chapter 10.

I know from experience how to market big stores. I've done it all my life. David Malpas, who was the Managing Director of Tesco, once joked to me: 'I will put you on the Board of Tesco, if you sort out point of sale.' By which he meant cardboard shelf-edge labels or tickets, because any retail business will be doing a price launch, something in the community, has just launched a new range of products and some major branded promotions, be doing some initiative such as a pet club, promoting its loyalty card and so on and on, all using printed cardboard. They do hundreds of campaigns at a time and basically, it's up to the human search engine to screen all that's irrelevant and hope it spots the relevant. But, of course, it's so busy screening out the irrelevant that it doesn't spot some of the relevant stuff either. So, by using digital connections and data, you can take a physical space and augment it with a digital layer. When you do that, you will move physical consumer spaces into the 21st century.

Providing reasons to be recognized

So by this stage I hope you are convinced of the power of connecting with customers as they shop with you – whether on or offline. Gaining a complete and data-based understanding of your customers is the primary objective in order that you can use that information both to serve customers and to run your organization better. Based on that, the primary objective then is to ensure that you are giving your customers a reason to connect with you every time they engage with your brand. This could be achieved in a multitude of ways so I've included a few ideas here:

Digitize traditional loyalty offerings

For any business already operating an analogue loyalty scheme, there is the opportunity to transform this into a digital, mobile-first version. The consumer benefits are that their rewards go into one wallet or app, where they can be tallied, and promotions stored for immediate and convenient access. Each time they shop, the consumer simply needs to identify themselves, typically by scanning their phone, to receive points and/or redeem offers/burn points in real time.

FIGURE 8.1 Example of an Untie Nots-powered challenge, illustrating the progress tracker, personalized to the individual

I would also advocate adding digital value into your existing proposition through deploying technology such as the Untie Nots solution detailed earlier in the book, which will provide you with another digital engagement opportunity for your customers (Figure 8.1). As the challenges they deploy are supplier-funded and have been proven to deliver incrementality, the risk to you as a business is absolutely minimal, but the potential upsides are huge.

The rest of my suggestions do not require a loyalty scheme to function but can be used to encourage the consumer to present their phone when in your stores or venues, offering a reason to be recognized. They are starting to complete the mosaic of connection opportunities I described earlier. All of these suggestions assume that the retailer, restaurateur or owner is connected to the Eagle Eye AIR platform or some digital way of confirming redemption so that the transaction can be tracked and linked back to a consumer identity. An essential component for their success is that consumers have to register to take part.

Do your own digital marketing

Do your own digital marketing to both owned and third-party channels. Rather than running a full-blown loyalty scheme, think of one excellent, relevant offer and make it always available via mobile. This offer can be triggered by device recognition at the store entrance, creating the connection as the customer starts their visit.

Create digital games

Create digital games that require the consumer to register in order to play. These games are typically played out of the store, often with a hierarchy of levels and prizes. Low level prizes could include free products or services redeemable on-site, with higher levels offering the potential to win larger discounts, holidays or cars, often funded by third-party partners.

Offer useful, digital services

Starbucks is a great example of a business that has created huge levels of customer engagement by offering utility to customers largely by making ordering and payment totally seamless through mobile. It does this both through its Mobile Order & Pay solution, as well as through its stored value payment method and automatic account top-ups. Removing friction in this way supports the business in driving a customer to visit one of its stores versus any of its competitors.

In-store offers

Have a few key, high-profile offers in-store that can be accessed through the digital connection (e.g. by scanning a QR code, touching an NFC-enabled label, accessing in-app, etc). Alternatively, this could be positioned as member-only pricing, accessible only for customers who register and scan their app when they make a purchase – as with the Tesco Clubcard Prices model discussed earlier. An alternative suggestion here would be to launch personalized pricing for digitally engaged members as opposed to flat-rate discounts, as Sainsbury's in the UK does with its My Nectar Prices proposition, which it launched in 2021.

Run continuity schemes

Engage customers in continuity schemes, e.g. spend £20 to get a stamp, collect five stamps and receive a free gift, where the earning of points and redemptions for gifts are handled through the phone.

Traditionally these have been run through cards and stamps, which now feels pretty dated and is disruptive to a retailer's front-end operation, which the retailer can ill afford in these times of increasingly squeezed productivity. As mentioned earlier, this is why the Untie Nots solution has proven to be so effective, with profitable, supplier-funded campaigns being deployed directly into the retailer's existing mobile app, driving significant digital engagement. For an organization that doesn't yet have a loyalty scheme in place in order to power the AI to deliver personalized stretch offers to customers, a more generic approach can be taken at first to establish the data connection from participating consumers, not just to the promotion but to their active basket. So, off the back of these continuity promotions you could start to build an owned database of customer IDs and use that to generate insight into the shopping behaviours of those customers.

Below is an example where a digital tweak to an existing marketing mechanic can open up a whole new way of going to market.

Stage 1 (12 weeks): Run a digital continuity programme. Build an owned database of participating customers.

Stage 2 (12 weeks): Use SMS or email to communicate with your new database, incentivizing the behaviour you seek through compelling offers and/or rewards for continued engagement.

Stage 3 (12 weeks): Run a second continuity programme, marketing this first to the owned database to try to activate previous participants, plus use external media to try to grow participation and therefore enlarge the database.

Stage 4 (12 weeks): Repeat stage 2 to the enlarged owned database.

Alternatively, Stages 1 and 3 could be a game or an app-based promotion. The point is that it's an alternative to a full-blown loyalty scheme. It may well be a digital tweak to marketing activity you already plan to do, but it has to be a thought through and invested programme. I am afraid it is naïve to imagine you can generate as much value from little investment and effort as your competitor who is spending 1 per cent. In my opinion, it is an inexcusable destruction of potential value to run the promotion but not bother to discover the identities of those who take part.

Mobile scan-as-you-shop

Create a mobile-based scan-as-you-shop model, replacing third-party hardware with the consumer's phone. This application has the enormous advantage of tracking the consumer's progress around the store from scan to scan and, therefore, can enable real-time offer engagement, based upon knowing not only the shopper history but exactly what is going into the basket during their current shop. That gives the retailer an unprecedented opportunity to understand and influence every step of a customer's journey around the store in real time.

Issue digital offers at till

Moving away from physical messages printed on customers' till receipts, it is also possible to issue digital offers or rewards at the till as part of the checking-out process, either as a 'thank you' for shopping or as a driver of the next shopping trip. Sainsbury's, that has a very strong focus on driving digital engagement with its mobile app, has created a great user experience that incentivizes the behaviour it seeks – getting customers to engage with its loyalty scheme by logging in to their Nectar app post-purchase. To achieve this, it prompts customers to visit the app by sending them a push notification immediately after they've made a purchase, offering them a mystery points bonus for doing so.

Use the phone

The phone can also be used to attempt to capture any feedback on the shopping experience. A very simple questionnaire once the customer has checked out may well capture data to be cross-correlated to shopping behaviour in order to understand what the drivers of satisfaction and dissatisfaction are.

A few of these elements put together, plus the connections outlined in the previous chapter, can come together as a 'mobile makeover'. However, as you would with any other refit, you need to make sure that you invest upfront to ensure that the makeover is a success. We explore the possibilities and implications of such a makeover in the next chapter.

IN SUMMARY

- Omnichannel is here – 90 per cent of customers combine digital and physical channels on the path to purchase.

- Businesses need to offer customers a digitally augmented experience when shopping in the physical store in order to capture data throughout their shopping journey and to use that to ensure that they get the most out of the fact that they've paid a visit.

- This digital layer will allow you to personalize the in-store customer experience in the same way that pureplay e-commerce businesses can, ultimately with a view to driving increased incremental spend alongside customer loyalty.

- When creating engaging reasons to be recognized for your customers, remember to always lead with the value proposition you're creating specifically for them, rather than simply offering a 'me too' solution.

Notes

1 Simpson, J, Kearns, D and Wagener, T (2022) Consumer preferences embrace a mix of physical and digital, Deloitte Digital, 25 January, www.deloittedigital. com/content/dam/deloittedigital/us/documents/offerings/offerings-20220125-insightiq-ccia-consumer-preferences-embrace-a-mix-of-physical-and-digital.pdf (archived at https://perma.cc/4WT9-4T5P)

2 Wright, J (2021) Winning in omnichannel, IGD, March, retailanalysis.igd.com/presentations/presentation-viewer/t/winning-in-omnichannel/i/10702 (archived at https://perma.cc/NQF6-RZD5)

3 Tesco (2021) Tesco opens new checkout-free store, 'GetGo', Tesco PLC, 19 October, www.tescoplc.com/news/2021/tesco-opens-new-checkout-free-store-getgo (archived at https://perma.cc/85JV-Z8U5)

4 Rowson, J (2022) @Jonathan Rowson, Twitter, 11 October, twitter.com/jonathan_rowson/status/1579959829950787584 (archived at https://perma.cc/V8Q2-4V7X)

5 Walton, C (2022) 5 Reasons why Amazon Go is already the greatest retail innovation of the next 30 years, *Forbes*, 1 March, www.forbes.com/sites/christopherwalton/2022/03/01/5-reasons-why-amazon-go-is-already-the-greatest-retail-innovation-of-the-next-30-years/ (archived at https://perma.cc/R8UC-29DX)

6 Walk-Morris, T (2022) Self-scanning stores to triple by 2027: report, *Retail Dive*, 3 August, www.retaildive.com/news/global-self-checkout-stores-triple-2027-report/628630/ (archived at https://perma.cc/YG7Q-3R6H)

7 Savvas, A (2021) Scan and Go will increase post-COVID shopping confidence, *Retail Systems*, 1 February. www.retail-systems.com/rs/Scan_And_Go_Will_Increase_Post_COVID_Shopping_Confidence.php (archived at https://perma.cc/ZQM7-8RWF)

8 Savvas, A (2021) Scan and Go will increase post-COVID shopping confidence, *Retail Systems*, 1 February. www.retail-systems.com/rs/Scan_And_Go_Will_Increase_Post_COVID_Shopping_Confidence.php (archived at https://perma.cc/U2HJ-BPV5)

9 IT Supply Chain (2021) Scan & Go goes mainstream as consumers turn to safer & more contactless ways to shop, *IT in the Supply Chain*, itsupplychain.com/scan-go-goes-mainstream-as-consumers-turn-to-safer-more-contactless-ways-to-shop/ (archived at https://perma.cc/J3HA-2JDM)

10 Savvas, A (2021) Scan and Go will increase post-COVID shopping confidence, *Retail Systems*, 1 February. www.retail-systems.com/rs/Scan_And_Go_Will_Increase_Post_COVID_Shopping_Confidence.php (archived at https://perma.cc/R7AG-JV57)

9

Mobile makeover

Although much of this book is about connection – using it to provide a digital layer, if you like, through which to experience the store – I am convinced that the core objective for winning in today's customer-facing physical spaces has to be via mobile: out of the pocket and in hand. This is because there are many customer-related advantages to mobile: it's personal to the consumer, they know how it works, it is their life, their memories and their connection to those they love and things they care about.

This is why, at its most basic level, the digitally augmented store has to put mobile at the centre of any transformation or customer engagement project, to create and capitalize on digital connection. The only way a store can offer the same levels of choice, speed, convenience and relevance available online is by using mobile to provide that digital layer: it can enable your customers to digitally locate both your stores and the products and services they offer in the real world; and, once inside, it can also be used to digitally enhance the physical search, browse and discovery phases of their shopping trips, wherever they are in whichever store, be it a flagship or pop-up, and whenever they decide to pay a visit.

Putting mobile at the centre of the customer connection strategy means that retailers can avoid adding more bespoke hardware to their existing POS-based operations that increases complexity, cost and inevitable obsolescence. My observation is that it is stark staring bonkers spending money to put customer-facing tech such as kiosks or scan-and-go guns into a store when we've all got more advanced tech in our pockets that it's up to the consumer to update and maintain. Invest in digitally augmenting the shelf edge, advertising screen or point of sale, so that engagement, redemptions or sales could potentially also take place anywhere in the store. But, whatever you do, make sure the delivery mechanisms are via digital touchpoints that can connect to people's mobiles.

In the same way as Tesco set out to make the Clubcard mailing 'the most valued piece of direct marketing junk mail', you need to apply the same strategy to mobile customer engagement in stores. You should aim to be your customers' most-valued app. You've got to be in it to win it. Mobile should be taking on a far larger role in your average retail store, restaurant and other customer-facing spaces by now.

Having examined some of the most important ways to digitally augment a store in the previous chapter, we can see how their main point of delivery to the customer is via mobile. With all of the shopping features and functionality available online, it is easy to see why mobile is an essential shopping companion in-store. We've explored how important an enabler mobile has become to bricks-and-clicks businesses at every stage of the shopping journey, not just in locating stores in a digital world, but also to provide a superior experience for customers while they are inside. Consumers say they use it to check or compare prices (perhaps as they're ROBO/webrooming or showrooming), to access offers or use loyalty schemes, as well as to access the retailer's website or app when they're in a physical store.[1] Plus, it provides store operators with the best available means of engaging with their customers when they're essentially a captive audience.

Competing with e-commerce

The whole point of equipping the store with digital connectivity, at till, through Wi-Fi, Bluetooth beacons or NFC and so on, is to enable customer connection in the physical world to rival what's available in the e-commerce world, because customers expect an omnichannel experience. They expect one brand in all its guises.

The common capability for delivering this is mobile. It is, therefore, the bridge we use to connect online to offline and give us an omnichannel view of our world in real time. This is exactly what it should do, in equal measure, for both retailers and their customers in-store.

Giving your customers a reason to get their phone out to engage with you when they're in your sales space is the best way to compete with online. Every bricks-and-clicks operator should therefore consider how features such as order tracking, ratings and reviews, user videos, recipe suggestions, offers and payment, as well as location-based check-in for click and collect, can be conveniently accessed via mobile.

This requires each retail channel to be equally digitally enabled and data driven to present a consistently compelling offer that can win at every stage of the shopping trip. The offer online must be attractive enough to have customers visit the store and, once there, has to live up to and augment the offer online. The use of mobile to digitally augment the physical parts of the trip is the only logical way to ensure that customer-facing spaces retain their role and relevance in 21st-century shopping, leisure and hospitality operations.

Refit for purpose

So, the technology is there. But how should retail, leisure and hospitality owners start to make sure that their sales, service and showroom spaces can deliver information and compelling offers at a time that's most relevant, in the moment, as customers are in or around the store, or at the shelf edge? I suggest the best way to think about digitally augmenting a store is as if it's a refit or remodel.

Most of us who've worked in retail will have been involved in projects called 'Refresh, Revamp, Renaissance' or some other pithily named refit programme. It may sound like semantics, but giving a refit programme a name aids external shareholder and internal focus, and ease of communication as well as measurement. It also focuses minds on the task at hand by putting the required commitment and potential returns in terms the business can understand.

E-commerce pioneer Stephan Schambach coined the term 'mobile makeover' and I commend it to you as the most useful way of winning hearts and minds over this type of investment. Regard it as a refit: allocate a budget, store numbers, then get on, roll out and measure the impact. Combined with a few popular physical upgrades, it could be a pretty cost-effective renovation, and isn't that the holy grail? Whatever works for you, it should be mobile, mobile, mobile – a digital connection enabling mobile delivery. Mobile-first, as Schambach says, is your customers' handheld remote to navigate the physical space.

Schambach's book, *Makeover: How mobile flipped the shopping cart*,[2] gave me the idea. Despite the obvious customer demand and business benefits, the businesses I talk to sometimes struggle to come to terms with the costs necessary to digitally enable their stores using a 'mobile first' approach. But, when you think of it as a refit or makeover, it doesn't sound so expensive. Certainly, at Tesco I was responsible for many such store refit programmes, where we spent many hundreds of millions refreshing the estate. Yet with a mobile makeover, set in this context, the costs will be much more manageable and, I argue, more impactful than a conventional bricks-and-mortar refit alone. Set against the cost of moving a bakery, café or other departments often featured in a major refit, a mobile makeover is significantly cheaper.

So, what do you need to digitally augment a physical sales space so that it is mobile-first? Start by working out how the bricks-and-clicks advantages of instant gratification and real-world interaction apply best to your proposition, while considering ways of matching and then exceeding customer expectations of product availability and information access set by online. In previous chapters, we've stressed the importance of the added value you can offer digitally. Any new mobile capabilities introduced must provide sufficient relevance, value and/or utility to support a coherent and consistent role of the store as part of a wider omnichannel presence. Also, you must remember that different customers want and need different things and therefore a range of mobile-engagement drivers will need to be applied to drive uptake across as broad a range of customers as possible.

Use mobile to be better, simpler and cheaper

A mobile makeover programme can digitally augment the store using a combination of a number of technologies. There are almost a baffling number of options but regardless of how you choose to do it, the benefits of connecting must be clearly communicated to the customer, and it must be incredibly easy for them to do. The ultimate aim should be to enable as many customer-facing digital touchpoints in a store as possible – at the till and shelf edge across both people and products – using the connection to generate greater data-based insight.

The ability to make-over stores to digitally enhance the customer experience via mobile is actually one of those fortunate confluences of events. Some might think that propositions such as scan-and-go just put an extra self-service burden onto the customer. But I would apply the principle of making service better, simpler and cheaper. It was the way that Tesco in its heyday ran its cost-reduction programmes and I introduced it to Eagle Eye too when I joined the company as CEO. It runs that you don't just try to do stuff cheaper – you look at it in the round and you first ask: Thinking about this particular product or service...

- How do I make this better for my customers?
- How do I make this simpler for employees?
- How do I make this cheaper?

Thinking in this way, what follows are six examples of ways to drive the mobile connection in-store, which I believe can satisfy all three criteria.

Use analogue tools to drive mobile engagement

A simple first step to driving the connection is to determine the benefits you're willing to offer your customers for connecting via mobile, and shouting about them wherever you can.

Walmart, for example, has advertised the (not entirely inspiring) benefit of eReceipts on its physical receipts with a QR code to seamlessly direct the customer to where to download the Walmart App. Similarly, it has used this medium to drive customers to sign up to its Walmart+ subscription scheme by offering a free 30-day trial for customers who scan their receipt and sign up. Other options in this category include incentivizing customers to scan codes at the shelf edge in order to unlock discounts, supplier-funded brand loyalty rewards, entry into competitions and more.

Empower customer self-service

One of the biggest opportunities for businesses in this space is to drive the mobile connection via the promise of utility – typically through the promise of a speedy and friction-free shopping experience. Looking at scan-and-go as an example, the solution should make checking out faster by introducing mobile self-service so customers can avoid queuing, it should be simple for employees to support (e.g. one dedicated employee covering multiple self-checkout tills) while reducing manned checkout costs for the retailer.

Nike has made great strides in this space, describing their in-store customer connection powered by mobile as the customers' 'ultimate shopping companion', designed to digitally augment the physical retail store. This delivers a better shopping experience for the end customer (e.g. providing access to exclusive offers, triggered rewards, product information and in-store service through concepts like scan to try on), in a way that is simple for employees to execute, at very low cost.

And it seems the strategy is working. We have long been told now that 'data is the new oil', but in its 2021 earnings call, Nike President and CEO, John Donahoe, talked about how having a direct, digital connection with the consumer is the 'liquid gold' that is driving higher profits (+16 per cent growth). Nike Digital, the brand's e-commerce sites and apps, grew 34 per cent in the same period, fueling its direct-to-consumer sales growth.[3]

> Increased digital engagement is translating into more repeat buyers, a higher buying frequency and increased average order value, ultimately driving higher lifetime value through membership.
>
> (John Donahoe, Nike President and CEO)[4]

The strategy is clear – using the digital connection, Nike is looking to grow membership numbers, increase customer engagement and grow direct-to-customer sales. I encourage any of you to visit, or at least look up online its flagship New York store where its strategy is made clear from the moment you walk through the door. The app is advertised everywhere, offering the customers utility through features such as Instant Checkout, Shop the Look and Scan to Try.

As Nike has demonstrated, using digital in the physical store also increases the amount of curation that can be achieved through merchandising. Using digital and/or interactive signage and shelf labels can boost conversion by giving customers more confidence in the purchase at critical decision points. Self-service access to pricing, product and provenance information, recipe, outfit and design ideas and so on can also provide a great link to exclusive digital content that can also attract online customers into the store. This obviously requires an app and/or mobile-optimized website, which opens the door to sophisticated multimedia engagement using AR to bring products to life at the shelf edge, or 'magic mirrors' that can superimpose clothing or backgrounds onto a customer's reflection, as just a couple of examples.

Deliver digital personalization

Starbucks invested ahead of the curve when it came to its strategic mobile makeover, ensuring that customers were both comfortable and compelled to use their phones while in-store because it powers a better, more personalized experience for them. In addition to the Starbucks Rewards loyalty scheme which lives and breathes in the mobile app, customers can also access utility in the form of customized drinks, mobile payments, advance ordering and access to playlists, as well as partner-based offers and rewards.

Barbara Spiering, Starbucks' VP Marketing Technology & Quality Engineering, said that its objective is for customers to 'feel as seen and known in all of our digital channels when they walk into the store because that's why people come in, they want to be seen and known from the digital, to the physical. We know who you are, and it's throughout the entire lifecycle. And that is really our goal, to create that connection.'[5]

Starbucks' mobile payment app now has more than 31 million users in the US, second only to Apple, and in Q2 2021, mobile orders made up 26 per cent of its transactions in the US, up 18 per cent from the year prior.[6] In 2022, it was reported that Starbucks held $1.6 billion in 'deposits' (unused credit and gift card balances), which means that the corporation now has more assets than 85 per cent of the banks in the USA.[7] The more it can drive usage of the app, the more data it generates on customers who are then sent personalized recommendations for additional products they might like, which delivers revenue growth.

Offer undeniable customer value

As I've mentioned previously, my advice is to always look to reward the behaviour you seek. So, if your ultimate objective is driving customers to connect via mobile, you have to determine what you're willing to 'give' in order to 'get' it. If you make that value proposition rich enough, and you clearly communicate it to your customers (again and again and again!), you will succeed.

As mentioned in Chapter 3, Tesco's Clubcard Prices proposition offers undeniable value for customers (Figure 9.1), which is most easily accessed via mobile and therefore has driven significant increases in digital adoption and more widely loyalty penetration over the last couple of years.

Sainsbury's Nectar Prices, only available for digitally engaged customers shopping in-store has also reportedly driven significant uptake of both the Nectar App and SmartShop scan-and-go offering.[8]

FIGURE 9.1 Tesco Clubcard Prices advertisement[9]

And of course, Pret a Manger's game-changing subscription pro-gramme, which is a 'no brainer' for any customer visiting Pret more than twice a week. A scheme that has now totally transformed its business through the power of the digital customer connection.

Make the weekly circular/flyer digital-only

In most grocery markets all over the world, the weekly flyer is still a hugely important driver of trade but I believe that a digital version of the flyer can unlock huge opportunity over and above what the traditional printed flyer can deliver. I've summarized what I believe to be the core opportunities in this area below:

- Personalization: move from mass to personalized offers as you transfer to digital. The efficiency of personalized promotions and the scale of the funds invested in flyer promotions will undoubtedly make a powerful combination.

- Agility: digital frees you from the weekly cadence of print and enables you to adapt to competitive and customer demands in real time.

- Immersive: harness the power of digital to give your customers more engaging and more valuable experiences – videos containing recipes or stories about provenance, etc can all be integrated to bring your flyer to life.
- E-commerce integration: as e-commerce continues to grow, a fully shoppable flyer where customers can easily add items to the cart becomes more important.
- Data: unlock a new stream of data to provide insight on how customers are engaging with this content in real time, enabling you to better demand plan, to optimize promotions on the fly based on performance, and to relentlessly A/B test to ensure you are always refining your approach in order to achieve your customer objectives.
- Unlock media revenue: as the digital flyer attracts more engaged users, it also opens up even more media monetization opportunities.

I think that retailers can and should try to learn from some of the big tech firms here – think Facebook, Instagram, TikTok. The transition from this paper-based experience into mobile has, in my opinion, generally been done very poorly. Typically, retailers have simply taken a glorified PDF of their circular and uploaded it onto their websites and into their apps. This creates a clunky and uninspiring experience for the end customer.

I think retailers should change how they think about this piece of content, moving away from simply showcasing a set of weekly price-cut deals to instead thinking about how it could develop to become a stream of content or a newsfeed for the customer. If you can shift your perspective in this way, what is currently a PDF could become an 'Instagram-esque' stream that is personalized, searchable, shoppable and more engaging.

Fortune favours the bold and I was pleased to see Giant Eagle announcing its plans to stop mailing its weekly ad circulars to consumers in its home market of Pittsburgh from March 2023, with plans to move 'from mailbox to inbox' across all its markets within the year. Explaining the reasons for this, Giant Eagle has said that 'we are actively evolving alongside our guests to meet their unique interests with personalized savings opportunities. An important part of this journey is our continued shift to an enhanced digital shopping experience where personalization can be more easily achieved.'[10]

The biggest retailers in France, including E.Leclerc, Carrefour, Monoprix, Franprix and Cora, have also said that they will either stop or significantly reduce the number of paper-based promotional catalogues being sent to customers during 2023. Alexandre Bompard, CEO of Carrefour France has said that 80 per cent of its marketing will be digital by 2024.[11]

Employees as digital advocates

Engaging and mobilizing your employees in-store to support your efforts in achieving the customer connection is of paramount importance. Thinking back to the concept that you manage what you measure, every store should be targeted and measured on the number of digitally connected customers it gets through the doors. I suggest that this should be a new role that is created – similar to the traditional Walmart Greeter – an employee whose job it is to welcome customers to the store and explain to them how and more importantly why they should establish a real-time digital connection. Technology should be used to make life easier for customers interacting with your organization in the physical world, and it should be the function of this new role to communicate that.

Once this mobile connection is in place, you can engage with your customers as individuals for free, whereas otherwise you've got to talk to them through Facebook, the daily newspapers and other advertising channels. Amazon talks to me frequently through email and push notifications directly into my app, so basically, it communicates for free. You cannot afford to allow one of your main competitors to have this cost advantage when you don't have to.

Digitally empowered employees

Now it's not only the digital connection that you have to drive with consumers, to successfully achieve your mobile makeover, you have to mobilize store staff so they can spend more time on the shop floor, offering assistance by accessing and sharing the same information available online with customers, using store-owned mobile tablets or phones. Mobile-equipped store staff could potentially save a sale if a product is out of stock in-store, for example, or 'queue bust' if traditional manned checkouts become busy. In addition to these more functional tasks, digitally empowered teams can combat showrooming and equip the store of the future with employees who are incentivized by digital technology to help customers, who have the capacity to share recipes and reviews, or even price match or apply special discounts or rewards.

Together with Google Cloud and Deloitte Consulting LLP, Kroger has recently announced that it is mobilizing its employees by embracing new cloud-based technologies, including data analytics, AI and machine learning, with a view to enhancing operating efficiencies to improve the end-customer experience. Jim Clendenen, Kroger Vice President of Enterprise Retail Systems, said in a statement that 'technology and digital tools are fundamental elements of how Kroger continues to improve the associate experience, which in turn, enhances the in-store experience for our customers.'[12]

Within the context of department stores and luxury retail this application of technology feels like even more of a 'no brainer'. Imagine having a top-tier customer who spends tens of thousands with you in one department, women's fashion for example, but when they go downstairs to buy luggage, they are ignored by your sales assistant who just assumes they are an 'average' customer, simply browsing the range. The goal here should be for in-store employees to be notified on their mobile tablets when a customer is nearby (these triggers can be set up using Beacons, for example, at the store entrances as well as throughout the store in key locations), highlighting that customer's value, key category interests, previous notable purchases, etc. This way, employees are able to invest their time in the best customers, and can provide a much more personalized service.

I spoke about the above to Al Henderson, Eagle Eye Chief Sales Officer, and he pointed out that the common thread across all sectors is that when customers visit a digital black hole of a store or restaurant to purchase a product or service, it's only when they go to pay and leave that its operator knows that that customer's been there. Instead, Henderson envisioned a casual dining example where the engagement ends at the POS but starts on entering the outlet. He said:

> I could pay a visit to my local restaurant and much more often than not, the manager won't know I'm there. I may place my order, eat, and it's only in the last few minutes of being there that you know who I am, that I want to redeem my birthday offer as I'm paying and then I'm going.
>
> All of the opportunity for you to personalize that experience for me has gone. Imagine if I had been encouraged to identify myself via Wi-Fi, Beacons, scanning a QR code, checking-in on my app, etc on arrival; you would have been able to serve me personally throughout my experience. You could so easily change my emotional feeling about your brand.
>
> Businesses like this need to create a way to help employees identify individuals at scale when they're in your venues. The digitally enabled example could power an experience where I turn up at the restaurant and, when you bring the menu over to me, you know it's my birthday. You also know I've been in five times in the last two months and every time I order Peroni beer – so, you could bring me a Peroni and say, 'Happy birthday, this is on us'. I've not told the staff it's my birthday. I've been identified on entry (via the Wi-Fi, Beacons, location services in-app, etc), which provides the relevant data direct to your employees either via the POS or in-venue tables or mobiles, which enables your employees to serve me in a personalized way.
>
> All of that can be powered by Eagle Eye, creating a real-time digital connection to the customer and to the point of sale, which allows you to make your customers feel special. That's an emotional engagement. I don't think you're going to get away with a personal experience that's 100 per cent enabled by digital, because you still need a human being to deliver the customer service with a personal touch. But that whole journey needs to be digitally enabled to improve the quality of engagement and make people's lives easier.

To app or not to app

In a recent earnings call, John Donahoe, president and CEO of Nike stated, 'we do not take lightly the choice made by consumers to put us in the most prized real estate that exists today: the home screen of their phone.'[13]

Thinking about the need to provide utility and value once the digital connection is established, you need a method of serving up content. To app or not to app is then the question, and I could not agree more with Donahoe – asking your customers to make space to give your brand a home on their phone is no small feat. Because of this, there is some debate as to whether it's better to curate consumer content via an app or direct the consumer to a mobile-optimized website. I think that if you are a high-frequency, high-volume business, it's worth aspiring to be one of the apps that people have and use, and if you choose to go down this route, you have to invest heavily in ensuring that the app contains so much utility for your customers that they opt to keep it and are compelled to use it. If you are a restaurant, speciality or fashion retailer that is visited a few times a year, I'd still recommend an app for your most loyal customers. But if you want a mobile site to offer a connection to infrequent customers, prospects and suspects, that may be more appropriate.

While the take-up of apps may not always be enormous, the engagement is spectacular. When talking about apps, I always point to JD Sports, which never misses an opportunity, on posters, sports ground perimeter advertising, store windows and in-store, to say some variation of, 'improve your experience with us by downloading the app'. This allocation of marketing funds and share of mind clearly demonstrates the huge value its management perceives from digitally connecting with its customers. Apps are neither difficult nor expensive to do and so if you determine that the right thing to do is to launch one for your brand, work as hard as JD Sports to drive sign-ups, and crack on and learn.

The digital echo chamber

At Eagle Eye, we refer to the siloed development of digital products and services as the 'digital echo chamber'. According to the *Oxford English Dictionary*, an 'echo chamber' is defined as 'an environment in which somebody encounters only opinions and beliefs similar to their own, and does not have to consider alternatives'. In many businesses the world over, digital echo chambers have cropped up as organizations believed that the only way to capitalize on the digital growth opportunity was to ring-fence teams and capabilities charged to deliver against it. What happens, however, is that these developments are often built and measured in silos where teams are using digital development to meet digital objectives, rather than business-wide or better still, customer-led objectives.

I am sure that, like me, you receive many marketing emails and social media ads highlighting new products, offers and specials. However, the digitally delivered offer almost exclusively refers to promotions that can be redeemed online, via a retailer's e-commerce store, even though at times I may not be more than 100 yards away from a physical branch of that retailer. This strikes me as daft. What I should receive is location- and context-aware engagement at a relevant point in the shopping journey, which says 'click here to shop' or 'click here to redeem in-store or online'. If I choose the in-store option, I should then be given a personalized digital coupon to present at checkout, which informs the business that I am a customer who was motivated by that communication and offer. This is exactly the same information the e-commerce division would capture. Moreover, in an omnichannel business, the store should share the successful engagement with its e-commerce counterpart while updating that customer's record with purchase history and preferences consolidated from both the in-store digital activation and any other engagement online. But this often doesn't happen.

It doesn't happen this way because the e-commerce marketing executive is too often operating in a silo, with a siloed budget, and is targeted to drive a specific amount of business to the retailer's e-commerce site. The fact that they have paid good money and expended effort to get this piece of communication in front of my eyeballs but then force me to shop using the retailer's minority, online sales channel just doesn't make any sense. Once a brand has got my attention, it should leverage its omnichannel advantage and make the offer accessible through both its site and its stores.

This is the biggest problem with the digital echo chamber. It under-values all of the great work businesses are doing in this space as, typically, the work touches only a small proportion of customers – early adopters of digital – and therefore the investment has a poor ROI. We suggest that instead, these businesses should refocus their energy on driving omnichannel engagement, which has the potential to impact every customer (Figure 9.2).

Moreover, every business I have ever come across that tracks these things will report (as the research referenced earlier in this book suggests) that its highest-spending customers are the omnichannel ones. Yet, to some extent, the poor consumer must battle against an operational set-up that militates against the cross-channel shopping behaviour that is the most valuable. For example, many businesses have separate e-commerce and store management platforms that don't talk to each other. Promotions earned in one place cannot be

FIGURE 9.2 Eagle Eye's digital engagement versus digital connection model

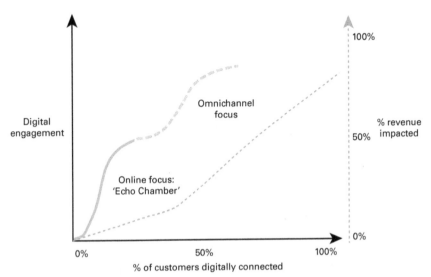

redeemed in the other. This is why digital performance marketing systems such as Eagle Eye have to be deployed, so that both channels recognize the customer and work as one.

While I absolutely acknowledge that focus and specialism work, we live in a digital world and consumers expect omnichannel experiences. While Eagle Eye's AIR platform can help deliver such experiences, the retailer using it will always be what I like to characterize as a swan – gliding gracefully over the surface of the water while paddling like crazy beneath – unless it consolidate its view of who the customer is and what they do across each individual channel.

Just as the retailer's view of customers must unify activity and engagement across every channel, its execution with digital must also be consolidated and consistent too. Having a single, centralized repository of knowledge on customers, combined with increasingly advanced marketing execution engines that can identify the 'next-best message' or 'next-best offer', connected to a platform that means the message or offer can be sent to exactly the right type of consumers, at the right time, and via the most appropriate channel, is what every business should aspire to have.

Digital cannot be siloed away. It has to be pervasive. It's the world we operate in and the way we must now go to market. To achieve this, all customer-facing spaces require a mobile makeover.

IN SUMMARY

- The core objective for any customer-facing business operating physical spaces should be to make shopping a 'phone out' experience.

- Mobile should act as the bridge that can be used to connect online to offline and give us an omnichannel view of our world in real time, both for retailers and their customers.

- Work out how the bricks-and-clicks advantages of instant gratification and real-world interaction apply best to your proposition and build this into your mobile-first strategy.

- Relentlessly communicate the value of mobile connection to your customers. If the 'give to get' is set at the right level, you will win.

- Data may be the new oil but having a direct, digital customer connection is 'liquid gold'.

- Don't silo digital investment. Focus on how digital can enable the best-in-class omnichannel experience for all of your customers.

Notes

1 Airship (2021) The Mobile Customer Imperative: A global consumer survey report, 8 December, grow.urbanairship.com/rs/313-QPJ-195/images/airship-2021-mobile-customer-imperative-consumer-survey.pdf (archived at https://perma.cc/WNE4-45TH)

2 Schambach, S (2017) *Makeover: How mobile flipped the shopping cart*, NewStore, Boston, MA

3 Kohan, S (2021) Customer engagement drives Nike profits pp 16%, *Forbes*, 20 December, www.forbes.com/sites/shelleykohan/2021/12/20/customer-engagement-drives-nike-profits-up-16/?sh=86a777f14520 (archived at https://perma.cc/UX4G-SLLB)

4 Williams, R (2022) Nike attributes digital revenue growth to demand across mobile apps, *Marketing Dive*, 30 June, www.marketingdive.com/news/nike-mobile-apps-SNKRS-digital-sales-growth/626285/ (archived at https://perma.cc/5CXM-6U28)

5 TechRound (2022) Starbucks marketing technology expert reveals customer personalisation strategy, 24 June, techround.co.uk/news/starbucks-marketing-technology-expert-reveals-customer-personalisation-strategy/ (archived at https://perma.cc/F3P3-MNDK)

6 McKinnon, T (2021) How Starbucks is using mobile apps to significantly increase sales, Indigo9 Digital, 10 June, www.indigo9digital.com/blog/starbucksmobileapps (archived at https://perma.cc/FKQ9-WLJY)

7 Moyle, L (2022) Starbucks: Banking & serving coffee, Fintech Talents, 19 July, fttembeddedfinance.com/starbucks-banking-serving-coffee/ (archived at https://perma.cc/J557-KFCB)

8 Sainsbury's (2022) Interim results for the 28 weeks ended 17 September 2022, 3 November, www.about.sainsburys.co.uk/news/latest-news/2022/03-11-22-interim-results (archived at https://perma.cc/Z7E7-YU65)

9 Tesco @Tesco (2021) Twitter, 6 July, twitter.com/Tesco/status/1412496260670574599 (archived at https://perma.cc/P5JE-2YSL)

10 Hamstra, M (2023) Giant Eagle ends mailed weekly circulars in Pittsburgh, *Supermarket News*, 6 February, www.supermarketnews.com/consumer-trends/giant-eagle-ends-mailed-weekly-circulars-pittsburgh (archived at https://perma.cc/7JRA-ZYWF)

11 Thompson, H (2022) Supermarkets in France to send fewer paper promo catalogues, *The Connexion*, 16 December, www.connexionfrance.com/article/French-news/Supermarkets-in-France-to-send-fewer-paper-promo-catalogues (archived at https://perma.cc/3X9N-32KX)

12 PR Newswire (2023) Google Cloud and Deloitte boost grocery associate productivity and improve the customer experience, 20 January, www.prnewswire.com/news-releases/google-cloud-and-deloitte-boost-grocery-associate-productivity-and-improve-the-customer-experience-301726406.html (archived at https://perma.cc/R7L3-Q39F)

13 Williams, R (2022) Nike attributes digital revenue growth to demand across mobile apps, *Marketing Dive*, 30 June, www.marketingdive.com/news/nike-mobile-apps-SNKRS-digital-sales-growth/626285/ (archived at https://perma.cc/AXD2-7QUF)

10

Marketing in the moment

I'm sure you've noticed that personalization is one of the key themes of this book. I firmly believe that it is impossible to run a world-class retail business unless you know who your customers are and can understand and react to their individual needs. As a general rule, when retailers think about personalization, the majority of them think fairly one-dimensionally about delivering offers to customers that they hope they'll find relevant based on what they've done before. But due to the acceleration of omnichannel shopping and advances in technology – specifically the ability for organizations to connect with customers in real time through the phone, as described in the previous chapter – I believe it's time to usher in the next phase of personalization, something which I call 'marketing in the moment'.

I believe that marketing in the moment will do for marketing what 'near me' did for search. It is retail marketing's next great transformation, with businesses finally gaining the ability to interact and engage with their customers in a contextually relevant way, not just online but in physical stores, when they're most primed to make their purchasing decisions. Marketing in the moment is all about recognizing that the customer journey comprises many different moments – singular intersections of time, intent and context. And moments matter – to brands, to retailers and most importantly, to customers.

What's different about marketing in the moment versus personalization as we know it now, is the ability to merge existing customer understanding with new contextual data points (e.g. location, time, environmental cues, loyalty status) to deliver unique content (an offer, reward, message, recipe, advert, free product, etc) to an individual customer at the optimal moment for that customer. Often these moments will be about influencing a purchasing decision but they can also be about positioning the retailer as the partner of the customer, offering utility and support to make the purchasing journey as convenient as possible.

Delivering contextually relevant offers and information is something that has been possible in the world of e-commerce for more than a decade. All the way back in 2012, Tesco started using Clubcard data to tailor online promotions depending on the type of customer on the site. Price-sensitive individuals would be shown offers on Tesco Value while the highest spenders were shown the Finest range, for example.[1]

Digital-first businesses have consistently worked to make the e-commerce experience more convenient and more relevant while the physical store has remained unchanged. Take Amazon for example, not only does it know every product or service I've ever bought from its site (as well as every other product I've searched for and not purchased), it knows where I am, where I live, what time it is, what device I'm using to shop with, how I got onto its site, and the list goes on. All of that information can be analysed and actioned in real time to enhance my shopping experience. The new opportunity and, I would argue, requirement to compete with digital pureplays is to take the learnings from e-commerce and apply them to your store network, layering new contextual data on top of your existing customer data so that you can understand more about each customer as a person and use that understanding to improve their every interaction with you.

When I think about marketing in the moment in its truest form, I see it as an ambition for businesses to be able to replicate the 'good old days' of shopping with your trusted local butcher or greengrocer but at massive scale. Before the advent of the supermarket, it was easy for a local grocer to know their customers by name, to offer them personalized product information and special deals based on what they knew about a specific customer and what was happening in the world around them; 'Hello Tim! Lovely to see you again. We've just had these Kentish strawberries delivered, they were picked this morning. I remember you said it was your daughter's birthday this weekend, why don't you take a punnet on us? They'll be lovely in the sunshine this afternoon with a glass of wine. Now, what else can I help you with today?' I believe that by harnessing the power of today's connected retail ecosystem and advanced analytical capabilities, retailers must seek to interact with their customers in just as familiar and as helpful a way, but via a whole suite of new channels.

The personalization matrix

Figure 10.1 shows a four-quadrant matrix of personalization that highlights where different omnichannel marketing programmes sit relative to a 'marketing in the moment' model.

Traditional, above-the-line offers sit in the bottom left quadrant, no. 1. These are in-store offers available to all customers (e.g. 25 per cent off fresh fruit and vegetables this weekend only) and

FIGURE 10.1 Eagle Eye's Marketing in the Moment model

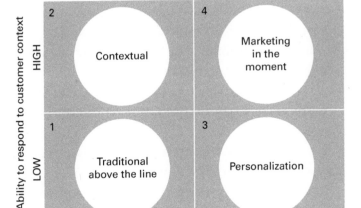

typically promoted through mass-market channels such as the weekly circular/flyer or in-store displays. Here, every customer receives the same offer via the same marketing tool(s), with no differentiation to reflect the context or the customer's own preferences.

Moving into more contextual offers, look at quadrant no. 2, which would include a business that has geofenced its stores to enable them to trigger messages and offers to customers when they enter the store (e.g. kids eat free today with every adult main meal purchased). Typically, these organizations are delivering a one-size-fits-all offer for every customer and are missing the personalization on top. In my view, the right question is not 'What should I do for every single customer who walks into the store?' but 'What should I do for this individual when they walk into the store?'

Retailers that are delivering personalized offers today can be found in quadrant no. 3, offering personalized content based on purchase history and the insights developed about preferences for products and rewards. However, almost all retailers still send their personalized offers through a single context (e.g. every Thursday at 1 pm), with no variation to reflect the customer's current situation, like whether they are about to shop or have just finished shopping, or what the weather is doing on that day.

In the top right quadrant, no. 4, sits 'marketing in the moment', a model where retailers deliver the optimal, personalized advertising message to a shopper at the most opportune time via the most relevant channel. It's delivered by combining several data points and analysing individual customer data within a larger context, including seasonality, time of day, product availability, and the retailer's goals for that customer. This model enables businesses to deliver entirely customized messages at the precise moment to best motivate the behaviour they seek.

Imagine a scenario where a retailer knew that a certain customer spent more money in the 'ready-to-eat meals' category than any other. When that customer goes to create a click-and-collect order on a cold afternoon for an early evening pick-up, their propensity for purchasing that category increases even further. 'Marketing in the moment' could identify and deliver an in-app coupon incentivizing the customer to trade-up to its winter special 'three course meal at home', while speeding up their shopping experience by immediately presenting them with the types of products they were hoping to purchase when they started their shop. This should make the customer feel 'known', developing their emotional loyalty to the brand.

Context – the missing piece of the puzzle

Advances in both digital technology and customer analytics and AI have led to a shift in the number of omnichannel retailers that are now able to execute personalized promotions, as per quadrant no. 3 in the above. Within the grocery space in particular, retailers have started on the journey to true personalization with some now sending customers a set of weekly offers in which both the products and the rewards are personalized for each individual customer. Retailers using this model can expect to see significant increases in both digital engagement and offer redemption.

This approach to personalized marketing can be incredibly effective, as described in a recent BCG study, 'The $70 billion prize in personalized offers',[2] but it fails to incorporate additional contextual information that can generate even greater business results for the retailer while significantly enhancing the customer experience. If you consider that the vast majority of personalized messaging currently being delivered via this single context – typically on one predefined day of the week, by email – without any variation to reflect the customer's current situation, the scope for improvement is still huge. If a customer receives a perfectly personalized offer the day after they complete their weekly shopping trip, that's a missed opportunity. Now of course, that's a simplified example, but precisely the kind of missed opportunity that a marketing in the moment model will help retailers to avoid.

Today, personalization is executed based on two Cs – customers and content. We know who you are and what you like so we'll send you this. Personalization of tomorrow will incorporate context to make this experience far richer.

In order to deliver against this, organizations should be seeking to incorporate real-time contextual data into their established DIAL processes. Merging historic customer data with current customer context will generate new insights, which should be actioned at the best time and via the best medium as dictated by the context. Predictive analytics may be able to suggest when a customer is most likely to visit your store next, and you should be primed to trigger the next best action as determined by the data for that customer 'in the moment', as they're walking into the store. I don't need to tell you how valuable it is to get your customers' attention and influence their behaviour at the precise time they're preparing to make a purchasing decision.

The first step is to start looking at what context-specific data you can build into your advanced analytical processes. At Eagle Eye, we have identified four key contexts, each getting closer to the customer:

- **Environment**
  - What's happening in the world right now for the customer, like sporting events, community events and the weather?

- **Location**
  - Where is the customer right there and then? At home, on the train, 100 metres from their local store, at the deli counter?

- **Activity**
  - Where is the customer on their journey with you? Are they writing a shopping list and browsing recipes? Viewing your mobile app in-store or shopping online? Have they just had a bad experience with you (e.g. late delivery of an e-commerce order)?

- **System**
  - Has the customer just triggered an action within the retailer's marketing and loyalty platforms? For instance, have they just transacted, the resulting impact of which means they have

moved up a tier within the loyalty programme? Did they just meet a stretch target as part of a personalized challenge? Did they just send a referral code to a friend, incentivizing them to sign up to the programme?

Using all of this contextual data available, personalized content can extend far beyond targeted offers and rewards. Totally unique messages could be triggered to two separate customers as they walk into the same store at the same time – one receiving a value-based notification making them aware of the top offers in-store today, while the other could receive a spend-stretch message to say that if they spend £35 or more they will have successfully achieved what's required to move up into the top tier of the retailer's loyalty programme, unlocking a host of new perks.

Creating the moment

So, how do you identify and create these engaging and highly personalized moments for your customers? We believe that moments sit at the intersection of the three Cs – customers, context and content (Figure 10.2).

FIGURE 10.2   Eagle Eye's 'three Cs' – customer, context and content, which are required to deliver marketing in the moment

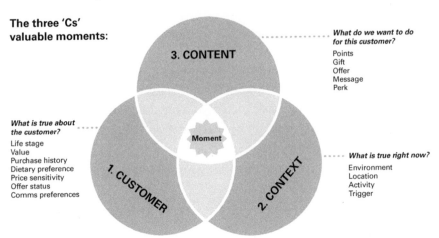

The three 'Cs' valuable moments:

3. CONTENT

What do we want to do for this customer?
Points
Gift
Offer
Message
Perk

What is true about the customer?
Life stage
Value
Purchase history
Dietary preference
Price sensitivity
Offer status
Comms preferences

Moment

1. CUSTOMER

2. CONTEXT

What is true right now?
Environment
Location
Activity
Trigger

In order to trigger these moments and deliver them straight into the hands of your customers, you have to start by creating and then maintaining compelling reasons for your customers to connect with you via mobile, as covered in the previous chapter. This will provide you with the same level of visibility and insight that e-commerce operations have used to improve their customers' experiences online, and also opens up a direct channel for you to use to engage and market to them in the moment. You may not always be able to price match, but what else can you offer customers, right there and then, to deliver value? It is precisely this immediacy, or the power of 'now' as I like to call it, that the store has over e-commerce competitors that this digitally enabled layer must enable.

The power of time is something I'm currently speaking to a lot of the world's leading retailers about, as the scope to advance personalization efforts considerably through integrating the additional context of time is huge. By moving away from delivering, for example, your weekly offers to all of your customers at the same time, to instead personalizing these to every customer, the potential to significantly increase the value you are able to provide to them, as well as the engagement that you'll likely see off the back of these communications, is enormous. And if there's this much richness in communication time, think about how much you can achieve when you start to integrate all of the other contextual triggers too.

For me, NOW!

As I write this, it is still amazing to me that this is a reality today. When I was running the Marketing team at Tesco, the ability to create this much value for our customers was something we could have only dreamed of. Thinking back to the early days of Clubcard, we successfully created an analogue customer connection. This connection was made at the end of, or just after, the customers' last shopping trip, and so didn't afford us the opportunity of influencing that trip. So, by default, our focus was always on the next trip at best, or more likely, the aggregate of trips over a 13-week period, which we could then respond to in the quarterly reward mailing. What is so brilliant about having a digital customer connection is that it unlocks the opportunity for you to influence the customer's behaviour as it's happening – in the now – wherever they are physically, as well as figuratively, in terms of the search, browse and discovery phases of their shopping mission. Personalized content moves from being just 'for me' to 'for me, now'.

I appreciate that this is no mean feat, so my recommendation is to just get started and if you do it soon, you'll be one of the very first. Recent research has shown that 84 per cent of digitally driven organizations cite the importance of becoming a real-time enterprise in order to meet customer demands, but only 12 per cent of businesses are actually using real-time data in a data-driven way.[3] So there is certainly an opportunity to gain first-mover advantage and I say there is no better way to learn than by doing. Unsurprisingly, I'd suggest that you use the DIAL framework to plan your next steps. Use the data that you have in the business (contextual or otherwise) to try to identify 'moments' where you can see you have the propensity to improve the customer experience while driving incremental revenue. Determine what contextual data you would need in your arsenal in order to be able to action contextually personalized insights, and start creating those moments.

In the hope that I can provide some inspiration, I've detailed a few examples below, focused predominantly on bricks-and-mortar retail, illustrating how these types of tactics could be deployed at each key stage of the customer journey.

Driving the visit

In an omnichannel world, location makes all the difference and so I would argue, is a great place to start. Nearly half of all Google searches now include local intent.[4] This means customers are considering location when they're online, planning their physical shopping trip. This is why I believe customer location data should be considered as important for businesses in the real world as 'near me' searching is an important utility that helps customers navigate their lives. But virtually all businesses know far more about their customers' movements online than they do about those same customers' activity in the real world. The objective here is to change that.

Retailers have a number of options available. If you have an app, ensure that customers are incentivized to have location services turned on in order that you can trigger messages when they're nearby. Use the information you're gathering on customers as they navigate the world in conjunction with all of the information you already know about them to determine the best content to serve them at a given moment, when they are considering shopping with you. For example:

1 **Predicting a moment:** Within your customer base there will be individuals for whom predicting when their next shop is going to happen is much easier than it is for others. You can use machine learning to identify these customers and their predicted shopping patterns and then use AI to determine the optimum time to send the communication to each customer. By issuing the exact right level of discount or reward for each customer to incentivize the behaviour you seek, you will drive significant engagement. You may have a customer who typically visits you every Saturday morning but you suspect they're buying their cupboard staples from a discount retailer as they very rarely appear in their basket with you. Therefore, you can send them a message on the Friday evening, offering them personalized discounts on your basics range alongside strong brand-quality messaging in order to incentivize them to come into store the next day and buy across a broader range of products. As they walk into the store, another notification can be triggered to either reiterate the message or to offer them a further incentive to stock up on basics while they're in-store.

2 **Competitor fight-back moment:** A price-sensitive customer is geolocated near your store in a mall where two of your competitors are also located. They receive a push message reminding them of the best deals in-store today, personalized to their preferences.

Maximizing the visit and optimizing share of voice in-store

So now you've got a customer into the store, but what can you do to enhance their experience while they're with you? Using marketing in the moment, retailers are encouraged to think about the physical shopping experience in the same way that e-commerce businesses do. In addition to your app, there is a whole raft of in-store technology, from geofences to Wi-Fi to Bluetooth beacons to NFC and more, which will allow you to collect real-time contextual data on when a customer walks into a store, enters a specific department, or is even engaging with a particular product. I also believe that integrating your marketing capabilities into your scan-and-shop technology is critical, as in doing so, you open up the ability to act exactly as an e-commerce business would – stretching spend, notifying customers of incomplete offers and recommending products – all while they build their basket in the store in real time.

Even in 2023, the vast majority of stores I visit are very noisy. Customers have become accustomed to simply filtering out the messages that aren't relevant to them, although this means they're likely missing some that are too. However, with a digital layer it is possible to personalize your headline marketing messages to individuals. For example, if you have had a major new pet-food launch, a remerchandise or a pricing roll-back, this can be marketed digitally to identified and permissioned pet-food buyers via their phone both during the online search, browsing and discovery phases of their shopping trips, as well as in the moment, on entering the store and at the shelf edge. In doing so, you can declutter your in-store messaging, can reduce marketing wastage and can significantly enhance the way you measure the impact of your campaign, ultimately getting to an ROI per customer:

1 **In-the-moment stretch:** A loyal customer who still has significant headroom walks into the store and receives a notification on their phone to say that they have a partially used continuity offer in their wallet. The message reads 'Did you know if you spend £62 you'll complete your challenge and get 1,000 bonus points?'

2 **Scan-as-you-shop moment:** A customer is using their mobile phone to conduct a shop in-store. As they add products to their basket, personalized recommendations are shared with them to ensure they don't miss out on any incomplete deals, for example. This upsell journey can of course happen across the retailer's digital properties too.

3 **VIP moment:** One of your top 5 per cent customers walks into the store. It's their birthday this month. 'Welcome back and happy birthday! We'd love to give you a gift! Swipe here to open your app and pick from three available gifts, or speak to any colleague in-store who'll be happy to help you choose!'

Rewarding the visit

Finally, what moments can you deploy to your customers once they've completed a purchase? Typically, these should be about thanking them for choosing to do business with you, offering added value through content and incentivizing the next visit:

1 **Points update moment:** After finishing a transaction, rather than scouring the end of the long paper receipt, the customer can receive a push notification, which says they earned 850 points on today's shopping and that they're 150 points away from receiving £25 off their next online purchase. The message can include a link to the retailer's e-commerce site, which has been curated to that individual's shopping history.

2 **Drive-to-digital moment:** Use printed messages at the checkout containing personalized offers and rewards, which the customer can only access if they download the app.

3 **Recipe-at-till moment:** At the checkout, the customer receives a push notification thanking them for shopping and directing them to a personalized recipe based on the contents of their basket.

The fourth C – Channel

In most of the examples above, I have detailed how these moments can manifest themselves in the physical store, as that is where I believe the biggest impact can be had. As I have said numerous times now, I believe that the future of shopping will be a 'phone out' experience and that this will enable businesses to power compelling, personalized journeys that customers are already becoming used to experiencing in the digital world. However, there is another C to consider when looking at launching a marketing in the moment strategy, which is of course, channel.

For any business looking to improve its marketing effectiveness, the first step has to be moving away from a channel-specific way of thinking to a customer-centric approach. In the same way that customers expect a consistent experience with your brand whether it's online, in-store or anywhere else, they don't want to be spoken to in a disjointed way across a variety of channels. You need a holistic approach to all customer communications, even when you start to integrate context into your personalization strategy.

For too long marketing has been siloed, with competing objectives set per channel – one team may be targeted on open rates, while another is focused on impressions and another is measured based on the revenue they generate from commercializing customer communications to suppliers. As I've mentioned before, you can't manage what you can't measure so you need to set your objectives (e.g. increase customer lifetime loyalty) and tirelessly and consistently measure the impact of what you're doing against them.

The execution challenge

The ability to offer this level of contextual personalization requires an ability to operate at real-time speed and at scale in order to deliver against what you've promised the customer in the moment. Real-time is a term that often gets bandied about but for clarity, what I mean when I talk about it, is the ability to personalize a customer's rewards (loyalty or other) while the customer is still at the checkout and before payment is made. For loyalty programmes, this differs significantly from the traditional model, where benefits are calculated after the customer has finished shopping.

With a real-time model, the loyalty engine adjudicates the shopping basket before payment is finalized, which provides a significant opportunity for marketing teams to execute 'marketing in the moment' to drive increased customer satisfaction. To do this, retailers need a method of delivering personalized rewards that can integrate seamlessly with the in-store POS – a very tall, if not impossible, task for legacy systems. Relying on promotions loaded at the POS will restrict your ability to deliver personalization at scale and therefore a purpose-built, cloud-hosted digital platform is necessary to make this a reality.

Both third-party and in-house solutions of this type can be costly to develop, maintain and innovate, especially if you want the same execution capabilities across all points of purchase – both physical POS and e-commerce. While there are clearly leaders advocating the benefits of an in-house approach, those taking this line are committing themselves to owning the challenges of innovation, channel fragmentation and evolving customer expectations.

To make the marketing in the moment model work, retailers need a powerful platform to connect with millions of context-rich data points that create moments that resonate with customers. As I mentioned back in Chapter 4, the Eagle Eye platform has been designed to do just this, acting as the 'retail nervous system', enabling the flow of decisions from the retail 'brain' into any connected customer touchpoint – including the POS – in real time. This provides businesses with the ability to manage, automate and track billions of unique customer communications all from one central platform.

The benefits of real time

The most obvious benefit of moving to a real-time approach is, of course, speed. Customers can then receive their rewards immediately, without waiting hours or even days for them to be processed. This boosts satisfaction and reduces the need for follow-up enquiries, easing the burden on your customer care teams. However, a near-real-time model – where rewards are received a few minutes after the transaction – also delivers speed. Speed alone, therefore, does not necessarily justify real-time integration. The investment needs to offer more than speed, and it does. I

FIGURE 10.3 Eagle Eye's 'power of real time' value matrix

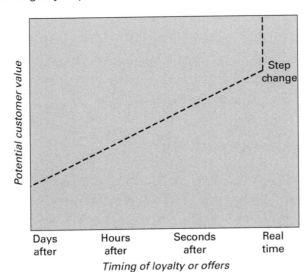

propose that the real-time integration to POS offers the scope for a significant levelling-up in the value that retail marketers can bring to customers through their ability to execute marketing in the moment (Figure 10.3). I've outlined some examples of this below.

Immediate benefits, not deferred benefits

Traditional loyalty programmes offer deferred benefits, such as points or vouchers for future purchases, through non-real-time platforms. Real-time platforms, on the other hand, allow retailers to offer immediate benefits like personalized discounts, bonus products and priority access to in-store services, enabling them to influence customer behaviour in the now.

There are several situations where offering an immediate benefit can be more effective versus something for the future and I've outlined a few examples below:

- In times of economic hardship, 'cash today' rather than 'a saving for tomorrow' can have much greater appeal so offering customers instant discounts can be very compelling.

- Driving engagement with new or lapsed customers can become easier with the power of immediacy.

- The power of 'now' becomes even more important in retail categories with lower visit frequency, so being able to offer the customer a saving or a reward that they can benefit from there and then can be crucial to driving conversion.

Omnichannel subscriptions – a new opportunity

We've already touched upon the fact that the subscription market has exploded over the last few years as consumers seek greater convenience and added value from the businesses they interact with. However, almost all omnichannel retailers that offer subscriptions focus on free delivery for online orders rather than finding ways to add value to in-store customers. This is principally due to the difficulty in integrating subscription platforms with in-store POS systems. With real-time integration, retailers can overcome this hurdle and get the flexibility to introduce a range of in-store subscription propositions.

Let's take the pioneering example of Pret a Manger's coffee subscription, mentioned briefly in Chapter 4. This gives customers up to five barista-made beverages a day for £30 per month. Pret now serves over one million subscribers per week, and the proposition has boosted Pret's market share and profitability since the pandemic.[5] In Australia, Woolworths' $59 per year Everyday Extra programme offers subscribers free products in their local stores, and the ability to save 10 per cent off one shop each month at Woolworths and Big W department stores.

As the economics of in-store subscriptions vary by category and retail proposition, the key to success is finding a sweet spot that keeps customers happy by delivering benefits of at least 150 per cent of fees, while also enhancing retailer profitability. Once you've got the subscription working, the ability to layer on marketing in the moment becomes an incredibly exciting opportunity. Take Pret, for example. If it sees in the data that one of its most valuable subscribers always buys a chicken salad with their coffee, it could trigger a message to them as they walk into store to offer them a discount or even a free trial of a new salad it thinks they'll like, extending the range of products they buy from Pret. Equally, it may have a subscriber who typically redeems three drinks per day, Monday to Thursday between 12 and 4 pm, but is never seen outside of that window. If the customer is opted-in to location services, they could be triggered whenever they're out of that time frame but within close proximity to a Pret, reminding them that they can come in to redeem a free drink, and potentially incentivizing them to trial other menu items that aren't on offer during the time they typically visit (e.g. breakfast).

Personalized offers for non-loyalty programme members

With real-time integration to the POS, you can look beyond just recognizing and rewarding your existing loyalty programme members, and take the opportunity to open up a dialogue with all your other customers. You may have a customer who has just paid for a full shop, including a range of food and toiletry products for children under the age of two. In the moment, you could print an incentive on their receipt, driving them to download your app, where they'll find a range of offers on key items in this category, or an invitation to your 'Kids Club' where loyalty members earn accelerated points on your whole kids range. Similarly, customers buying into local and seasonal produce could be sent information about product provenance, their carbon footprint, or rewards for shopping more sustainably. The options are endless and once you successfully achieve that initial engagement, you can simply follow the DIAL model so you can deliver more of what they want.

IN SUMMARY

- 'Marketing in the moment' will do for marketing what 'near me' did for search – unlocking the power of contextual personalization.

- Delivering personalized and contextually relevant experiences to customers has been happening online for more than a decade, and so bringing this capability into the physical store will enable bricks-and-mortar operators to effectively compete with digital pureplays.

- To execute a 'marketing in the moment' strategy you need to be able to send personalized content to customers based on what you know about their historic behaviour as well as their current context.

- This approach unlocks the opportunity for you to influence the customer's behaviour as it's happening – in the now – wherever they are physically, as well as figuratively, in terms of the search, browse and discovery phases of their shopping mission.

- Retailers need to stop executing and measuring direct-to-customer communications in silos. Set your overarching objective and continuously measure and optimize against it.

- Ensure you have the technical infrastructure in place to enable you to execute against your 'marketing in the moment' strategy, namely unlocking the ability to personalize the customer experience in real time at every point of purchase, whether digital or physical.

Notes

1 Tesco (2012) Philip Clarke speaks at the Global Summit of the Consumer Goods Forum 2012, 25 June, www.tescoplc.com/news/2012/philip-clarke-speaks-at-the-global-summit-of-the-consumer-goods-forum-2012/ (archived at https://perma.cc/P62C-H29R)

2 Abraham, M, Callersten, A, Bak, S and Kalthof, R (2021) The $70 billion prize in personalized offers, Boston Consulting Group, 14 September, www.bcg.com/publications/2021/personalized-offers-have-a-potential-70-billion-dollar-growth-opportunity (archived at https://perma.cc/YTM9-6H5U)

3 Goldsworthy, C (2022) Cookies, compliance and customer data: preparing for a privacy-first future, Segment, 24 June, segment.com/blog/cookies-compliance-customer-data/ (archived at https://perma.cc/6NRG-PRV5)

4 Safari Digital (2023) 18 Local SEO statistics that matter in 2023, 12 January, www.safaridigital.com.au/blog/local-seo-statistics/#:~:text=46%25%20of%20all%20searches%20on,search%20marketing%20for%20Google%20searches (archived at https://perma.cc/F6RH-6DB8)

5 Jolly, J (2022) Pret returns to profitable operations with strongest sales outside London, *The Guardian*, 4 July, www.theguardian.com/business/2022/jul/04/pret-returns-to-profitable-operations-with-strongest-sales-outside-london-covid (archived at https://perma.cc/SED7-C93P)

11

Monetizing the customer connection

As I hope I have made clear time and time again throughout this book, I believe there is huge power in knowing who your customers are and having a direct connection to them. To capitalize on this power, businesses need to be able to create personalized calls to action through compelling content to continue to engage their customers throughout their journeys, wherever they happen to be.

One thing I haven't mentioned in this book to date is the cost of running a loyalty programme. This has been intentional as I believe that the value generated off the back of a well thought out customer proposition means that your scheme will easily pay for itself. Even if you had to pay for the entire scheme yourself, it would be worth it. However, the good news is, you probably don't have to. There are significant commercialization opportunities involved once you've got customers engaged in your offering, which this chapter explores in more detail.

Most, but not all, retailer loyalty programmes contain a 'base earn' element – this is the foundational part of the 'give to get' exchange. A common example would be 'earn back 1 per cent of your total spend in points'. Although this may not seem like a huge amount at the outset, when you are operating at profit margins of perhaps 2–3 per cent, giving 1 per cent of total sales back to customers in points as a 'thank you' is a very expensive commitment! Of course, the loyalty business model is such that the power of the programme enables organizations to make better decisions across all areas of their business and thus, is worth its weight in gold. However, there are ways to offset the costs associated to this value exchange, as well as to unlock new revenue streams.

Monetizing customer data

The direct-to-customer connection and first-party data that retailers collect as a result of running loyalty or broader customer engagement programmes is hugely valuable. As I covered in Chapters 4 and 5, this data can and should be used to help these retailers make better, more informed and customer-centric decisions across all areas of the business including product range, merchandising, prices, promotions, personalized marketing and more.

Compared to their retail partners, consumer packaged goods companies (CPGs) typically live in a very data-poor world as the majority of their products are sold by retailers, rather than through direct-to-customer channels. Despite this, CPGs understand the power of customer data and so, for many years, retailers have been monetizing this opportunity. They do this by charging suppliers to access their customers' purchasing data across the categories those suppliers operate in (e.g. Coca-Cola will see the entire carbonated soft drinks category data), typically via dedicated self-serve platforms which are provided by the retailers' third-party analytics partners (e.g. dunnhumby, IRI, Quantium, etc). This enables the CPGs to make better, more customer-centric decisions regarding how best to price, promote and range their products with that specific retailer based on how its customers shop the category. Without this information, the CPGs have no choice but to make one-size-fits-all decisions spanning all of their retailer partner businesses, or to make them based on gut-feel rather than using hard facts.

Done well, this is a win–win for the retailer that can open up a new revenue stream off the back of its loyalty offering by commercializing this customer data, while building better, more collaborative working relationships with its supplier partners, aligning on what they can do together to serve the end customer in the best way.

Monetizing loyalty promotions

Once retailers have monetized the 'D' and 'I' parts of the DIAL as explained above, there also becomes an opportunity to open up a new revenue stream focused around the action that CPGs want to take off the back of the insights that they've generated.

The most commonly initiated action plan once CPGs have the data light switched on is to build a more effective promotional strategy in partnership with the retailer, including both mass and targeted offers.

Mass offers are typically run as bonus points-type promotions available for all loyalty members when they buy a specific product (e.g. '200 bonus points on any Coca-Cola 2 l'). The objective of these is to drive engagement in the loyalty offering by funnelling suppliers' promotional funds into points-based trade-driving offers rather than traditional price-cut discounts. They are typically displayed at the shelf edge (in-store and online), as well as potentially marketed on other channels such as the weekly circular.

In this example, the supplier – namely Coca Cola, would typically be liable to pay for all of the bonus points being offered to the customer as part of this promotion over and above the 'base earn', for which the retailer would be responsible. Occasionally, retailers also charge a handling fee in order to process the points, which means that the supplier could be charged ~15 per cent more than the base value of the points – this obviously helps to offset the cost of the base earn too. Using the data after the end of the promotional period, suppliers will be able to measure the impact of the offer and use that learning to determine the next best activity to run.

Targeted offers on the other hand are typically points promotions that are sent either to segments of customers or individuals (e.g. one customer might receive '150 points when you buy Diet Coke 330 ml × 6' and another might receive '50 points when you buy any Coca Cola 500 ml'). The objective of these types of offers is to deliver the right offers on the right products to the right customers with the right level of reward to incentivize the behaviour both the retailer and their supplier partners seek. Using the customer data, suppliers will be able to create compelling campaigns based on their own objectives, which align to the retailers' own strategy (e.g. drive trade-up in the category, incentivize trial of new products, increase purchase frequency, etc). The same rules would apply here regarding suppliers paying for bonus points awarded to customers and the ability for them to measure the campaign's success.

This may sound straightforward, but when retailers are running true personalization programmes as part of their loyalty offering, they could be delivering hundreds of millions of personalized points promotions per week – both own-label and brand-funded. In order to be able to manage this effectively, you have to have the right infrastructure in place, both to be able to allocate the right offers to the right customers, which they can redeem across all channels, as well as to accrue the points funds awarded to customers back from suppliers.

At Eagle Eye, we have built the capability to do this at massive scale. Using our Wallet functionality, we allocate offers to individual customers at any cadence a retailer desires, including in real time. We could allocate one brand-funded offer to 10 per cent of a retailer's loyalty base in support of a new product launch, or could allocate hundreds of millions of unique offers determined by the retailers' analytics capabilities to millions of customers' Wallets at the same time.

Due to the real-time integration at the POS as described in the previous chapter, customers can redeem these offers whenever and wherever they choose, following which we can 'burn' the offer in the Wallet, meaning it is no longer available for use.

When it comes to accruing funds back from suppliers, we offer the capability to automate this by enabling CPGs to draw down on their own account of points (or any other loyalty currency), which they pre-purchase from the retailer. This means that as soon as a supplier offer is 'burnt' at the POS, Eagle Eye can call the supplier's points account and debit the required number of points, crediting them to the retailers' account. This effectively makes the problem of post-promotional funding calibration disappear, with both the retailer and its suppliers able to see a real-time log of balances, debits and credits for all points-based marketing activity.

The retail media explosion

> Retail media is digital advertising's third big wave. Following the search ad market led by Google and the social ad market led by Facebook, this third wave led by Amazon is now cresting. (Andrew Lipsman, Principal Analyst at Insider Intelligence)[1]

According to Andrew Lipsman, we are now in the third wave of digital advertising. The first wave, led by Google, was driven by its understanding of what people search for to determine what else they might be interested in. The second wave, led by Facebook, was all about knowing what you like and what you talk to your friends about and using that to determine the best ads to serve you. This third wave, driven by Amazon, is all about knowing what you actually buy, and being able to influence that through ads when you are in the process of making a purchasing decision. An audience with intent to purchase is the gold standard.

As part of the third wave, the world of 'retail media' has exploded. Now, although retail media has absolutely been one of the biggest buzzwords in this space in the last couple of years, it's certainly not all new. Retailers have been monetizing their portfolio of assets to CPGs for decades – think floor stickers, in-store radio, sampling, shelf talkers, posters and more. The primary purpose of all of this activity is to influence the customer 'in the moment', at the point of purchase. Due to the five key factors detailed below however, retailers have taken the next step and have taken their retail media offering further, moving into the digital world.

1 The Amazon effect

One of the biggest stories in marketing over the last few years has been the rise of Amazon to become the third player in digital advertising, behind only Google and Facebook. In the first nine months of 2022, Amazon's ad revenue had already surpassed revenues made from Prime and Prime Video, as well as its other audio and e-book subscriptions,[2] with its ads generating $38 billion in 2022, which is expected to grow by 20.8 per cent in 2023.[3] Retailers have looked on as this rapid market domination has taken place and have been looking to see how they can get in on the action.

2 The growth of retail e-commerce

This has been a trend that has been happening for decades now but was of course accelerated in a way that none of us could have predicted by the pandemic. This means that retailers have a bigger audience of known customers with whom they have a direct digital connection. And although e-commerce provides customers with more choice about how and when to shop, offering greater convenience, it is still less profitable to run versus a traditional store network. Again, retailers looked to Amazon and saw that high-margin ads were potentially a way to change that.

3 The growing importance of first-party data

The changes in customer privacy laws and the imminent phasing-out of third-party cookies has rapidly transformed the advertising industry. The introduction of laws such as GDPR and CCPA have made it necessary for businesses to be transparent about their data collection practices, putting the power in the hands of the owner of the data – the end customer. The phasing out of the third-party cookie will mean that it will no longer be possible for businesses to track customer behaviour across different websites and platforms, significantly limiting the potential for businesses to execute personalized online ads based on an individual's browsing history.

This has created a significant opportunity for retailers that recognize the value of the first-party data that they've generated as a result of their loyalty offerings and the growth of their e-commerce businesses. Like Amazon, they now have a significant owned customer database to whom they can run their own digital marketing programmes but, more importantly in this context, they can commercialize access to this audience to brands, providing them with the ability to advertise to their customers, enabling them to influence the path to purchase.

4 The introduction of new technologies

Developments in technology have meant that retailers and their brand partners are now able to seamlessly reach and engage with consumers online in a personalized way across their owned and third-party properties. Primarily, this has been via the development of programmatic advertising technologies that have automated the buying and selling of ad inventory in real time. In addition to this, innovations that enable contextual targeting to increase the user experience by serving ads based on, for example, a customers' browsing history or their location etc, as well as dynamic creative optimization have also advanced the space significantly, making ads more relevant, more effective and more appealing for brand advertisers.

In addition, as discussed throughout this book, retailers' analytical and AI capabilities have also significantly improved in recent years, meaning they can determine the right content to send to the right customer and go on to action those insights in record speed.

5 Providing accurate measurement

For brands looking to advertise, the opportunity Amazon presents is unique versus its two key competitors, Google and Facebook, as it

FIGURE 11.1 The Amazon advertising model

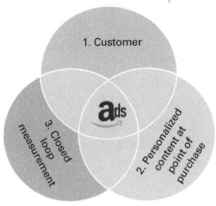

can enable the personalization of ads at the point of purchase, the impact of which can then be measured based on whether a customer goes on to buy the product or not.

Retailers have realized that they can take a leaf out of the Amazon playbook as they also have these three capabilities: owned first-party customer data, the ability to personalize ads at the point of purchase and the ability to offer closed-loop measurement (Figure 11.1).

Accurate and transparent measurement is absolutely critical to the success of this business model. Albertsons has talked recently about its work in this space to drive better collaboration with its supplier partners. During an NRF panel in January 2023, Kristi Argyilan, Albertsons' Senior Vice President of Retail Media said that it is working towards having 'an API for our measuring capability that can then plug into bigger marketing mix modelling that a lot of our clients are doing.'[4] This greater transparency would enable brands to truly understand the impact of the media dollars that they're spending, not just with Albertsons but in the wider context of their overarching media strategy. This is hugely valuable and will ultimately result in more CPG dollars flowing through to Albertsons versus its competitors if it has a first mover advantage here.

The future of retail media

It's clear that the retail media industry has now really hit its stride, with many grocers – both large national chains as well as smaller, regional players – having launched their own retail media networks (RMNs) to capitalize on this opportunity.

As reported by the latest WARC Media analysis, global spending on retail media is expected to climb 10.1 per cent in 2023 to $122 billion, which will mean that it is the fastest-growing media channel.[5] This proves that retailers with a direct connection to their customers who are permissioned to receive marketing are in a significant position of power as brands will pay to be able to get the right messages in front of the right customers, especially when those retailers can close the loop between ad view and product purchase to prove the impact on performance.

This is going to be transformative for the industry, as confirmed by Walmart recently. Just over two years following the launch of their RMN, Walmart Connect, the business is reporting huge successes, with ad sales growth of 30 per cent from 2022 to 2023.[6] In March 2023, John David Rainey, its CRO, said that 'Today, the vast majority of our overall profits are attributable to in-store brick-and-mortar in the U.S. If you fast forward 5 years, we are much less dependent on that as an income stream than some of these other faster-growing parts of our business.'[7]

When thinking about retail media and the opportunity it presents, I advise retailers not to forget where this all started, in their stores, where at least 70 per cent of their sales are likely still happening. To be effective, retail media needs to be omnichannel, utilizing integrated strategies across all your available channels and touchpoints to create a seamless, cohesive and personalized customer shopping experience.

The opportunity to digitize in-store media is huge and still largely untapped. If you go back to the digitally augmented store and the mobile makeover, media should simply be another customer engagement tactic and commercial proposition that you can layer on top of your current offering. The ability to target ads to customers while they use scan-as-you-shop, as well as the capability to use connected shelf coupons that unlock personalized offers for customers who scan them in-store are two incredibly compelling use cases for brands, which could completely transform the physical shopping journey due to their power to influence customers 'in the now'.

Think customer first

For me, the big watch out for retailers moving into this space is to ensure they continue to act in the customers' best interests. Don't be tempted to go for the quick buck, monetizing your customers by spamming them. Think instead about how you can use these new capabilities to make your customers' lives better and easier and their loyalty will surely follow. This is not just the right thing to do, but the sensible thing commercially. If you chase the advertising revenue over and above trying to solve individuals' needs you will rapidly lose the interest of the audience that you have worked so hard to engage. Then you will have neither happy customers nor growing ad revenues! It's lose–lose. This means you need to think about the whole marketing mix (both ads and sales promotions) and create a personalized capability that means customers get a valuable experience and brands get a good return on investment.

On its website, Amazon proudly claims that it strives to be 'Earth's most customer-centric company';[8] however, as I write this, I have opened a web browser on Amazon and searched for a specific product – the Scoot and Ride Scooter (for any parents or grandparents of toddlers – take a look, they are fantastic!). The first image I see and the first three associated results are advertising a different brand of scooter, which doesn't meet my needs as it's for much older children. The following three results are also 'sponsored', and again, show only irrelevant products that I do not want, nor have I searched for. Only the seventh product I scroll down to is the one I have asked them to display. I'm not sure about you, but this couldn't feel like a less customer-centric experience. Amazon knows exactly what I'm looking for because I have told it, but it consciously goes out of its way to be unhelpful, cluttering my view with products that I'm simply not interested in as a way to monetize my attention.

What's the learning here? Most likely, it's to carry on doing what you're doing – focusing on understanding your customers and using your knowledge in order to be helpful, serving their individual needs as best you can. Customers want conversations, not interruptions, so don't interrupt them with irrelevance when they're trying to find a specific product that you stock. Instead, start the conversation. 'Is this a gift? Do you know it comes with a matching helmet? People who bought it also loved these products'. The watch out is to not let yourself get bent out of shape by trying to apply some of these monetization tactics to your business that could result in you taking your eyes off the customer. If you stay on their side and build your business around them, you will undoubtedly gain their trust and earn their loyalty.

As retail media grows, organizations should look to move beyond banner ads and sponsored product searches to create more personalized, more useful and more entertaining experiences that improve the overarching experience. It's my hope that in the near future ads won't look like ads, they will feel like entertainment because it's an ad that I want to see and engage with.

The big sales promotion miss

As I stated at the outset in the first chapter, the world of advertising has really capitalized on the digital opportunity, while the world of marketing, particularly sales promotion, lags woefully behind. If I was still doing my old retail marketing job today, my focus would absolutely be on how to change this. The world of promotions is still incredibly analogue and fragmented and it shouldn't be.

If you think back to the nervous system analogy I introduced in Chapter 4, my vision would be that everything that gets presented to any of my customers, be it a promotion, a reward, a third-party partner offer, an advert or anything else for that matter, is personalized and flows through this same system in the same way. Every piece of content presented to a customer should be data driven, personalized and consistently available across all channels and touchpoints.

My co-author told me that, a number of years ago when she was working with a large grocery retailer that was just about to launch a loyalty programme, she sat down with the marketing director and together, they wrote down the 'golden rules of customer communications'. This was the standard that was to be set for the scheme from launch and these rules would be adhered to every time a customer communication was being planned. The first, and she says, most important rule was that 'every communication that goes out to our customer base must contain something of value'. For them, this didn't mean that every communication contained a promotion or a reward, although many of them did, but it was an opportunity to sense check the fact that yes – sending an email with recipes written by a celebrity chef to a segment of customers who were undoubtedly home cooks, based on the products they consistently bought, was a good idea as this content was of value to them. The same went for sending VIP customers information about early store-opening times during the Christmas holidays, should they want to beat the queue.

I think this is an excellent barometer and one more of us should think about more often. We are all living busy lives and being bombarded with content across every device. Wouldn't it be wonderful if everything we received from the brands that we engaged with was of genuine value to us? And the same goes for ads. It's my belief that as the owner of the customer, you are responsible for filtering the world you present to them to make it as relevant and as useful as possible, so apply the same stringent processes that you would regarding promotions to all the other content that you present to them.

Creativity rules

When speaking to Simon Andrews, media expert and founder of Addictive! agency about this in early 2023, he said that he still thought the biggest miss in digital media was all about creative:

> We know that the single thing you can do in communications to have the greatest impact is the creative. Google has proven that 70 per cent of ad campaign performance is based on the quality of ad creativity but in the digital world, it's still often thought of as an afterthought. It is the place where people spend the least time at the moment but is the area which has the greatest potential.

When I think about this in its simplest terms, it seems to me that brands and retailers have been working in the digital echo chamber again, running digital campaigns in a digital silo, rather than having a consolidated, omnichannel approach.

Digital is simply another execution engine (as direct mail was when I was running the Tesco Clubcard mailings, for instance). Businesses still have to do all of the other work that is required to run a fantastic marketing department, before they should even think about executing campaigns direct to the customer. This means determining your culture, your mission, your values, etc, just as we did when we wrote the Clubcard Customer Charter as detailed in Chapter 3. Only once you have decided upon the business you want to be, should you start to think about how you want to get that across to your customers creatively.

Now, what I won't deny is that things have become more complicated. When I was managing Tesco's marketing budget I knew I had to get our press ads to work in newspapers, TV ads had to resonate with terrestrial TV audiences, and the Clubcard mailings had to be designed in a way that would generate excitement among our many millions of members when they received them on their doormats four times a year.

Nowadays, what you do on your own website will need to be very different to what you might do on TikTok, which should be different to what you do on Facebook, which is different to what you do on Google and what you do directly on email, and the list goes on and on. There are more customer touchpoints than ever before, and you need to appear like a consistent organization across all of them, while flexing your creative muscles to ensure that the right content is resonating with the right individuals in the right places. This is why it's so important to get the foundations right first or else you're in danger of simply confusing your customers, or worse, damaging your reputation. Do the work, set your own 'golden rules' and live by them.

And remember, it's not all bad news. First of all, you own your own audience that you know a huge amount about. This is incredibly valuable. In addition, the speed at which businesses can move today has increased beyond recognition, while the costs associated with performance-based versus traditional mass marketing have come down significantly. Many of you reading this wouldn't believe how much I used to have to spend to communicate with my customers just once per quarter when running the Clubcard quarterly statement programme, and how far in advance I had to plan what I was going to say. Once those statements had been sent to customers, it would then take many more painful weeks of waiting before I could see the data that would determine whether I'd said and done the right thing or not. Thankfully, this is absolutely not a problem that exists any more. Businesses now have the ability to use their data to craft personalized messages to their customers, which they can action 'in the moment', and almost instantly can start to see exactly what is and what isn't working. This means they can focus their time and efforts doing more of the things that do work to ensure they're always turning the DIAL.

IN SUMMARY

- Loyalty programmes offer retailers huge value implicitly, but they also provide potential revenue-generation opportunities.

- Use customer data to build closer and more collaborative relationships with your suppliers.

- Think customer first – always try to be as useful and relevant as you can, regardless of what the content is that you're sharing with your customers.

- Customers want conversations, not interruptions. Engage with them as they navigate their shopping journey with you, don't spam them!

- Digital is a means of execution. Live in accordance with your values and ensure that every piece of content you put out into the world is data driven, personalized and consistently available across all channels and touchpoints.

Notes

1 Lipsman, A (2022) LinkedIn, www.linkedin.com/posts/andrew-lipsman-10b2162_retailmedia-amazonadvertising-activity-6866860892923977728-XtOU/ (archived at https://perma.cc/ZKR7-BR3B)

2 Del Rey, J (2022) Basically everything on Amazon has become an ad, *Vox*, 10 November, www.vox.com/recode/2022/11/10/23450349/amazon-advertising-everywhere-prime-sponsored-products (archived at https://perma.cc/CP94-66Z7)

3 Adgate, B (2023) Global ad revenue for print struggles, as total ad revenue nears $1 trillion, *Forbes*, 7 March, www.forbes.com/sites/bradagate/2023/03/07/global-ad-revenue-for-print-struggles-as-total-ad-revenue-nears-1-trillion/?sh=436262c3275a (archived at https://perma.cc/956X-YTYG)

4 Bigora, P (2023) What's ahead for retail media in 2023? *Grocery Dive*, 30 January, www.grocerydive.com/news/whats-ahead-for-retail-media-grocery-in-2023/640705/ (archived at https://perma.cc/53RE-SETV)

5 Huang, C (2022) Retail media to be the fastest-growing channel in 2023, reaching $122bn, WARC, 12 December, www.warc.com/content/paywall/article/warc-curated-datapoints/retail-media-to-be-the-fastest-growing-channel-in-2023-reaching-122bn/en-GB/148817? (archived at https://perma.cc/VF7C-64CK)

6 Cavale, S and Kumar, U S (2023) Walmart will derive more profit from services, ad sales in next 5 years - CFO, Reuters, 7 March, www.reuters.com/business/retail-consumer/walmart-will-derive-more-profit-services-ad-sales-next-5-years-cfo-2023-03-07/ (archived at https://perma.cc/KY7Z-XG2M)

7 Cavale, S and Kumar, U S (2023) Walmart will derive more profit from services, ad sales in next 5 years - CFO, Reuters, 7 March, www.reuters.com/business/retail-consumer/walmart-will-derive-more-profit-services-ad-sales-next-5-years-cfo-2023-03-07/ (archived at https://perma.cc/6NM3-4QV8)

8 Amazon (nd), Who we are, www.aboutamazon.com/about-us#:~:text=Amazon%20strives%20to%20be%20Earth's,Earth's%20safest%20place%20to%20work (archived at https://perma.cc/SA2B-M72Z)

12

The culture of loyalty

Throughout my career, I have seen time and time again that culture eats strategy for breakfast. However, when a business has a brilliant strategy that is excellently executed thanks to winning teams who are responsible for maintaining a world-class company culture, then you are really firing on all cylinders.

I have been lucky enough to have experienced this twice in my career, something which, in my view, is incredibly rare. Both at Tesco and now at Eagle Eye, our culture is entirely central to our success and was/is the enabler of us delivering against our strategy. Because of this, I wanted to include this new chapter in the second edition of my book, which focuses on culture and how it can manifest itself to make you win with both your teams and your customers.

It all starts with you

I have mentioned Fred Reichheld a number of times throughout this book as his work has had such a significant impact on my life. Despite this, there is one thing I fundamentally disagree with him on. In his first book, *The Loyalty Effect*, and later in *Winning on Purpose*, he argues that to earn loyalty you need three things: loyal customers, loyal employees and loyal shareholders. He suggests that all organizations should put their customers first to drive the other two outcomes. Not so, I say. I believe that everything has to start with you; we are, after all, our own favourite subject. Earn the loyalty of your teams and the rest will follow. Loyal teams are responsible for all the value you create for your customers and your shareholders. Put them first, think deeply about them, thank them and reward them for what they do and they will do more of it, faster, as loyal employees become more productive.

At Eagle Eye, our company culture is, I believe, our secret sauce. We recruit, retain, reward and remove people based on whether they align to what we call our 'Purple' way of being. Being 'Purple' means living and working in accordance with our values – Excellence, Integrity, Teamwork, Innovation, Passion and Kindness. These are not just buzzwords that are written in an employee handbook (although we do have one of those – a Purple Playbook that every employee is gifted on their first day in the business, which provides an introduction to the way we do things and why we do them that way), they are lived and breathed throughout our organization on a daily basis. We have a group of Values Champions based across all corners of the globe who are responsible for capturing and sharing stories of our individual and collective Purpleness throughout the company, celebrating employees at every level of the organization who are continuing to embrace and enhance our culture.

I believe that it is these values that drive our always-on dedication to creating value for customers, which breeds customer loyalty, (our customer retention rate is +99 per cent), which delivers incredible shareholder value. It is this that makes our business incredibly unique. It was fantastic to see my retail crush of the moment, Target, speaking about its shared beliefs when I was at NRF's Big Retail Show in January 2023. Its CEO, Brian Cornell, spoke of how he believes the company's huge successes, highlighted in Chapter 7, is all down to its culture.

In a panel discussion focused on leadership and culture, Cornell and some of his leadership team spoke about how they always start with their people. Cara Sylvester, EVP and Chief Guest Experience Officer stated:

> I would say my most practical piece of advice is when you care for your team first, they will care for your guests, for your customers, for your

community. Every single one of us, all 400,000 team members, plays a critical role in ensuring that our guests have an amazing experience. Our guests actually feel our culture when they're walking through our stores or interacting with us.[1]

In his summary, Cornell went on to say that culture 'isn't just something that just sits on the wall'.[2] It has to be owned, embraced and lived out across every part of the organization for it to truly bear fruit in driving the business forward. I couldn't agree more.

Galvanize your teams

A core part of having a successful company culture is having a clearly stated mission that your teams can get behind. This should be the reason they show up every day, and the benchmark for how they make empowered decisions about what to do/how to prioritize their work.

This book is all about creating winning stores in a digital world and I hope that, by this point, you have gained greater clarity for how you might apply some of this thinking to your own business. But you can't do it alone, you have to galvanize your teams around your mission, and make it absolutely central to everything you do.

It's my belief that your mission should be to serve a higher purpose than just to be the best supermarket, drugstore, pet shop or whatever line of business you're in. As mentioned earlier, at Tesco, our strategy was 'To create value for customers to earn their lifetime loyalty'. This logically enabled it to follow the customer and their money into financial services, mobile and e-commerce, as well as embracing international expansion. Had our mission been 'To run the best grocery stores in the UK', this wouldn't have been so logical.

At Eagle Eye, we are on a mission to help businesses earn the loyalty of their customers through the power of personalization. We live to create value for our clients by solving their problems with our technology, which means they can deliver better, more personalized marketing to their customers that is simpler for their teams to execute and cheaper for them to run. This is all underpinned by our belief that following the Golden Rule – treating people they way they want

FIGURE 12.1 Eagle Eye's customer promise

Our customer promise

We deliver*
a service we are proud of

Security by design gives you peace of mind when it comes to your crown jewels – your data

Stability No downtime for us means no downtime for your customer strategy

Speed Our ability to execute at lightning speed means your customers can get value in real time

Scalability More scale means more capacity for you to do more to delight your customers and keep them coming back

Support Our Eagle Eyes are monitoring our service 24/7 so you don't have to – but we're here for a chat anytime if you need us

We care*

*
The words our client chose, when asked to describe what we were like to work with

We're transparent*

Share We'll always communicate openly and honestly with you, even when it's difficult

Simple We strive for simplicity and seek to demystify the complex

Sensible We price fairly and transparently

We try*

Status quo We thrive on challenging the status quo to innovate and do things better, simpler and cheaper

Satisfied? We love to hear your feedback because it makes us better. We promise to act on it so give it freely!

Success Long-term, trusted partnerships are our thing

We win when you win

to be treated – is what sits at the very heart of personalization. Our goal is to deliver a service we are proud of, and when it comes to our front-line teams, this manifests itself in our Customer Promise (Figure 12.1), the standard that we set ourselves to ensure that we are focused on achieving this through creating the maximum value for our customers by delivering our technology to solve their specific needs. Like our values, this promise is lived and breathed throughout the organization, it is our North Star, it is what we build and measure our company objectives and key results (OKRs) around and is what makes us proud to work here. Because we care.

So, what might this mean for your business? Perhaps in reading this book, you have taken a decision to launch or refresh your existing loyalty proposition as you have become even more convinced of the power of the one-to-one customer connection. If so, then I would urge you to go all-in. If you look at the best-in-class programmes globally, you will see that the leaders in this space are businesses that have become loyalty companies, they are not simply companies that happen to operate loyalty schemes. Starbucks is a loyalty company. Tesco is a loyalty company. Loblaw is a loyalty company. Woolworths Australia is a loyalty company. But these are certainly the outliers. What they've done to drive their success –from both a loyalty and a wider business point of view, is to make their connection to their customers central to everything they do. Loyalty is the thread that binds their propositions together and is the KPI that they all continually try to optimize against.

Speaking to Matt McLellan, VP at Asda, responsible for loyalty, personalization, monetization, media and data partnership about the business' new scheme, Asda Rewards, he confirmed the central role that front-line team members have in its success. 'We have really had to enthuse the entire organization to get them behind the loyalty programme. We have been working to change our company culture since launching the scheme, getting all of our colleagues to be cheerleaders for our new, leading proposition.' And it's working: five months after launching, Asda was seeing around 40 per cent of sales linked to its Rewards programme; however, the best performing stores are far exceeding these levels, and these were the stores with the greatest colleague take-up.

I would recommend that any business operating a loyalty scheme makes the impact of its initiative palpable to front-line teams through the creation of an employee rewards proposition. This can sit on top of your existing programme, with internal users essentially being segmented so that you can offer them enhanced perks to further incentivize their usage. I would suggest that for every significant new product launch, relevant employees receive a free trial or discount on that product, redeemable through their loyalty app, to encourage digital engagement in the programme and to enhance their knowledge regarding all the products available in the range so that they can pass that knowledge on to customers when needed.

Another opportunity is to use employees as a test bed for new promotional or marketing activities. They could receive the planned marketing communication weeks prior to the planned customer go-live, with the results measured to determine whether the proposition needs tweaking before its official launch. This way, colleagues in-store will also be able to provide expert customer service, answering any questions regarding the proposition because they will have already experienced it themselves.

Appoint your gardeners wisely

To deliver a great culture you have to have great managers. The single most important thing about creating an exceptional place to work is how your manager treats you. We believe that great teams need great leaders – at Eagle Eye we call ours 'Gardeners'.

I discovered this concept when reading General Stanley McChrystal's book, *Team of Teams*. McChrystal was the military commander of the Joint Special Operations Task force in Iraq in 2003. He found that the largest, best-funded military operation in the world was being thwarted by an enemy that, although smaller and less well trained, was winning due to flexibility and speed. *Team of Teams* was his response to this, which was based around transparent communication and decentralized decision-making. In the book, McChrystal claims that their fortunes were transformed because of the 'Team of Teams' way of working, rather than due to any particular part of their strategy.[3]

By working together in teams bound by trust, with a clearly understood mission, the role of the gardener is to enable 'empowered execution' – a place where everyone is given the freedom to work and make decisions in the way they see best.

I encourage you to train your managers to lead like gardeners – preparing the ground, selecting the seeds, watering and feeding them and keeping up with the weeding to ensure your seedlings aren't overwhelmed. Gardeners can't change the DNA of the plants they grow, but they can select the right varieties and make sure that they have the right conditions for growth – a safe environment with light, water, nutrients and where they're not eaten by slugs.

One single gardener can grow more than they can eat from a small piece of land. Leadership, in my view, is as much about nurture and encouragement as it is about strategy and direction.

At Eagle Eye, we run what we call our Gardener's Club – a weekly meeting focused on helping our senior leadership team become better managers. Some sessions are dedicated to learning (together, we have read and taken actions from a whole host of books including McCrystal's *Team of Teams*, Simon Sinek's *Start With Why*, Steve Peters' *Chimp Paradox* and of course, Fred Reichheld's *Loyalty Effect* and *Winning on Purpose*, to name a few), others to some of the practical elements around people management including hiring, training, career development, etc, as well as it acting as a safe space for managers to brainstorm, ask for advice from each other and to become a better and stronger team. This has had a fantastic impact on our business and so I would recommend to anyone reading that they think about what their version of a Gardener's Club might look like within their organization.

Earn your customers' trust

I think that one of the ways omnichannel businesses can beat the Amazons of the world is because they can be more trusted. Would you trust vitamins you bought from Amazon's marketplace, for example, compared to the health and wellness chain, Holland & Barrett? That's where the role of a brand within the channel becomes important. How do you excel in this area? The first step is by ensuring that you maintain a coherent brand presence that spans every physical and digital touchpoint a customer may encounter throughout their shopping journey. This omnichannel consistency has a very important role to play in engendering brand and retailer trust, as well as loyalty.

The next step has to be in understanding your customers. You will only be able to stand out and earn the trust and loyalty of those you serve if you are able to demonstrate how well you understand them. You must use this knowledge to build meaningful connections through relevant, personalized messages and offers. As I mentioned earlier, in Chapter 6, it is Asda's Matt McLellan's belief that 'using the data to be as helpful and as relevant as possible is what matters'. I believe that this notion of being helpful is really where omnichannel retailers can step up and ultimately, out-Amazon Amazon.

If in doubt, ask

In this world of advanced analytics, AI and machine learning, I believe that businesses often forget that the data doesn't always have to provide the answer; in many instances, the customer can. Despite all the advances in data science, predicting what people are going to do, or what they want or need is still very difficult. Humans are complex! Now, I hope you've realized by now that I am a huge proponent of using data to run all aspects of your business in a more customer-centric way, however, getting that 'data' directly from the customer can sometimes be a better, simpler and cheaper way of getting to the same outcome.

I received an email from Fortnum & Mason recently, which made me think of just this. The purpose of the communication was to ask whether I wanted to opt out of Mothering Sunday related news as it understands this time of year can be difficult for some people. The email was short, to the point and polite, and despite the fact that I did not want to opt out of these messages, struck an 'emotional' loyalty chord with me as it further cemented the fact that I believe it is a good business that puts its customers first.

My co-author shared a similar example with me recently from children's retailer, Pehr, which, when you get onto its website, asks you to self-select a persona: 'I'm a parent', 'I'm expecting', 'I'm gifting'. Answering that question triggers an offer for 15 per cent off your first order – this is the 'give to get'. As with the Sephora example I mentioned in Chapter 6, this enables Pehr to start to personalize the experience when the customer is still in the browsing phase, enabling it to offer a better, more curated service as a result.

Speaking to Terry Leahy about this, he suggested that more physical retailers 'should be looking for ways to get instant feedback. You should ask them what they want when they're in store or why they're there. Engage with them and help them to do some of the customer research for you!' He absolutely has a point here and I believe that this is something that could be easily addressed via the mobile makeover in the digitally augmented store, again, equipping retailers with another tool in their arsenal to compete with online. Once you're able to capture this kind of data in real time, it becomes possible not only to run a branch-based business in a more agile way, but also to start tailoring the in-store marketing communications accordingly, where digital gives you the flexibility to execute integrated digital and physical marketing campaigns and promotions in a much more agile, flexible, dynamic and cost-effective way than printed point-of-purchase materials requiring a six-week lead time ever can.

Don't stop

Establishing and maintaining a culture of loyalty is a life's work. This is not a 'one and done' mission. If you really want to rally your employees behind your mission to serve your customers in the best possible way to drive their lifetime loyalty, then you can never stop. Retail is relentless, you are only as good as your last transaction, so you have to keep your mission in sight and continue to pursue it across every facet of the organization. Remember, the goal should be to be a loyalty company, not simply a company with a loyalty programme.

A year or so after the launch of Tesco Clubcard, the vast majority of transactions that were flowing through the checkout were associated to an individual customer. Our loyalty card penetration was more than 70 per cent. A great achievement. This provided us with enough data to use to run the business better and to start making our first moves towards personalization. But did we stop there? No. Every single quarter, we would roll out the tables at the front of every store and man them with employees charged with motivating customers to sign up to the scheme. In most cases, the customers were already members but every now and then, someone would walk into the store who wasn't, and we would be able to clearly communicate the value of Clubcard to get them to sign up right there and then. Now, nearly 30 years later, it is still pursuing its mission of 'creating value for customers to earn their lifetime loyalty' through initiatives such as Clubcard Prices, which, as discussed earlier, has driven loyalty penetration back up to record levels.

Thinking about this idea of never giving up, I am reminded again of *The Social Dilemma*, the Netflix documentary I mentioned in Chapter 8. The ability that retailers have today to analyse and action data-driven insights at scale is something that I could never have dreamed of in the early days of Clubcard, however, there is still scope to do more. Compared to the likes of Facebook, Google and TikTok, retailers are still miles behind in terms of the quest for continual data-driven optimization against clearly set KPIs. I would recommend anyone reading this to watch or even rewatch the film but thinking about how you could use the power of data and AI to serve your customers better by being more helpful and more relevant. Again, it is the application of this kind of strategy that I believe will enable omnichannel retailers to out-Amazon the Amazons of this world.

Because you can

The final thing I wanted to leave you with here is really inspired by Reichheld. When speaking about the importance of following the golden rule, he states, 'every time you treat someone right – the way you would want to be treated if you were in their shoes – you are building your reputation and making the world a better place, one life at a time.' I love the idea of actions building and strengthening our characters, like practising a golf swing or playing the piano.

Now you might be sat here reading this, thinking 'but what on earth has this got to do with my business?' And my answer, just like David Malpas' answer to me regarding launching Clubcard, is 'we have to do this, because we can'.

As leaders, we have the ability to enrich the lives of those we touch, simply because we can. I would suggest that this starts with your own teams and colleagues, creating great places to work, but should extend as far and wide as possible, because it can. For me, the promise of personalization is not just a marketing buzzword, it is something that businesses should aspire to do to improve the lives of their customers, however big or small.

We all know that doing good is good business, and being in the fortunate positions that we're in, I believe we should drive to do more good, because we can. At Eagle Eye, we have partnered with a fantastic charity called 52 Lives, run by the ever-inspiring Jamie Thurston. 52 Lives aims to change the life of at least one person every week of the year while inspiring people to be kind, as they believe kindness has the power to change lives and to change the world for the better. Every week, 52 Lives chooses someone in need of help, and shares their story across their network and in the media, requesting what that person needs. Supporters of the charity from all over the world then spread the word and offer the help they can. It is a brilliant organization that puts the power of personalization into a whole new context. I would encourage you to look them up and, if you can, help them change a life.

Our partnership with this amazing charity has also been amazingly beneficial for us as a team. We have rallied together on numerous occasions over the last few years – both virtually and physically – to think of innovative ways to raise funds for 52 Lives. This has involved gardening, cycling, litter picking, painting, running, hair dyeing and even burpeeing together, all of which has significantly strengthened us as a team.

IN SUMMARY

- Culture eats strategy for breakfast. As leaders, it is our job to establish and work with our teams to maintain a winning culture that enables you to excellently execute your strategy.

- Your team members are responsible for all the value you create as a business. Put them first and they'll look after the rest.

- Rally your teams around your clearly stated mission and don't give up. There is always room to be better so optimize wherever and whenever you can.

- Earn your customers' trust by being as relevant and as helpful to them as you can while they navigate the world around them.

- Follow the golden rule and seek to improve the lives of everyone you come into contact with. Because you can.

Notes

1 Redman, R (2023) Target's Brian Cornell: Company culture 'part of who we are', *Winsight Grocery Business*, 17 January, www.winsightgrocerybusiness.com/retailers/targets-brian-cornell-company-culture-part-who-we-are (archived at https://perma.cc/9ULC-7LSG)

2 Redman, R (2023) Target's Brian Cornell: Company culture 'part of who we are', *Winsight Grocery Business*, 17 January, www.winsightgrocerybusiness.com/retailers/targets-brian-cornell-company-culture-part-who-we-are (archived at https://perma.cc/CJ9U-J4LZ)

3 McCrystal, S (2015) *Team of Teams: New rules of engagement for a complex world*, Penguin, USA

Lessons learnt

I hope you agree by now that I have made a compelling, or at least an interesting, case for getting digitally connected and being data driven.

I firmly believe I am directionally right, if wrong in some of my specifics. Some elements may just not be for you, and that's fine. But one thing I am absolutely clear about: this is not a zero-sum game. It is incontrovertible that we live in a digital world and, to be a winner, you have to find your place in this world.

So, in summary, what I have tried to do is pick out what I believe are the non-negotiable elements of an omnichannel journey and one golden rule:

1 **The golden rule.** Treat people the way you would like to be treated.

2 **Know your customer ('*Who* did it?').** However you do it, you must get the identity of as many of your customers as you possibly can.

3 **You manage what you measure ('*What* did they do?').** Once you know who your customers are – what do they do? Data capture, analytics and, increasingly, AI should be a core competence of any business in the digital age. (Remember 'DIAL'.)

4 **Establish a digital connection (Get connected).** Give your customers many compelling reasons to connect to your business via mobile. The prize is enormous: a personalized real-time channel for your marketing, and it's free.

5 **Operate an omnichannel presence (Follow the customer).** To win in the future you need a great mobile-optimized website and app, and digitally enabled and augmented stores, offering your customers a joined-up complementary experience that can be located digitally, online and offline.

6 **Gain a single customer view (Recognize me).** All customer-related data sources need to be brought together in one place, so you fully understand their relationship with you, including the combination of channels and touchpoints they use during their shopping journeys.

7 **Personalize offers (Offers just for me).** Big Data, AI-based analytics and a mobile connection enable one-to-one marketing. The greater the level of personalization, the greater the relevance you can deliver and the more success you'll have for a lower cost.

8 **Market 'in the moment' (There's no time like the present).** As well as relevance, consumers love utility – especially at the point of need. An offer delivered in real time – now, that I can use now – can transform the power of your marketing.

9 **Reward the behaviour you seek (Incentivize and thank).** Make sure the service, message, promotion, reward or offer you design drives the behaviour you're looking for. Offers to drive frequency are different from those that drive spend and are different again from when you're simply saying 'thank you'.

10 **Move the dial (Performance-driven marketing).** Remember that a hugely successful, targeted promotion resulting in a 100 per cent increase in sales to only 10 customers won't necessarily register with the business. Learn by doing, start small and use digital scale and traceability to expand the test-and-learn process rapidly. Make sure the business can see and feel the impact by doing enough of it, and involve your front-line staff.

11 **My strategy (The new normal).** This isn't your 'digital' strategy, this is your strategy. Make sure you step outside of the digital echo chamber and bring your vision to life for your business in a digital world.

12 Doing good is good business. Wherever possible, seek to enrich the lives of those you come into contact with. Why? Because you can.

It's will, not skill

Although this subject can appear sophisticated, tech dependent and jargon laden, it's actually quite simple. Do you have the will to recognize your customers as individuals and serve them as such? Pursue this with every ounce of your corporate being and the skill will surely follow.

INDEX

The index is filed in alphabetical, word-by-word order. Numbers in main headings are filed as spelt out in full; acronyms and 'Mc' are filed as presented. Page locators in *italics* denote information contained within a Table or Figure.